T

MW00952821

PREPARED FOR THE COLUMBIA COLLEGE PROGRAM OF TRANSLATIONS FROM THE ORIENTAL CLASSICS

THE LUTE

Kao Ming's *P'i-p'a chi*

Translated by
Jean Mulligan

toExcel
San Jose New York Lincoln Shanghai
NEW YORK
COLUMBIA UNIVERSITY PRESS
1980

The Lute: Kao Ming's P'i-p'a chi

Published by toExcel by arrangement with
Columbia University Press

For information address:
toExcel
165 West 95th Street, Suite B-N
New York, NY 10025
www.toExcel.com

ISBN: 1-58348-283-0

LCCN: 99-62479

Printed in the United States of America

Translations from the Oriental Classics

Contents

Acknowledgments

My very deepest gratitude is felt toward Professor David Roy of the University of Chicago, whose contributions to this book are immeasurable. He guided me through every stage of my doctoral dissertation on *The Lute* from first reading of the play to final polishing; without the benefit of his vast learning and the patience and enthusiasm that constantly inspired me, I do not see how the work could have been completed.

Professors T. H. Tsien and Lois Fusek, also of the University of Chicago, and Professor J. I. Crump of the University of Michigan gave valuable suggestions and encouragement during the preparation of the dissertation. Completion of the final work was aided by advice from Professor Cyril Birch of the University of California at Berkeley, Professor Irving Lo of Indiana University, George Kao of the Chinese University Press, and Professor C. T. Hsia of Columbia University.

Finally, I wish to thank my parents, Louise and J. Kenneth Mulligan, for their support and faith through the many years it took to complete the work.

Introduction

The Lute is among the greatest achievements of Chinese drama. Since its composition in the Yüan dynasty by the scholar-official Kao Ming, its beautiful songs, vivid characters, and forceful moral message have won critical acclaim and popular devotion through the centuries. One of the first plays written in the *ch'uan-ch'i* form (the very first according to some commentators), it became a model for later playwrights and greatly influenced the development of the genre. In recent times, it was a topic for debate in the People's Republic of China, where it was analyzed for its social significance in terms of its portrayal of traditional morality.[1]

It is important too in the history of Western appreciation of Chinese literature. A. P. L. Bazin's French translation in 1841 was probably the first translation of a *ch'uan-ch'i* play into a Western language. About a hundred years later, Will Irwin and Sidney Howard wrote a musical based upon the play. Titled *Lute Song* and starring Mary Martin, it had a successful run on Broadway in 1946. Although a Westernized adaptation, the play preserved a good deal of the flavor of the original and provided American audiences with an introduction to traditional Asian drama.

Despite its artistic and historic significance, no full English translation of the play has been available. Now the English reader will be able to appreciate this landmark work—a prototype of a major genre and a masterpiece of world drama.

THE PLAY AND ITS GENRE

The story of *The Lute* is based on elements dear to the Chinese populace and conventional in Chinese drama. A bright and conscientious hero, Ts'ai Po-chieh, has spent his youth in study for the civil service examinations, the traditional means by which even the poor and humble could become members of the highly esteemed official class. When the final examination in the capital is announced, however, he is reluctant to go because of an equally pervasive ideal in the culture, filial piety. His parents are aged, and he balks at leaving them with no other support than that of his young wife, Wu-niang. It is only out of obedience to his father, who insists that he attempt to win glory for the family, that Ts'ai finally sets out for the capital. Once there, he wins first place in the examinations. Now the most coveted marital catch in the empire, he is coerced by the powerful Prime Minister Niu, supported by the emperor, into marrying his daughter and taking up residence in his mansion.

While Ts'ai lingers on in the capital, finding it impossible to return home, his hometown Ch'en-liu is ravaged by famine. Wu-niang's valiant struggles to provide her parents-in-law with food are in vain, and they die one after the other. She sets out for the capital to find her husband and inform him of his parents' deaths, along the way playing her lute and singing as she begs for alms.[2] Reunited, they return, along with Mistress Niu, to Ch'en-liu to carry out the traditional three years of mourning by the parents' graveside. The play closes at the end of this mourning period with Ts'ai about to return to the capital to resume his official career, after he and his wives have received an imperial commendation for their filial and virtuous conduct.

The plot itself, with its emphasis on filial piety and success through study, is a conventional one that has been the basis for a good number of plays and stories in traditional Chinese literature. Kao Ming's special contribution is his sensitive exploration of the conflicts involved in realizing these values and his portrayal of the bitter contrast between the suffering of the common people and the luxurious life of the elite. In addition, he developed to its full potential the multifaceted form of the *ch'uan-ch'i*, writing with equal skill lyric songs, comic skits, descriptive prose, and scholarly argument.

The *ch'uan-ch'i* form, actually the maturation of an earlier folk genre called southern drama, emerged in the late fourteenth century. Of extreme length (averaging forty or fifty scenes, which must have required several days to perform in full), the plays are composed of songs, dialogue, and action. The plots, generally romantic and moralistic in tone, are often based on traditional stories and history. The form differs significantly from the Yüan *tsa-chü* or northern drama, which is better known in the West because of a number of major translations and studies. Some of these differences will be pointed out in the description of the *ch'uan-ch'i* that follows.

Songs were considered the most important element of the plays, and critics evaluated authors above all on the quality of their lyrics. The authors selected tunes from an existing repertoire of several hundred, fitting their lyrics to the metrical demands of each particular tune. *Ch'uan-ch'i* plays generally used the southern tunes of their homeland; contemporaneous commentators described this music as slow and langorous, as opposed to the livelier, somewhat raucous, *tsa-chü* tunes.

The *ch'uan-ch'i* writer was free to use a number of singing combinations in his plays, unlike the *tsa-chü* composer, whom convention bound to assigning all songs to the single lead character. In *ch'uan-ch'i,* a song could be shared by two or more characters, either by singing together or by each singing several lines in alternation. A set of songs was often similarly shared; two or more characters sang separately different lyrics to the same tune, each song being followed by a brief chorus in which all joined. The author, again more free than his *tsa-chü* counterpart, could change modes and rhymes with each new song. It was in his songs that an author generally expressed the most intense emotions of his characters, but the flexibility of musical conventions in the *ch'uan-ch'i* made it possible to frame even ordinary conversation or exposition in song.

The spoken dialogue of the plays was written in a wide range of styles, from the colloquial speech of the time to extremely flowery parallel prose and poetry.

Colloquial speech was used in much of the conversation and monologue, but its most distinctive use is in comic passages. All of the early extant plays are enlivened by episodes of comedy scattered throughout. These passages provide welcome relief from the emotionally charged and often didactic main action of the play, and would also have entertained members of the audience who were not educated enough to appreciate the literary language of the songs and polished prose. Some of these skits are quite lengthy (as in Scene Sixteen of *The Lute*) and only loosely related to the plot. The characters appearing in them are often very minor ones, on stage only for these episodes. In keeping with their style of speech, they are generally of a social status beneath the middle- or upper-class heroes and heroines, including such figures as servants, monks, vagabonds, thieves, and petty officials.

At the other extreme are passages of parallel prose (an ornate traditional literary form in which pairs of sentences are balanced grammatically against each other, usually containing many learned allusions and flowery phrases), philosophical and historical discourse, and poetry.

Parallel prose is used primarily in description. Because no scenery was used on the Chinese stage, the author had only the words of his characters to describe the settings unseen by his audience. *Ch'uan-ch'i* writers delighted in using this elegant style to describe such high-class pleasures as sumptuous palaces and luxurious feasts (as in Scenes Nine and Fifteen of *The Lute*) and the beauties of nature. These elaborate passages were excellent showcases for the author's literary skill and erudition, but because of their distinctive grammatical form and frequent allusions are difficult to render into effective English.

Almost as elegant are the high-flown discussions of philosophy and history to which the characters are prone. It is not unusual for even uneducated servants to cap each other's quotations from the classics. Conflicts over moral dilemmas form the basis of most of the plays, but one suspects that such discussions are sometimes included as much for their intrinsic interest and proof of the author's erudition as for their relevance to the plot.

Poetry is an important element in the plays; both major traditional forms, *shih* and *tz'u* (the former uses lines of equal numbers of syllables, the latter unequal lines) are used throughout. Conversations as well as monologues are often set in poetry, which is generally written with more care than the often rote poetry of the *tsa-chü* plays. In addition, almost every scene ends with a four-line poem in the *shih* form, and many scenes begin with either a *shih* or *tz'u* poem. Characters occasionally express themselves in an informal style of folk poetry.

Our knowledge of the third element in the plays, action, is

more limited. Chinese stage directions are most often very general; the most common is the single word *chieh*, a dramatic term that means simply to perform an action or gesture. When we read these texts we can only guess at what action would be appropriate whenever the term is used. Some actions *are* specified and appear in the plays frequently. *Ch'uan-ch'i* actors are often called upon to cry, fall down, or choke on food; it is likely that the Chinese theater had developed particularly effective pantomimes for these actions, and authors made a point of including them in plays. *Hun chieh* is a more general term used to describe any type of comic action; *ta chieh* indicates fighting or hitting actions. Although the directions are vague, the plays probably included lengthy dramatic fighting performances and slapstick mimes—lively visual entertainment that is lost in the written text. *The Lute,* because of its subject matter, includes no battle scenes, but these were a key element in many plays. The genre occasionally includes dancing, as in Scene Three of *The Lute.*

With such variety in level and style of language and modes of presentation, the *ch'uan-ch'i* form is significantly different from the compact Yüan *tsa-chü.* Rich with realistic detail, description of the sights and sounds of settings, and elaboration of the background and issues of the stories portrayed, the *ch'uan-ch'i* plays give a complex and detailed portrait of society. It was, of course, the length of the form that both allowed and demanded of its authors such varied and complex creativity. The effect has aptly been characterized as "a kind of symbiosis of drama with novel."[3]

The length of the *ch'uan-ch'i* form demanded not only variety of style, but also complexity of plot to engage the audience's interest through some forty or fifty scenes. The plots are far more involved than those of the simple and direct stories on which the *tsa-chü* are based. At least two characters (usually a man and woman) play major roles in the story; the most characteristic pattern is alternating scenes in which the two play out their separate fates. A subplot of a second pair of characters is sometimes added, and comic skits are often lengthy enough to stand as miniature plots in themselves. Historical events are also presented in some detail.

The origins of the plots can generally be traced to tradi-

· tional stories and fiction, earlier plays, or historical incidents. Study of the five major early plays extant,[4] along with hundreds of fragments from southern plays,[5] reveals a striking similarity in the essential plot elements of many of them. Four of the five early plays, including *The Lute*, tell of a young man's rise to success, separation of husband and wife, and conflicts centered around a proposed or actual second marriage. It is easy to see the meaning of such stories to the audience of the time: people dreamed of winning the supreme honor of official position and yet feared the family conflicts— through separation in space and status—such success could cause. But the authors treated this basic theme in widely different ways (for example, in their attitudes toward second marriages), and it is likely that this basic story was used partly because of its compatibility with the *ch'uan-ch'i* form. Separation of husband and wife provided the perfect dramatic situation for lyric songs of loneliness and longing that had already become a standard theme of *tz'u* and *ch'u* poets, and it created the pattern so effective in these long plays of switching back and forth between the separate experiences of hero and heroine.

These standard plots—in particular the strands dealing with conflicts over second marriages—were also excellent frameworks for expressing a theme with which all five of the early plays are deeply concerned: conflict between principle and authority. In all these plays, the younger generation is firmly committed to the basic moral values of the society—marital faithfulness, respect for education, filial piety, and loyalty to friends and family—and struggles to uphold these standards against the immoral and often materialistic demands of the elder generation to whom they owe obedience. As in romantic stories of the West, the heroes and heroines of the Chinese plays are often pressured to desert their original sweethearts or spouses to marry rich and powerful mates. Young women struggle against family members—parents or elder brothers; men are coerced by powerful members of the society, like Prime Minister Niu in *The Lute*, who demands that Ts'ai marry his daughter.

Didactic as the themes may be in their stress on the conventional values of the age, the plays are best classified as come-

dies in their treatment of these potentially tragic themes.
Happy endings were, as far as we know, an unbroken convention. All five of the major early plays end with grand reunions
in which as many of the major characters as possible are
brought together to rejoice in the fortunate working out of
their problems. In four, the virtuous heroes and heroines are
further blessed with commendations from the emperor. Not
only are heroes and heroines rewarded with success; even
villains are treated with tolerance. Petty villains who are not
family members may be punished, sometimes harshly, but the
dominant relatives themselves are always let off lightly. Despite the intense conflicts throughout the plays, there is a ten-
dency to shy away from unyielding blame of the elder generation. In the "comedies of errors," *Thorn Hairpin* and *Ladies'
Secluded Chambers,* for example, all conflicts are resolved
through lucky coincidences; young lovers separated from each
other are saved from their struggle against remarriage by
finding that the new mates offered them are the very same to
whom they were striving to remain true. In others, the villains
are forgiven both because they repent of their past errors and
because they are family members; the heroine of *The White
Rabbit* takes no vengeance on her cruel brother out of respect
for their dead parents. The plays are particularly cautious
about placing blame on parents. In *The Thorn Hairpin,* it is a
stepmother who plays the villainous role, and in *The Lute*
Ts'ai's father is not an evil man, but merely mistaken in his
demands. Fortunate resolution of conflicts, merciful redemp-
tion of villains, and joyful reunion characterize the happy
world of the *ch'uan-ch'i* plays.

THE AUTHOR

The creation of the *ch'uan-ch'i* form received little attention
from the scholars of the time, perhaps because of its folk origins. It has taken a good deal of effort to establish tentative
authorship attributions for even the most famous of the early
plays. With *The Lute* we are more fortunate. Although some
critics believe that the present play is merely a revision of an
earlier folk play, all agree that Kao Ming of the Yüan dynasty
is either its author or its editor. Not only has his name been

firmly attached to the play throughout history, but it has been possible to reconstruct the basic outlines of his life.[6]

Kao Ming (*tzu,* or courtesy name, Tse-ch'eng) was born about 1305 during the period of Mongol rule in China. His family were scholars and poets living in retirement in the southeastern province of Chekiang. Local histories suggest that Kao's father died at an early age and that Kao served his widowed mother with exemplary filial devotion.

Kao's official career began late and ended early, lasting in all only about ten years. He obtained his final *(chin-shih)* degree in 1344 when he was about forty. His first appointment was as district judicial officer in Ch'u-chou in his native province, where he established a reputation for ability and integrity among both the people and the gentry. Kao's short period of government service was curiously intertwined with the activities of the pirate Fang Kuo-chen, who terrorized the Chekiang coast during this time. In 1348, Kao was recruited as an advisor to the government naval forces sent to subdue the pirate. It was an unhappy experience; at odds with his commanding officers, he left the post disillusioned with official service and is quoted as telling friends that he finally understood the warning of his elders that official success marks the beginning of anxiety and trouble. After several more years' reluctant service in various posts, Kao was offered a position with the former pirate Fang, who had become a powerful warlord. Kao refused the summons and, putting an end to his official life, disappeared to the village of Li-she, where he took an apartment and lived in retirement, writing *The Lute.*

Kao took no part in the political uprising that led to the Ming dynasty and return of the empire to Chinese rule. He died not long after declining an invitation from the new emperor, a great admirer of *The Lute,* to accept official appointment with several of his good friends at work on the official history of the Yüan dynasty.

Today Kao's one masterpiece is considered to be *The Lute,* but during his lifetime he was most noted for his poetry in the *tz'u* form, only one example of which has been preserved. Fifty of his poems in the *shih* form have survived in various anthologies.[7] A second *ch'uan-ch'i* play has been attributed to him, but it is not extant and there is reason to believe that the attribution is erroneous.

Kao Ming lived under the harsh domination of Mongol conquerors. His native province of Chekiang, where the Southern Sung capital had been located, was most oppressed of all. Economic hardships brought on by the Mongol rule were intensified by a series of natural disasters in the province, and it is likely that Kao Ming had experienced the suffering about which he wrote in *The Lute*. A secondary hardship for the ambitious literati class was their exclusion from their traditional ideal of government service; it was not until 1342, just three years before Kao Ming took his *chin-shih* degree, that the civil service examination system was officially reinstated and Chinese scholars allowed a limited role in the rule of their country.

The distrust of official service that underscores *The Lute* is a natural product of the author's personal experiences and background. Though scorn for worldly success is a convention in Chinese poetry, Kao Ming's words from one poem ring true: "Don't speak of the affairs of the city and marketplace / For success and fame make slaves of men."

SOURCES OF THE PLAY

The Lute, like most *ch'uan-ch'i* plays, has its source in popular legend and history. But the origin of this play is uniquely significant to its understanding, for it helps to explain both the author's moral attitude and a number of weaknesses in the plot that have been sharply criticized through the ages.

The story of a young scholar named Ts'ai who deserted his family to win official success, and his wife named Chao, who struggled to care for her parents-in-law, was already popular in the Southern Sung dynasty. The poet Lu Yu (1125–1210) alluded to an obviously reprehensible Ts'ai in these lines:

While the sun sets amidst ancient willows on the Chao family estate
An old blind man, drum in hand, tells his tale.
After one's death, who can control the talk?
The whole village listens to the song of Ts'ai Chung-lang.[8]

Several lists of plays from the Chin dynasty (1115–1234) or somewhat later include titles of plays also based on the surnames Ts'ai and Chao. We know these stories were moral tales

that warned against the lure of fame and fortune and the forsaking of family duties. One is described as "The old story of
Po-chieh, who abandoned his parents and forsook his wife
and was killed by a bolt of lightning."[9] A later reference
suggests that the virtuous heroine Chao was killed under the
hooves of her prodigal husband's horse.[10]

As the story developed through time, it took a curious turn.
The villainous Ts'ai, a fictional character, became identified
with a historical figure, Ts'ai Yung (133–192) of the Han dynasty. It was an unjust stigma to place on the highly principled
Ts'ai Yung. He was devoted to his mother, taking care of her
through years of illness and fulfilling the mourning rites of
dwelling for three years by her grave. In sympathetic response
to such filial piety, it was said that Heaven sent tame rabbits
and trees with linked branches to grace her grave.[11] In addition, he was a master of the philosopher's instrument, the
ch'in. This stringed instrument has a special meaning in Chinese culture; the ability to play and compose—or even appreciate—its music is a sign of superior character. Many popular
anecdotes tell of Ts'ai Yung's musical abilities, several of which
are alluded to in The Lute.

Ts'ai Yung was only slightly less honorable in his official career. Like many famous scholars in Chinese history, he went
through occasional periods of reluctance to serve and falls
from grace. But it was only his service to the tyrannical
usurper of the throne, Tung Cho, that tarnished his reputation in history. Although Ts'ai accepted appointment under
him reluctantly, he became a trusted advisor and, according to
popular history, the sole mourner when Tung Cho died. Traditional accounts place no blame on Ts'ai for his actions, but
the people may have seen his role differently. There is evidence that they began to cast blame on Ts'ai for his service to
a tyrant, and this attitude made it more likely that he would
become a villain in popular stories. A Ch'ing critic, Niu Hsiu
(d. 1704), suggests that because Ts'ai Yung's conduct was
flawed by disloyalty (service to a usurper of royal power), dramatic treatments added the stigma of unfilial behavior to his
character. This may well have been a factor, but probably the
more important reason was that Ts'ai Yung's name was well
known to the populace, and it was easy for confusion to arise

between the name of the fictional character Ts'ai Chung-lang
(Ts'ai the second son) and the name and title of Ts'ai Yung,
Ts'ai *Chung-lang-chiang*.

Whatever the reason for it, the fact that Ts'ai Yung had
become a villain in popular literature doubtless influenced
Kao Ming's creation of *The Lute*. The reputation of an honorable scholar-official had been unjustly defiled with the crime
of unfilial conduct, and I believe Kao Ming was moved to clear
his name. He included in his play a number of references to
the life of the historical Ts'ai which make it clear, sometimes at
the price of considerable anachronism and weakness of plot,
that the hero of the play is indeed Ts'ai Yung. He lives in
Ch'en-liu, is appointed to the position of *i-lang*, and plays a
ch'in carved from *wu-t'ung* wood salvaged from a stove. The
tame rabbits and trees with linked branches that surround the
graves of Ts'ai's parents at the end of the play are the same
auspicious signs said to grace the grave of Ts'ai Yung's
mother.

Although he based his work on previous plays that cast Ts'ai
Yung as a villain, Kao Ming reinterpreted the story to portray
Ts'ai as a victim of circumstances. If it is true that Kao hoped
to clear Ts'ai Yung's reputation, the play is still far more than
a simple apology; its universal appeal lies in its more subtle
meanings. Earlier fiction and drama concerning Ts'ai and
Chao apparently portrayed the two in absolute terms, as does
much popular literature: one was a heartless villain, the other
a glorious heroine. Kao Ming may have felt the value and
challenge of creating a new interpretation of the story in
which the issues involved could be more honestly explored
and its central characters drawn in a more realistic and humane way.

Our examination of earlier treatments of the story of *The
Lute* leads to a question that has been much debated, particularly by modern critics. Just how much did Kao Ming contrib-
ute to the play that bears his name? Some have gone so far as
to suggest that Kao should be considered not the author, but
merely the reviser of an earlier folk play; they maintain that
he had only to add a number of scenes and modify others in
order to exonerate his hero, and they cite inconsistencies in
the play as proof of his careless editing. As further evidence,

they point to references to popular legend and mythology which they feel Kao himself, as a scholar, should not have included and which must therefore be remnants of the original text.[12] Reading the play itself, with special attention to the author's treatment of inconsistencies of plot and development of artistic unity, is the best way to refute this theory.

THE PLAY AS LITERATURE
ARTISTRY

The Lute's power to move readers is attested to by the fact that it is among the most widely anthologized of Chinese plays. In China, favorite scenes from plays have been traditionally read or performed individually, and *The Lute* contains dozens of scenes whose poetry and humor make them natural selections for such appreciation. But the play also possesses a unique beauty and strength as a whole. This artistic unity, the result of the author's studied creation of structural patterns and images to bind the play together, is Kao Ming's most significant contribution to the form.

Kao Ming's attention to unity is particularly exciting for its application to the *ch'uan-ch'i* form—a form not compatible with, for example, the tightness that rules Greek drama. The length of the plays encouraged discursiveness. Further, because the most valued element in a play was its songs, authors sometimes designed scenes less for their relevance to the plot than as settings for the type of songs they wished to compose. For example, a number of plays include scenes of celebration that are not really called for by the plot; when such plays were performed at holiday parties, as was the custom, the audience's festive mood would have risen as the actors on stage urged each other to drink and make merry. A final obstacle to unity was the origin of many of the plots in legend or popular history. Authors of the essentially rational and down-to-earth plays were often at pains to explain the fantastic elements in the stories they used. And the *ch'uan-ch'i* writers had little to draw upon for models of artistic unity in fictional works; the novels of the time and even later are notably episodic in form and style.

The Lute's characteristic unity begins with its basic structure, a pattern of alternating scenes that contrast the life of Ts'ai in the capital with that of his family in Ch'en-liu. Again and again, the author sets scenes of their suffering in hunger and fear against Ts'ai's life of luxury. In Scene Nine, Ts'ai is toasted at the imperial feast of congratulation; in Scene Ten, his family begins to suffer from famine. In Scene Eighteen, Ts'ai marries the prime minister's daughter in a lavish ceremony; in Scenes Nineteen and Twenty, the famine in Ch'en-liu reaches a terrible intensity, and Mother Ts'ai dies. In Scene Twenty-five, Ts'ai rejoices at the news in a forged letter that his family is well; in fact, his father has died in the preceding scene.

This contrasting pattern at once provides a structure for the long play and underscores its emotional force—Ts'ai's abandonment of his family to ever-increasing suffering. Much of its power comes from the author's use of dominant symbols and images that reoccur throughout the play to express the bitter gulf between life in capital and at home. Particularly forceful are his concrete symbols of food and clothing and images that relate to rise and fall or heights and depths.

In the second scene, Ts'ai's parents urge him to "climb to the clouds," a conventional metaphor for reaching a high position. In Scene Eight, Wu-niang sings:

> You may ascend to the high clouds;
> I only fear your parents are returning to the yellow earth.

This contrast between ethereal heights and earthy depths is constant throughout the play. Sometimes it is framed in literary clichés: Ts'ai plucks the cassia in the moon (passes the examinations), marries the moon goddess (Mistress Niu), and soars like the *p'eng* bird over a span of thousands of miles (wins success effortlessly). His family, meanwhile, faces the threat of dying and becoming corpses in the ditches or descending to the Yellow Springs beneath the earth. The symbolic contrast is also embodied in dramatic situations. In Scene Twenty-six, Wu-niang carries dirt in her skirt to build the grave mound where her parents-in-law lie buried; in the following scene, Ts'ai and his second wife admire the full moon in the luminously clear sky of mid-autumn.

Symbols and images relating to food pervade the play. They are especially moving because of their concrete relation to its most crucial events and themes: it is starvation that most threatens the Ts'ai family during the son's absence, whereas Ts'ai's new status rewards him with exotic and expensive foods (camels' humps and bears' claws). The famous twentieth scene, in which Wu-niang compares her husband to fine grains of rice and herself to the worthless husks she eats to maintain her strength, gains much of its poignancy from its relation to the actual diets of the two.

Kao Ming also makes frequent explicit contrasts in which food is the central symbol. In Scene Nine, Ts'ai is stricken with guilt at the thought of his family's poverty while he is being treated to a lavish feast:

> As cups are passed, my heart's stricken by its old pain.
> The wine may be sweet—but how hard to swallow!
> They—all alone with no one to offer even pulse and water;
> I—here amid the clamor of passing cups.

In the following scene, Mother Ts'ai reminds her husband of how he wanted Ts'ai's rise to high position, the fruits of which he assumed the whole family would enjoy:

> You planned that the three sacred meats and five tripods we'd be
>   offering day and night;
> And now who will bring you a single sip of rice soup?

A key duty of filial piety is to supply one's parents with food, and these symbols and images thus gain added significance. Ts'ai's failure as a son is most often expressed as his failure to save his parents from hunger, while Wu-niang's heroism lies above all in her struggle to find food for them. Mistress Niu suffers her own failure as a daughter-in-law as being unable to offer her parents-in-law "even a single cup of tea." It is not hunger alone that kills Mother and Father Ts'ai, but the pain they feel at Ts'ai's neglect and Wu-niang's sacrifices. Mother Ts'ai dies, stricken by guilt, when she realizes she has wrongly accused Wu-niang of hoarding food; Father Ts'ai refuses medicine both because his son is not there to taste it first (as decreed in the Book of Rites) and because he is ashamed to accept it when Wu-niang has only husks to eat.

Clothing is no less pervasive a symbol in the play; not as essential to the survival of the Ts'ai family as food, it is used primarily as an expression of status. Ts'ai's success—both in dream and in reality—is often represented by his change of attire. He dons new green robes (clothing of a successful candidate), is wrapped in purple with a belt of gold (noble attire), and longs to return to his hometown wearing brocade (a triumphant native son). His devotion to a humble life of filial service is meanwhile expressed in his desire to wear the motley clothes of Old Lai (to provide amusement for his parents) and keep to scholar's cap and robes. Wu-niang's poverty is embodied in her cotton skirt and thorn hairpin, as is her loneliness in her bridal gowns growing dusty through lack of use. Clothing symbols, like those relating to food and rise and fall, are a means by which the author builds a structure of contrast between the capital and Ch'en-liu.

These dominant symbols and images reach their full power in the final scenes of the play. *The Lute,* despite its happy ending, with a grand reunion and the imperial commendation customary to *ch'uan-ch'i* plays, leaves a feeling of underlying tragedy not often found in Chinese drama. Although Ts'ai and his two wives are left to a life of comfort and harmony, Kao Ming does not allow the audience to forget the sadness of the deaths of Mother and Father Ts'ai; this sadness is conveyed through a return to the pervasive images of the play. In two final scenes, set at the graves of Ts'ai's parents, Ts'ai and his two wives mourn over the tragic contrast between the son's rise to fame and fortune and his parents' fall to death beneath the ground. Ts'ai sings to them:

> Because I was unable to return to my hometown,
> You have had to return to the yellow earth.

Images of food also reoccur to call up the suffering the parents endured. Wu-niang sings in Scene Forty:

> What value have these offerings to the dead?
> If only we had been able to offer food to the living!

The three refuse wine offered by their neighbor Chang, ashamed to drink when they reflect on the parents' starvation. Finally, the clothing motif serves to emphasize how tragically different was the outcome of Ts'ai's trip to the examinations than that for which the family had planned:

So sad to see how, dressed in faded hemp, he bows before the
grave!
He wasn't able "in clothes of brocade to return to his hometown."

To this dominant structure of contrast is added a second
pattern; seasonal imagery underlies the play and also contrib-
utes to its unity. Descriptions of the seasons not only relate to
the thematic contrast between the capital and Ch'en-liu, but
also dramatically express the main action of the play—the decline in happiness and fortune of the Ts'ai family.

The action of *The Lute* takes place over a period of about
eight years, but the author depicts a single cycle of seasons.
The play opens in spring, the first season of the Chinese year
and a time filled with as many joyful connotations in Chinese
culture as in the West. Scene Two depicts an idyllic celebration
in beautiful weather as the Ts'ai family congratulate one another on their good health and domestic happiness. This is the
image of humble contentment to which the later develop-
ments of the play provide a bleak contrast.

In the next scene, set in the Niu residence, spring is about
to pass. While the servants frolic in the garden, making the
most of their brief gift of freedom and the fine weather,
Mistress Niu, following the dictates of her strict upbringing,
shows herself unmoved by the end of spring. The juxtaposi-
tion of the Ts'ai family's lighthearted enjoyment of spring and
Mistress Niu's aloofness from its beauty introduces the contrast between the capital and Ch'en-liu that is so central to the
play. At the same time, the passage of spring suggests the
beginning of the falling action of the play and, appropriately,
it is in this scene that the origin of the tragedies is in-
troduced—Mistress Niu's marriageable status. Scene Twenty-
two is the next scene dominated by a seasonal mood; Ts'ai
spends a hot summer day in the courtyard of his new father-
in-law playing the *ch'in* to express his grief. The long days and
aimless ennui of summer are an appropriate setting for Ts'ai's
growing passivity as his life in the capital drags on.

Scenes Twenty-six and Twenty-seven occur in autumn and
again present contrasts between the capital and Ch'en-liu. In
the former, Wu-niang, alone in the mountains, buries her
parents-in-law; the withered trees and chill winds of autumn
intensify her loneliness. In the latter, Mistress Niu persuades

her new husband to admire the beautiful light of the mid-
autumn moon as they drink fine wine brought by their servants. The cycle of seasons ends as Ts'ai and his wives mourn
by his parents' grave in Scene Forty. The bitter cold of winter
accentuates their grief, while the white snow that covers everything suggests the expiation of Ts'ai's sin of unfilial conduct.

In each scene, seasonal images underscore the mood and
themes of the action. But the cycle of seasons is equally important in providing a symbolic statement of the tragic development of the play as a whole and in forming an underlying pattern that unifies the work.

Appreciation of the artistic unity of *The Lute* will help to
clarify Kao Ming's position as true author of the present play.
However, critics who maintain that he merely patched up an
earlier play were less troubled by any lack of artistic qualities
in the work than by a number of serious flaws in the plot.
Readers of the translation will undoubtedly notice these weaknesses, and some prior discussion may be helpful.

The most serious flaw in the plot—for it weakens the very
core of the motivation of the play—is Ts'ai's failure to send
help, or even news, to his family during his long stay in the
capital. No matter how great the distance, the celebrated First
Winner could easily have found a friend or paid a messenger
to take word home. And Ch'en-liu was actually only a few
hundred miles from the capital, not the thousands of miles the
characters in the play always sigh over. Here is an example of
the problems that arose from the unusual motivation of the
author in composing this play—to clear his hero of a crime he
had never committed. Kao Ming named Ch'en-liu as the
hometown of the Ts'ai family because the historical Ts'ai
Yung had come from there. But Kao Ming did his best to alle-
viate such weaknesses. Ts'ai's constant laments at the difficulties of communication are supported by the action of the play.
As early as Scene Six, Kao prepares for the difficulty when
Ts'ai tells Wu-niang that he fears letters may not get through.
Once in the capital, Ts'ai spends his life in abject fear of his
new father-in-law, afraid to confide even in his upright new
wife. When he does finally try to send a letter and money
home, he is cheated by the messenger. Even the powerful
Prime Minister Niu and his daughter find it impossible to cor-

respond during her stay in Ch'en-liu. And the arduous journeys of Wu-niang, Li Wang, and Niu make the distance a concrete hardship that gives meaning to Ts'ai's complaints. Kao Ming's intention was to portray his hero as a truly filial son helpless to carry out his deepest ideals, rather than as the hypocritical weakling modern critics sometimes call him.

Other, less serious, inconsistencies—Prime Minister Niu's insistance on marrying his daughter to a man who is unwilling, and the ambiguity about whether he knows Ts'ai is already married; Ts'ai's failure to recognize that the fake letter he receives is not in his father's handwriting—can be explained similarly as problems with which the author failed to deal adequately in recasting an old story in a new form.

Though the play's unity is one of its unique strengths as an innovative work in its genre, the author's attention to variety of effect should also be noted. He makes full use of the *ch'uan-ch'i* form's wide range of techniques for maintaining audience interest through the long plays: shifts in level of language used (either to highly literary parallel prose or colloquial speech full of slang phrases); development of miniature comic plots or subplots; and relaxation of the serious mood through, for example, comic or lyric passages. His use of comic passages is perhaps the best example of Kao Ming's skill in creating variety. He includes lengthy passages in Scenes Three, Six, Nine, Eleven, Sixteen, Twenty-one, Twenty-five, Thirty-three, and Forty-one. Comic relief is thus quite evenly distributed in the first half of the play, intervals between such passages ranging from two to five scenes, and then considerably reduced during the second half, providing only occasional release from the tragic events that are unfolding.

THE MEANING OF THE PLAY

Truly, a tale without moral teaching,
No matter how finely written, is useless.

Surely these often quoted lines from the prologue of *The Lute* give us the right to expect that this play, composed with such skill, expresses some important views of its author.

An initial search for such moral teaching is somewhat frustrating. Chinese drama, on the whole, follows the principle of retribution; reward of the good and punishment of the bad demonstrates the standards of morality on which these plays are based. In *The Lute*, however, it is difficult to name a villain—and even more difficult to find one who suffers punishment. Ts'ai Po-chieh, the original villain of earlier plays and stories, is a passive victim of circumstances rewarded in the end with a bright future as a high official and husband of two devoted wives. Father Ts'ai, who ordered his son to attend the examinations, is portrayed sympathetically, most movingly in his loving concern for Wu-niang. It is Prime Minister Niu, of course, who is most responsible for the tragedy of the Ts'ai family because of his insistence on keeping Ts'ai in the capital; his overbearing and snobbish nature qualify him for the villain's role. But he too has redeeming qualities—love of his daughter, dedication to public service, and a change of heart that leads him to repent of his past errors. Although he suffers because of the separation from his daughter, the play ends happily for him as well with his daughter and Ts'ai about to return to the capital to resume the life he had planned for them. Blame for the suffering and death of the Ts'ai family is not squarely placed on any one person.

To understand something of the author's philosophy, we must look to the play's more subtle themes. Another line of the prologue which states that the author wishes his play to be judged on the basis of whether "sons are filial, wives are true" is a better starting point.

The Lute has generally been considered to be a play about filial piety. Discussion of it, by both traditional and modern critics, has often focused on the issue of whether Ts'ai Po-chieh actually deserves the title "filial son" bestowed on him by the author. It is clear that, despite Kao Ming's failure to solve some problems in Ts'ai's motivation remaining from earlier popular treatments in which he was portrayed as a villain, the thrust of the play is a demonstration of Ts'ai's filial devotion and its ultimate fulfillment. A more complex question remains—the *nature* of filial piety. *The Lute's* conflicts are between different interpretations of this virtue so important in traditional Chinese culture.

Two major conflicts in definition of filial piety underlie the play. The first is between the duty of obedience to one's parents and that of reproving them when they are in error, even acting against their will when necessary for their own good. Ts'ai alludes to a saying of Confucius, "In serving his father and mother a man may gently remonstrate with them," as support for his resistance to his father's command to attend the examinations, but finally submits with filial obedience, even though he fears his absence will imperil the lives of his parents.

A second conflict is more fully developed and lies at the heart of the play. Ts'ai and Wu-niang both believe that the essence of filial piety is personal care of one's parents; Ts'ai quotes both the Book of Rites and Confucius: "Every son should warm his parents' bed in winter and cool it in summer, at evening settle them in bed and in the morning inquire after them"; "As long as his parents are alive, he doesn't travel far away." To Father Ts'ai and neighbor Chang, the greatest filial piety is to bring glory to one's family by winning fame and fortune. Father Ts'ai also finds confirmation in the classics, quoting the Book of Filial Piety: "Establishing oneself in the world and practicing the way of right so that one's fame is known to later generations is the means of bringing glory to our parents; it is the culmination of filial piety." Ts'ai finally submits to his father's command and leaves to pursue the fame and wealth demanded by the second definition of filial piety.

The play provides no resolution to the conflicts it presents. The search for fortune and fame to bring glory to one's parents is never firmly condemned; even Wu-niang, in Scene Thirty-three, appreciates the desire of parents for their son's worldly success. But the emotional force of the play is strongly on the side of the humble life spent at home in service to one's parents. Wu-niang's appeal to our sympathies in her courageous struggle and the contrast between the family's suffering and the son's life of luxury make the second concept of filial piety—raising the family status by becoming an official—seem hollow.

Kao Ming's attention to the question of the proper conduct of women, though not as important a theme as a son's filial duties, is also interesting in its study of conflicts. The word *hsien*, translated in the line from the prologue quoted above as "true," actually has a much broader meaning. Applied to women, it denotes not only faithfulness and propriety, but also the fulfillment of duties toward husband and parents-in-law. The play embodies two conflicts in the fulfillment of these duties.

In much the same way as sons, women have a duty to be deferential toward parents, husbands, and parents-in-law, and the conflicting duty to remonstrate with them when they are in the wrong. Wu-niang rebukes her husband for deciding to leave for the capital and even considers arguing with her parents-in-law. Mistress Niu dares not discuss her reservations about marrying Ts'ai with her father, but she is bold enough to berate Ts'ai for his unfilial conduct and reprove her father for refusing to let the two of them go to Ch'en-liu.

A second conflict Wu-niang alone must face is between the propriety of remaining secluded at home and the demand to provide for one's parents-in-law. Wu-niang breaks the rule of seclusion several times. She is scolded by an official when she comes to request grain from the public storehouse, but, although trembling with shame, she knows that her impropriety cannot be condemned: "The rule of seclusion is for ordinary times—what point to speak of it now?" Her trip to the capital, traveling thousands of miles unchaperoned, is most unseemly—and has been criticized by traditional commentators such as Li Yü—but is the only way she can bring her husband back to the parental grave.[13] Unlike the conflicts over filial piety, the play shows little ambiguity about the author's attitude toward the conduct of the two heroines. It is clear that he applauds both their outspoken criticism of husband and father and Wu-niang's bold struggles to save her parents-in-law and bring her husband home.

The rewards and hardships of official service are another subject that the author explores with some complexity. On the one hand, official service is a noble duty toward emperor and country. Chang Ta-kung emphasizes this aspect when urging Ts'ai to attend the examinations, as does the emperor in his denial of Ts'ai's petition to leave office. The officials who actually appear, however, do little to earn respect. Prime Minister Niu is dictatorial and snobbish. Successful candidates in the examinations brag of their plagiarism and use of substitutes to

pass. The head of Ch'en-liu oppresses the poor, steals grain
from the public storehouse, and complains, in turn, of vic-
timization by higher officials. The lofty ideals of public service
expounded by Chang and the emperor are certainly not seen
in action.

For the officials themselves, a government career is a mixed
blessing. The comforts Father Ts'ai imagines for his son do
indeed become a reality and are sumptuously depicted in such
scenes as that in which Ts'ai is feted for his success. But official life is not always glamorous. Ts'ai's unhappiness in his
new life is caused only partly by the guilt and worry he feels
over his family; in Scene Twenty-nine, he sings of the con-
straints and tension of official life, while in Scene Thirty-six he
complains of the lack of leisure to pursue the occupation he
still loves most, study. By comparison, the simple country life
Ts'ai and his family enjoyed in Scene Two seems idyllic. Even
though the play ends with Ts'ai about to resume his career, its
dominant feeling is a strong distrust of the official life. The
main action of the play—the suffering and death of his
mother and father—is, after all, indirectly caused by Ts'ai's absence. This is a most forceful indictment of a government career.

Kao Ming's scepticism of traditional ideals is further expressed in his characteristic mocking of conventional clichés.
Most frequent are ironic references to the happiness study
and success in the examinations are supposed to bring. The
most common cliché, "He returns to his hometown in brocade," expresses the dream of every young man living in obscurity to return in triumph from the examinations. Ts'ai wins
the greatest success in the examinations, but the clothes he
wears on his return are mourning robes. Similarly, a maxim
quoted several times exhorts young men to apply themselves
to study; books, it says, are the key to attaining wealth, fame,
and beautiful women. Again, Ts'ai achieves all that the maxim
promises, but in Scene Thirty-six, he realizes that his very excellence at study has cost him all he held most dear.

The author also mocks the traditional romantic ideal of the
perfect match between "brilliant man and beautiful lady," as
exemplified in a marriage between a high-ranking winner in
the examinations and a young lady from a powerful family in

the capital. In the prologue, Kao Ming mentions stories based
on such marriages in a disparaging manner, and the play viv-
idly depicts the strained relations between the "ideal young
couple," Ts'ai and Mistress Niu.

Like many of the *ch'uan-ch'i* writers, Kao Ming maintains a
strong respect for the moral sense of the younger generation;
The Lute ends with their victory over the mistaken demands of
their elders. Father Ts'ai comes to accept his blame in sending
Ts'ai to the examinations, though too late to save his own life,
and Prime Minister Niu repents both of forcing Ts'ai and his
daughter into marriage and of refusing to let them return to
Ch'en-liu.

Ch'uan-ch'i plays are, after all, written to be wept and
laughed over, loved as much for their music and poetry as for
the stories they tell. We need not demand of this play a concrete moral or complete philosophy. But we can find and appreciate qualities of the author's mind characteristic of him.
Humane, broad-minded, and independent, Kao Ming took a
simple story originally cast in terms of absolute right and
wrong and created a play that explores the complexity of the
issues involved. Conflicts between different interpretations of
traditional morality are sensitively drawn, and one of the most
important goals of the Chinese scholar, official success, is
questioned. He points to the potential hollowness of traditional ideals and gives moral victory to the younger generation.

THE CONTRIBUTIONS OF KAO MING

The Lute was long considered to be the prototype of the
ch'uan-ch'i form, and Kao Ming the creator of that form. But
study has shown that the genre was probably already well established at the time *The Lute* was written. Four other major
plays identical in form and style remain to us from that
period, and three extant southern plays that precede *The Lute*
are clear forerunners of the form.[14]

Kao Ming's contributions are, nevertheless, of major significance. Although other plays contemporaneous with *The Lute*
embodied morals, only Kao Ming stated that this was the main
purpose of drama. And his play is without doubt the most

serious of the early *ch'uan-ch'i* plays. Only in *The Lute* are the issues on which the conflict centers explored in a complex way (the meaning of filial piety and the social forces that block its fulfillment), and only in *The Lute* does severe and irrevocable loss occur (the death of Ts'ai's parents, the tragedy of which underlies the last scene of the play). Kao Ming developed a form for entertainment into a vehicle for the expression of serious themes. He also raised the artistic level of the genre. He was innovative in his creation of methods to unify his play; no other early *ch'uan-ch'i* drama uses the sustained imagery and structural patterns that bind *The Lute* into a cohesive whole.

The play is also a skillful synthesis of literary and colloquial diction. This combination has been the subject of some criticism, both laudatory and pejorative; while some critics praise the poetic heights of such scenes as that in which Ts'ai expresses his sorrow through a series of learned allusions to stories about the *ch'in*, others feel that the most valuable scenes are those using the simple language of the people, such as the famous scene in which Wu-niang forces herself to eat rice husks. Whatever their relative merits, Kao Ming was able effectively to combine elements that appealed to the people and those that were prized by a learned, sophisticated audience.

The composition of *The Lute* did not represent the birth of the *ch'uan-ch'i* form. But Kao Ming expanded its potential for the artistic expression of serious moral themes, thus bringing it to a new stage in its maturation.

ON THE TRANSLATION

For my translation I used the excellent text edited by Ch'ien Nan-yang, published in Shanghai in 1960. As well as being carefully annotated, this edition is based on what is widely accepted as the most authentic copy of the original play, the Ch'ing scholar Lu I-tien's handwritten copy of a Yüan edition.

Some explanation of the conventions used in traditional Chinese play texts, as well as the modifications I have made, may be useful to the reader.

Of the three elements of the text—speech, song, and stage directions—the first requires little explanation. Various types of speech, such as parallel prose and poetry, are not labeled as such in the text, but I have identified the parallel prose with a small ornament to give the reader a clear sense of the texture of the original. Poems in the *tz'u* form, originally a musical one, have traditional titles indicated in the Chinese texts and given here in romanization.

Titles are also included for the tunes of the songs, and there are a number of variations which should also be mentioned. It is common for *ch'uan-ch'i* plays to present a series of songs written to the same tune but using different lyrics. I have indicated the title at the first occurrence only, using the designation "same tune" for subsequent songs. Where the form of the tune has been altered slightly in its opening phrases, I use the designation "same tune with a modified opening." Since the traditional titles for the songs and *tz'u* generally are unrelated to the lyrics used in the play, I have not translated those titles.

Several more complicated singing arrangements are also indicated in the translation. When one character sings part of a song and a second character then takes over, I have used the phrase "CHARACTER (*continues the song*)." Sometimes each song in a sequence, sung to the same tune, is followed by a brief chorus in which all characters join; for this I have used the phrase "They repeat the chorus above" for each repetition. Songs are often interrupted with prose dialogue. When a second character breaks into a song with a short spoken comment, both the character's name and the spoken part are set off in parentheses.

Understanding of the stage directions used in the text requires some knowledge of the Chinese system of role types. Actors are classified into a number of types according to the nature of the roles they play. The actors used in *The Lute*, a description of the type of role played, and the characters they assume in the play are listed below:

Sheng. Male lead, generally young (Ts'ai Po-chieh).
Tan. Female lead, always young (Chao Wu-niang).
Wai. Secondary male role, usually an older man (Father Ts'ai; Prime Minister Niu).
Ching. Secondary or subordinate role, male or female; often comic (Mother Ts'ai, Mu-mu, many minor characters).

Ch'ou. Subordinate role, male or female; generally comic (Hsi-ch'un, village head, many minor characters).
Mo. Subordinate male role and stage manager (Steward, eunuch, many minor characters).
T'ieh-tan. Secondary female role, always young (Mistress Niu).

It is these role titles, rather than the name of the character being played, that are used in the stage directions. For the sake of clarity, I have amended these directions; at the first entrance of an actor I give both the name of the character he or she is playing and the role title, and in subsequent appearances only the name of the character.

A second modification I made was to place tune titles within the parentheses that indicate the stage directions; in the original, these titles are placed above the *tz'u* or song being performed. I have also sometimes combined several stage directions into one set when the original text listed them separately.

One feature of the stage directions I have been careful not to alter. Although specific actions, such as crying and falling down, are sometimes noted in the original text, the majority of the directions are indicated by the single word *chieh*. I have translated this as "with a gesture" or "performs an action," avoiding the temptation to supply more specific directions that may be suggested by the context of the play.

Two problems of translation require special discussion. The first is the wide variety of titles and modes of address used in the play. I have been rather free in translating these; for example, I have used the title "sir" for a number of different polite forms of address and have eliminated one personal style of address (*Niang-tzu,* meaning "young girl," for Wu-niang). Passages involving Wu-niang and her parents-in-law presented a special problem. The terms for in-laws often proved too cumbersome in lines of poetry and too formal in direct address. I often substituted "father," "mother," and "daughter," which are more effective in expressing the closeness of the relationship between a married woman and her husband's parents, with whom she lives, and also better fit the syntax of poetry. Finally, married women were often called by their maiden names. The daughter of Prime Minister Niu is consistently called Niu Hsiao-chieh (Miss Niu) even after her marriage to Ts'ai; I have adopted the term "mistress" for this usage.

The Chinese language is rich with set phrases, the use of which would often make little impression on the native reader; the question always remains as to how literally such phrases should be translated. Although it may seem that I have been somewhat too explicit in rendering what are often mere clichés, in many cases a literal rendition seemed desirable to preserve the parallelism used in the original or the effectiveness of a series of related images.

NOTES

1. The papers and discussions of a conference held in 1956 to discuss the social and artistic significance of the work were published in book form. Much of the argument centered around the question of where Kao Ming's sympathies lay—with the common people or the aristocracy. See Chü-pen yüeh-k'an she (Drama society monthly), *P'i-p'a chi t'ao-lun chuan-k'an* (Special volume on the discussion of *P'i-p'a chi*) (Peking: Jen-min wen-hsüeh ch'u-pan-she, 1956).

2. I have adopted the translation "lute" for the *p'i-p'a* from previous translations. A small stringed instrument, the *p'i-p'a* is now most commonly translated as "guitar" or "balloon guitar."

3. "Some Concerns and Methods of the Ming *Ch'uan-ch'i* Drama," in Cyril Birch, ed., *Studies in Chinese Literary Genres* (Berkeley: University of California Press, 1974), p. 229.

4. The other four are *Yu-kuei chi* (Ladies' secluded chambers) by Shih Hui (late Yüan); *Sha-kou chi* (A dog is killed) by Hsü Chen (fl. 1368); *Ching-ch'ai chi* (The thorn hairpin), attributed to K'o Tan-ch'iu (late Yüan); and *Pai-t'u chi* (The white rabbit) by an anonymous writer of the late Yüan period.

5. These fragments of southern plays are collected and discussed in Ch'ien Nan-yang, *Sung Yüan hsi-wen chi-i* (Reconstruction of play texts of the Sung-Yüan period) (Shanghai: Shanghai ku-tien wen-hsüeh ch'u-pan-she, 1956), and Lu K'an-ju and Feng Yüan-chün, *Nan-hsi shih-i* (Reconstruction of fragments of southern drama) (Peking: Harvard-Yenching Institute, 1936).

6. The primary source for this biography of Kao Ming is Ch'ien Nan-yang's documented biography in his edition of the *P'i-p'a chi* (Shanghai: Chung-hua shu-chü, 1960), pp. 231–44.

7. Kao Ming's extant poetic works are included in *P'i-p'a chi t'ao-lun chuan-k'an*, pp. 334–48.

8. The poem "Hsiao chou yu chin-ts'un" (Traveling by small boat to a nearby town) is in *Lu Fang-weng shih chi* (The poetry of Lu Yu) (Shanghai: Commercial Press, 1929), *chüan* 19.

9. Hsü Wei (1521–1593), *Nan-tz'u hsü-lu* (Notes on southern drama), in

Chung-kuo ku-tien hsi-ch'ü lun-chu chi-ch'eng (Collection of studies of classical Chinese drama), 10 vols. (Peking: Chung-kuo hsi-chü ch'u-pan-she, 1959), 3:245.

10. A modern P'i-huang play alludes to Wu-niang-tzu, who was denied by her husband when she reached the capital and who "met with the horses' hooves." See *Hsiao shang fen* in *Hsi-k'ao* (Drama study) (Shanghai: China Library, 1916).

11. Ts'ai Yung's biography is in *chüan* 90 of the *History of the Latter Han.*

12. Chao Ching-shen is the most convincing advocate of this theory in *Yüan Ming nan-hsi k'ao-lüeh* (Research on Yüan-Ming southern drama) (Peking: Tso-chia ch'u-pan-she, 1958), pp. 49–52; a number of the participants at the 1956 conference on the play also supported this theory.

13. Li Yü (1611–1679), *Li-li-weng ch'ü-hua* (Comments on plays by Li Yü) (Shanghai: Ch'i-chih shu-chü, 1927), p. 12.

14. These three plays, recently discovered as part of the imperial compilation of 1408, *Yung-lo ta-tien,* are discussed most fully in Tadeusz Zbikowski, *Early Nan-hsi Plays of the Southern Sung Period* (Warsaw: Wydawnictwa Uniwersytetu Warszarskiego, 1974).

THE LUTE

Titles:[1]
The rich and exalted Prime Minister Niu
The kind and just Chang Kuang-ts'ai
The pure and constant Chao Chen-nü[2]
The loyal and filial Ts'ai Po-chieh

[1] The function of the titles (*t'i-mu*) is unclear. In later *ch'uan-ch'i*, they were often placed at the end of the first scene or at the end of the play; late editions of *The Lute* place these titles at the end of the first scene, where they become the closing poem.
[2] The designations *kuang-ts'ai* and *chen-nü* are never used in the text of the play. The neighbor Chang is always referred to by the respectful title *Ta-kung*. The *Morohashi Dictionary* defines the term *kuang-ts'ai* as equivalent to *hsiu-ts'ai*, holder of the first degree. While the descriptive title *chen-nü* (virtuous woman) appears nowhere else in the play, it does appear in the title of an earlier play on the same subject, *Chao Chen-nü Ts'ai Erh-lang* (The virtuous woman Chao and Second Son Ts'ai). Perhaps Kao Ming has retained the original titles from that play.

SCENE ONE

(*The* mo *actor enters and recites to the* tz'u Shui-tiao ko-t'ou):

An autumn lantern brightens kingfisher blue curtains.
By my night table I look through rue-scented volumes.
From today back to ancient times,
So many kinds of tales!
Countless romances of beautiful ladies and brilliant men,
Miraculous immortals, mysterious demons—
All trifling stories worthless to read.
Truly, a tale without moral teaching,
No matter how finely written, is useless.
As for plays,
To please people is easy,
To influence them hard.
But those who deeply understand
Will look with different eyes.
Don't be concerned with the clowning and jokes,
Nor examine the modes and count up the tunes.
Consider only whether sons are filial, wives are true.
Hua-liu has just galloped forth alone;
What common horse would dare to join the race?[3]

(*He recites to the* tz'u Ch'in-yüan ch'un):

The beauty Mistress Chao,
The scholar Ts'ai Yung,[4]
Had been husband and wife but two months.
Then yellow placards summoned the wise scholars of the land.
His parents' strict command
Forced him to attend the capital examination.
In one try, First Winner in the land,
He took a second wife, Mistress Niu;
Bound by fame and profit, he did not return.
In years of famine
His parents both perished.
How pitiful it was!
How pitiful Mistress Chao in her struggle!

[3] Hua-liu was one of the famous steeds of King Mu of the Chou dynasty, reputed to be able to run a thousand *h* in one day (a *h* is equivalent to about a third of a mile).

[4] Yung is the given name of the hero, Po-chieh his *tzu* or courtesy title.

She cut off her perfumed hair to provide burial for her parents-
    in-law,
And carried earth in her skirt
To erect the grave mound.
Expressing her sorrows on a lute,
She journeyed to the capital city.
Filial indeed was Po-chieh!
How virtuous was Mistress Niu!
So moving was the meeting in the study!
They dwelt in a mourning hut by his parents' grave,
The man and his two wives,
And imperial commendation brought glory to their home.[5]

---

[5] Prologues like this in which the author makes a general philosophic statement and gives a rough outline of the plot became standard features of *ch'uan-ch'i* plays.

SCENE TWO

TS'AI PO-CHIEH (*played by the* sheng *actor, enters and sings to the tune* Jui-ho hsien):

Ten years now I've kept company with a study lamp.
For brilliant talent and profound learning,
Don't sing the praises of the illustrious Pan and Ma.[1]
And now the forces of the cosmos being all in tune,
It's time for Hua-liu to gallop forth,
And fish to be transformed to dragons.[2]
I sink in thought:
How could I leave my parents' side?
With all my heart I'll serve them,
Merit, fame, wealth, and rank
I'll leave to Heaven's will.

(*He recites to the* tz'u Che-ku t'ien):

Hardly worthy of praise, the great talent of Sung Yü,[3]
And Tzu-yün's scholarly fame is far too high.[4]
Already the star of literature K'uei casts its rays over thirty
    thousand feet,[5]
And the *p'eng* bird rides the wind over a span of ninety thousand
    miles.[6]
With the skills of a statesman,
And ability to govern the world,
What difficulty could I have rising to high position in Jade Hall
    and Golden Horse Gate?[7]

[1] Pan Ku (32–92) and Ssu-ma Ch'ien (145–c.86 B.C.) were famous historians of the Han period.
[2] According to legend, fish which were able to pass over the gorges at Ho-chin were transformed into dragons. The phrase is used a number of times in the play to symbolize success in the examinations.
[3] Sung Yü, probably of the third century B.C., is most famous for his descriptive poetry in the classical *fu* form.
[4] Tzu-yün was the *tzu* (courtesy name) of Yang Hsiung (53 B.C.–A.D. 18), famous for literary scholarship.
[5] The star K'uei rules literary endeavor; its radiance is thus an auspicious sign for success in the examinations.
[6] The philosopher Chuang-tzu wrote of a giant *p'eng* bird that could soar to a height of ninety thousand *li.*
[7] The Jade Hall was the name of a government office during the Han period; Golden Horse Gate was the entrance to the imperial palace during the same dynasty.

But to fulfill my desire to amuse my parents as did Old Lai in
    motley clothes[8]
I must keep to my student's cap and carry out a son's duties.

(He continues in parallel prose):

 I'm drunk on the Six Classics and have mastered one by
one the Hundred Philosophers. I've penetrated the
mysteries of everything from ritual and science to each
form of poetry and prose. I've fathomed the essence of all
studies from divination and astrology to music, philology,
and mathematics. My talent for government is
extraordinary, and I live in an enlightened and
prosperous age. "Study in youth and put it into practice in
maturity," it is said, and I long to rise to a position as high
as the clouds a thousand miles up in the sky. But they also
say, "At home, be filial; in society, respectful as a younger
brother," and how could I leave the side of my white-
haired parents? It's better after all to devote myself to my
parents' service, even if I can offer only pulse and water,
and to accept my lot of eating only pickled food and salt.

How true the saying, "Carry out filial piety in your own life
and leave the reward to Heaven." Besides, I delight in my
marriage of two months. My wife, Wu-niang of the Chao
family, is a native of Ch'en-liu. Her manner is elegant and
refined, and her beauty surpasses that of all others. Virtuous
and reserved, she is truly worthy to be entrusted with our
family rites. I rejoice that our marriage is harmonious and
that my father and mother are healthy and content, and I
recall a line from the Book of Poetry, "We make this spring
wine to increase their years."[9] Now I'm happy that my
parents, though aged, are still in good health, so on this spring
day, we drink wine beneath the blossoming trees in
celebration of their long life. I told my wife yesterday to
prepare things, but I'd better hurry her up. Wife, set up the
wine and invite my parents to come out!

[8] Lao Lai-tzu of the Warring States period was a paragon of filial piety; in his seven-
ties himself, he used to dress in variegated clothing and imitate a child at play for the
amusement of his parents.

[9] James Legge, translator and editor, *The Chinese Classics*, 5 vols. (Hong Kong: Hong
Kong University Press, 1960), vol. 4, p. 231 (hereafter 4:231). In this and subsequent
references to the classics, I have used my own translations in the text.

(WU-NIANG, *played by the* tan *actor, answers from backstage.*)

FATHER TS'AI (*played by the* wai *actor, enters and sings to the tune* Pao-ting-erh):

> To our home in a quiet lane
> Spring has brought forth fragrant plants
> And we're at ease on this bright, fine day.

MOTHER TS'AI (*played by the* ching *actor, enters and continues the song*):

> Men grow old, their white hair not as before;
> Spring returns, year after year the same.

WU-NIANG (*enters and continues the song*):

> How delightful—today the new wine's matured,
> Before our eyes, flowers everywhere opening like brocade!

(*They finish the song together*):

> We hope year after year to be together,
> Under the blossoms, pouring out spring wine.

MOTHER and FATHER TS'AI: Son, why did you invite us out?
TS'AI: Though a man's life may last a hundred years, even that is too little time. You two have had the good fortune to live to the age of eighty, and I am "happy yet apprehensive."[10] And now with spring so lovely and nothing to disturb our tranquillity, I wanted to celebrate with you.

MOTHER and FATHER TS'AI: Fine!
TS'AI (*sings to the tune* Chin-t'ang yüeh):

> Through curtained chambers, gentle breezes pass;
> In secluded apartments, daylight lingers.
> Mornings, the air holds a slight chill.
> My parents are still with me;
> I rejoice, but worry too.
> I only hope that my parents, for a hundred years,
> Will be like the flowers and willows of May.

(*They sing the chorus together*):

---

[10] The quotation, from the *Lun-yu* (Analects) of Confucius (Legge, 1:171), expresses the idea that although one is happy about the long life of one's parents, one is also worried over their failing health.

Pour the spring wine!
Listen—under the blossoms, our voices raise in song,
As together we celebrate long life.

WU-NIANG (*sings to the same tune with a modified opening*):

We've joined together
As husband and wife.
A new bride, ever bashful,
I take the cup, aware of my own blush.
I fear I'm not capable of being mistress of the family rites,
And feel unworthy to serve with dustpan and broom.
My only wish is that my husband and I will grow old together,
Always in the service of his aged parents.

(*They repeat the chorus above.*)

FATHER TS'AI (*sings to the same tune with a modified opening*):

White hair covers my head,
Red flowers fill my gaze.
And my heart is shaken by the thought of passing years.
It's only time I fear;
Ever hastening us on, it can't be stopped.
I hope only that yellowing books and blue lamp
Will soon be exchanged for a gold seal tied to purple ribbons.

(*They repeat the chorus above.*)

MOTHER TS'AI (*sings to the same tune with a modified opening*):

And yet, a worry:
By our gate, hidden in bamboo and pine,
Mulberry and elm trees are covered in dusk;
Next year will they still endure?
Alas, the single iris stalk
And solitary cassia flower!
I hope only that those trees with branches linked
Will soon put forth new twigs to grow even stronger than the
    old.[11]

(*They repeat the chorus above.*)

[11] The plant images used in this song are interpreted as follows: Because the sun is traditionally said to sink in mulberry and elm trees, these trees signify evening and thus "the evening years" of one's life. Both the iris stalk and the cassia flower are symbols of children; the lines refer to Ts'ai, an only child. Trees with linked branches are a traditional symbol of a harmonious couple and here represent Ts'ai and Wu-niang. Finally, it is said that the new branches of the *wu-t'ung* tree grow stronger than its trunk; such branches represent worthy descendants.

TS'AI (*sings to the tune* Tsui-weng-tzu):

> I turn my head;
> In a flash the rabbit and crow rush past.[12]

WU-NIANG (*continues the song*):

> I rejoice at the health of our parents,
> And thank Heaven for its protection.

TS'AI (*continues the song*):

> It's true:
> Untroubled, our happiness!
> Who could have greater joy than ours today?

(*They sing the chorus together*):

> Congratulations to all!
> Pour the wine, and raise your voices!
> We celebrate long life.

FATHER and MOTHER TS'AI (*sing to the same tune*):

> However humble,
> A man should bring glory to ancestors and descendants.
> My son, go climb to the clouds,
> Race your horse a thousand miles.

TS'AI (*continues the song*):

> Please listen to my belief:
> Real happiness is found in garden and field;
> What need to be a marquis or duke?

(*They repeat the chorus above.*)

TS'AI and WU-NIANG (*sing to the tune* Chiao-chiao ling):

> Spring blossoms brighten our patterned sleeves;
> Spring wine fills our golden cups.
> Our one desire is year after year to be together.
> Father and mother, husband and wife, each to the other lifts a
>   cup.

FATHER and MOTHER TS'AI (*sing to the same tune*):

> Ever true to each other, the young husband and wife—
> We hope it will last forever.

---

[12] The crow represents the sun, the rabbit the moon; thus, the line describes the rapid passage of time.

Before us the beauty of "blue mountains thrusting blue through
   our door."
And see the rippling of "green brook girding our field with
   green." [13]

(They sing together to the tune Shih-erh shih):

The blue mountains, the green brook, always remain;
The green springtime of a man's life can never return.
So enjoyment is the wisest plan of all!

(Closing poem)
FATHER TS'AI:

Whenever you can, take wine and sing loudly.

MOTHER TS'AI:

Understand that life can't last forever.

TS'AI and WU-NIANG:

Stacks of gold have no real value;
A family's carefree joy is worth far more.

(They exit.)

---

[13] The lines are from a poem, "Shu Hu-yin hsien-sheng pi," (Inscribed on Mr. Hu-yin's wall) by Wang An-shih (1021–1086). See *Wang Lin-ch'uan ch'uan-chi* (The collected works of Wang Lin-ch'uan) (Shanghai: Commercial Press, 1935), *chian* 29, p. 3.

SCENE THREE

STEWARD (*played by the* mo *actor, enters and recites in* shih *form*):

Wind carries incense fragrance through the outer yard;
Sunlight moves flower shadows up the tranquil court.
Days are long, people at leisure and free of care,
All is silent, but for the oriole's cries.

I am a steward in the mansion of Prime Minister Niu. In
wealth and rank, the prime minister fits the poem:

Only Heaven is higher than he;
No mountain is as tall.
When he lifts his head, the red sun is near;
When he turns around, white clouds lie below.

What are his wealth and rank like?

(*He continues in parallel prose*):

 His power dominates the central court and his wealth
could empty the imperial park. Sunlight gleams on his
smooth highway, and frost shines on his painted halberd.[1]
Outside his door flows a river of chariots; within his walls,
the towers of his mansions rise like a range of mountains.
His vermilion towers for viewing the moon are twelve
stories high, and the embroidered curtains that encircle
his beautiful young ladies are fifty miles long.[2] The
elegance of his gardens, filled with perfume and silk, I
can't begin to describe. The splendor of his courtyards,
glimmering with pearls and feathers, I have no words to
express. How delightful it is to ride in his "shiny
lacquered chariot, pulled by a plump golden bull! Within
its tasseled screens, it's so warm that a rooster would think
it a morning in spring."[3] Everybody who moves about in

[1] Special roads were laid for the use of the prime minister and his guests. In T'ang
times, only officials in the three top ranks were permitted to display decorated hal-
berds outside their gates.

[2] The line refers to two men of the Tsin dynasty who competed with each other in
the display of wealth. Both had embroidered curtains made, one man's stretching for
forty *li*, the other's for fifty *li*.

[3] The lines are from the *tz'u* "Ch'un hsiao ch'ü" by Wen T'ing-yün (ninth century).
See P'eng Ting-ch'iu, compiler, *Ch'uan T'ang shih* (Complete T'ang poetry), 12 vols.
(Peking: Chung-hua shu-chü, 1960), *chüan* 577, p. 6708. (*Ch'üan T'ang shih* is
hereafter cited as *CTS.*)

his ornamented halls, goblets of wine in hand, wears
purple ribbons and gold and sable in their hats. And
those arrayed in rows before embroidered screens,
playing flutes and strings, are beautiful ladies adorned
with rouge and powder. On tortoise-shell mats, the
precious incense burns—day after day like the Festival of
Cold Food![4] Within glass doors, silver candles
glow—night after night a Feast of Lanterns!

In such a Paradise, of course there must dwell a divine
beauty lovely as jade. Enough of the wealth and rank of
Prime Minister Niu! Let me tell instead of the virtue of
our young mistress. Her manner is beautiful and graceful,
her lovely face has not a single fault, like a piece of
beautiful jade without one flaw. Retiring and modest, she
has a heart so pure it could never be stained by a speck of
carnal desire, like a piece of clear ice pure to the core.
Though she grew up among piles of pearls and
ornaments, she delights in plain and refined adornment.
From childhood she was surrounded by row upon row of
silk gowns, but she dislikes extravagant display. Sounds of
music and rhyme appall her; her only wish is to sit and
sew. She loves this pure seclusion and remains all day in
the ladies' chambers. She laughs at those who wander in
search of pleasure; even in spring, why would she wish to
leave the inner apartments? When begonia flowers are in
full bloom, she'd never ask, "How many more opened last
night?" Willow catkins may scatter from the trees, but she
won't wonder, "How long will spring remain?" To know
her innermost feelings, there is none but the bright moon
casting its rays through her latticed window. To win a
delicate glance from her eyes, there is only the soft breeze
swaying her kingfisher curtains. She'll never be like Wen-
chün, infatuated with a dashing Ssu-ma Hsiang-ju.[5] Like
Te-yao, she'll choose an upright Po-luan.[6] Most
remarkable of all is her knowledge of ceremony and
literature—a true scholar who's deprived of a chance to
win official rank. Her virtue and deportment should
entitle her to wear the cap of a real gentleman. Truly, the
offspring of a prime minister! If only she were a man!

[4] The Cold Food Festival marks the beginning of the spring Ch'ing Ming holidays
during which family graves are visited. Only cold foods are served on this day.

[5] The young widow Cho Wen-chun eloped with the Han poet Ssu-ma Hsiang-ju
(179–117 B.C.) after hearing him play the *ch'm* at her father's home. She is alluded to
several times in this play as a woman deluded by romance.

[6] The thirty-year-old Meng Te-yao of the Han dynasty, asked why she had never
married, said she was waiting to find a man as worthy as Liang Po-luan. When he
heard of this, he proposed. Here Te-yao is used as an example of a woman who is
prudent in choosing a husband.

But there's no lack of young aristocrats competing for her hand in marriage. Do you understand?

(He recites in shih *form):*

Once the Jade Emperor's immortal scribe,
She was banished to earth by a speck of carnal thought.
Don't wonder at the divine orchid fragrance that pervades her body;
A trace of heavenly incense lingers still in her clothes.

Hey, what's this? How come the old housekeeper, Mu-mu, and the maid, Hsi-ch'un, are dancing by?

MU-MU and HSI-CH'UN (*played by the* ching *and* ch'ou *actors, enter dancing and sing to the tune* Yen-erh wu):

Closed within door after door,
We cannot help but complain.
To seek husbands
We have no way.
When will I be able
With a husband,
Side by side, two by two, to dance the Wild Goose Dance?

STEWARD: How are you, Mu-mu?

MU-MU: Good afternoon, Mr. Steward.

STEWARD: How are you, Miss Hsi-ch'un?

HSI-CH'UN: Good afternoon, Mr. Steward.

STEWARD: Let me ask you something. You never came out to have fun like this before—why are you so happy today?

HSI-CH'UN: You have no idea how my mistress makes me suffer! She won't allow me one carefree step or let me speak a word about men. How I suffer! My lady, maybe *you* don't want a man, but *I* do! She tells me I should be like her and won't even let me laugh. Today Heaven took pity on me. With thousands of schemes and wiles, I persuaded the mistress to give me an hour to play in the garden. Ah! Why shouldn't I be happy?

MU-MU: As for me, how wrong I was not to plant the seeds of good fortune in my former life! That's why fate brought me here as a maid. I can't begin to tell you! I've grown old here, and not one day have I been able to smile. Today the master's away, so I came out to amuse myself a little.

STEWARD: I see. No wonder you're happy!

MU-MU: You, sir, wait on the master—"rooster meets rooster," while I serve the young lady—"hen meets hen."

STEWARD: I think the phrase, "The male phoenix is alone and the female phoenix still single," describes it better. Madame, Hsi-ch'un is young—she can't be blamed for having spring fever. But at your age, how does such talk sound?

MU-MU: You old brute! Don't you know that autumn eggplant bears fruit late? That late bloomers produce flowers in the end? "So I'm old! I'm like a date—the outside's wrinkled, but the inside's good." Don't you know about Old Lady Li of East Village? She was seventy years old, her head completely bald, but her one wish was to marry. People asked her, "Why would an old woman like you want to get married?" She made up a little poem which answered them nicely.

STEWARD: How did it go?

MU-MU:

> To live seventy years has always been rare;
> If I don't marry now, when will I?
> As a new bride, I can let down my hair,
> And see on the bed the big mallet lie.

STEWARD: That's scarcely proper!

HSI-CH'UN: Then there was Old Lady Chang from West Village. She was sixty-nine years old, but one old man saw how good-looking she was and wanted her. She asked him to make up a poem, and he made a good one.

STEWARD: What was it?

HSI-CH'UN:

> Don't let youth pass you by!
> The bed goddess is the bed god's mate.
> Husband and wife within red curtains lie;
> On the pillow two watermelons wait.

MU-MU: Let's stop chattering. Today we managed to get some time to play, and it sure wasn't easy. Now that we've run into the steward here, we should play a game together.

HSI-CH'UN: What game?

MU-MU: Kickball.

STEWARD: No good!

MU-MU and HSI-CH'UN: Why not?

STEWARD (recites to the tz'u Hsi-chiang yüeh):

I was always superb at singles,
And famous since youth at three-man games.
But now I'm old and my legs are sore;
I won't rush around with the club any more.
Why stain fine shirts with sweat?
Or ruin gauze stockings with dust?
Kickball is a sport for lads,
Not for lovely ladies like you.

HSI-CH'UN: How about playing "Grass Fight?"
STEWARD: That's no good either.
MU-MU: Why?
STEWARD (*recites to the previous* tz'u):

You'd tear up the grass growing in fragrant lanes,
Break off the flowers covering carved railings.
If you have not the cunning to move a gentleman's heart,
Why waste all that effort for naught?
You'd arouse delicate orioles and chattering sparrows,
Awaken frivolous butterflies and reckless bees.
And if you should discover those "double-bed pinks,"
How fast your innocent hearts would be led astray![7]

HSI-CH'UN and MU-MU: Let's swing.
STEWARD: Now that's fine!
HSI-CH'UN and MU-MU: Why do you like swinging so much?
STEWARD (*recites to the previous* tz'u):

Sweat like perfume glows on ladies' skin of jade;
Embroidered skirts ripple like bright-colored clouds.
So delicate the lovely hands that grip the rainbow ropes!
What a fine painting such a scene would make!
The game that started among the barbarian tribes in the North
Is now the sport of aristocrats in the imperial park.
Young ladies disorder the blossoms on the wall;
They seem half divine in their play.

HSI-CH'UN and MU-MU: Well then, let's swing! But where is the
swing?
STEWARD: You can't expect to find a swing in this garden! The
master would never permit it, nor would the young mistress
approve. If we ever had one, it would have been dismantled
by now.
HSI-CH'UN: Well, we'll just have to make a swing ourselves

---

[7] The birds, insects, and flowers mentioned all have erotic connotations.

then. We can take turns—two of us will be the swing, and the other ride.

STEWARD: Who's first?

HSI-CH'UN and MU-MU: You go first, sir. We'll be the swing.

(They form a swing for the STEWARD.*)*

MISTRESS NIU *(voice is heard from offstage)*: Mu-mu, where did you put my *Biographies of Virtuous Women*?

*(*MU-MU *and* HSI-CH'UN *release their grip, letting the* STEWARD *fall.)*

STEWARD *(getting up)*: You tricked me!

MU-MU: Now it's my turn.

HSI-CH'UN and STEWARD: Get on, Mu-mu!

(They swing her.)

MISTRESS NIU *(voice is heard again)*: Hsi-ch'un, what have you done with my sewing box?

*(*HSI-CH'UN *and the* STEWARD *release their grip, but* MU-MU *doesn't fall.)*

STEWARD: You two are making a fool of me!

HSI-CH'UN: My turn! Hurry up!

(They swing her.)

MISTRESS NIU *(played by the* t'ieh-tan *actor, enters and says)*: "Don't trust in the virtue of the seemingly virtuous; guard against the evil of those who appear good."

(The STEWARD *and* MU-MU *release their grip and run away.)*

HSI-CH'UN *(not noticing* MISTRESS NIU*)*: Come on! Where have you gone? You're cheating me out of my turn!

MISTRESS NIU *(grabbing* HSI-CH'UN *by the ear)*: You little wretch! You have no self-respect at all. All you ever want is to play around and make a racket.

HSI-CH'UN: But how can people help playing?

MISTRESS NIU: What do you mean?

HSI-CH'UN: You see, even the swing-stand is still jumping about!

MISTRESS NIU: You little wretch! All I said was that you could go out and amuse yourself for a few minutes. Who gave you permission to make such a racket?

HSI-CH'UN: My lady, I am named "Spring Sighs."[8] When I see spring passing, the sadness of spring arises in me; how can I help feeling unhappy?

MISTRESS NIU: What's this sadness of spring that you feel?

HSI-CH'UN (*in parallel prose*):

 At dawn, I saw the cold wind, *su-la-la,* scatter whole curtains of willow down. At noon, I saw the light rain, *hsi-ling-ling,* destroy treefuls of plum blossom. A moment of song from pairs of yellow orioles, then the sudden cry of cuckoos.

Watching such a spring pass, how can I not be unhappy?

MISTRESS NIU: Spring goes as it will. Why should you be unhappy? Let's go in and do some needlework.

HSI-CH'UN: Ah! With weather like this, who wouldn't want to go out and have fun? Now you tell me to go and do needlework. I can't stand it!

MISTRESS NIU: Ladies are not permitted to play games. For us, what is there to do but needlework? Yet you won't follow the standard of keeping to secluded chambers.

HSI-CH'UN: My lady, you have thousands of boxes of fine clothes; pearls and kingfisher feathers cover your head. What do you lack, that you want to give yourself such trouble?

MISTRESS NIU: You little wretch! You find that strange? It was your fate to work for a living. Why concern yourself with what I own or don't own?

HSI-CH'UN: Well then, I'll leave you and go serve somebody else, carry love messages back and forth for her, and get a chance to have some fun myself! While I'm in your service, if a man happens by, you don't even let me raise my eyes. The other day was so fine—flowers red, willows green—it would even have moved the heart of a dog or cat, but *you* weren't moved a bit. Today at the end of spring—birds crying, flowers falling—who wouldn't feel sad? Yet you're not bothered in the least! It's really hard for me to live with you, my lady.

[8]*Hsi-ch'un* translates as "regretting [the passing of] spring."

MISTRESS NIU: You little wretch! Are you crazy? I'll tell my father, and he'll give it to you good.

HSI-CH'UN: Please take pity on me! I'm depressed, and can't help talking this way.

MISTRESS NIU: Don't you see?

(*She sings to the tune* Chu Ying-t'ai chin):

> Green leaves become shade,
> Red petals fall like rain—
> Nothing of spring remains.

HSI-CH'UN (*continues the song*):

> I hear that in the western suburbs,
> Chariots and horses still gallop about.

MISTRESS NIU (*continues the song*):

> Could that compare to our screen of willow down,
> Or this courtyard of pear blossoms?

(*They finish the song together*):

> What beautiful weather, this time of the spring festival!

(*They recite to the* tz'u Yü-lou ch'un):

HSI-CH'UN:

> The spring festival, we begin to wear unlined clothes.
> How can I bear being closed within when days are long, and people at leisure?

MISTRESS NIU:

> My pure heart isn't bothered at all;
> I'm ashamed to watch those drifting cobwebs and flying catkins.

HSI-CH'UN:

> Behind embroidered windows I try to sit and sew,
> But suddenly hear the orioles and sparrows chattering in pairs.

MISTRESS NIU:

> People with cool heads can't relate to so much warmth!
> Just let spring pass as it will!

HSI-CH'UN: Is there any way to put an end to my sadness?

MISTRESS NIU (*sings to the tune* Chu Ying-t'ai hsü):

Take those scenes of late spring,
Cast them off to the river's eastward flow.

(HSI-CH'UN: The cry of birds, the fall of blossoms—it *must* disturb you!)

Though the cuckoo cries itself into old age,
Red flowers fly till trees are bare,
There's no cause for spring depression.

(HSI-CH'UN: If you're not depressed, do you want to go out and have some fun?)

No, never!
Women mustn't leave their secluded chambers;
How could they go seek flowers and thread willows?

(HSI-CH'UN: If you don't go out and have fun, I'm afraid you'll waste away.)

My flowerlike face—
How could I let it waste away because of spring?

HSI-CH'UN (*sings to the same tune with modified opening*):

A spring day:
Just see the swallows fly in pairs,
Butterflies form in rows,
Orioles chatter as if in search of companions.

(MISTRESS NIU: You belong to the human world; why talk about birds and insects?)

But more, beyond the willows, painted wheels,
Under blossoms, carved saddles—
Young men everywhere in search of pleasure.

(MISTRESS NIU: This wretch! You're a woman; why talk about what young men do?)

It's hard to bear—
My lonely room, cold without a man,
And I'm looking for a mate.

(MISTRESS NIU: Wretch! You're actually thinking about men!)

The way you talk,
I must remain single all my life!

MISTRESS NIU (*sings to the same tune with a modified opening*):

Can you understand?
Why is it I don't roll up the pearled screen,
But sit alone, loving this pure solitude?

(HSI-CH'UN: Pure solitude! Pure solitude! How depressing!)

A thousand pecks of depression,
Or a hundred kinds of spring melancholy,
Won't easily weigh down my eyebrows.

(HSI-CH'UN: I suspect you won't always feel like this.)

Don't worry!
Let spring come year after year;
My pure heart will always be the same.

(HSI-CH'UN: I bet a dashing young man will come along and charm you.)

This Wen-chün
Will never be trapped by Hsiang-ju's song.

HSI-CH'UN (*sings to the same tune with a modified opening*):

It will be some time
Before I believe that you're really so pure to the core
And I have no cause to doubt you.

(MISTRESS NIU: Why can't you pull yourself together?)

I think how the evening clouds
Are being cast off to the east wind
And I feel such pain I can't bear to look upon the past!

(MISTRESS NIU: Why don't you follow my example?)

The way I see it,
You're an immortal from Petal Hall or Cornelian Park,
With nothing in common with those of us seduced by the dust of
    the world.

(MISTRESS NIU: Well then, come with me to do some needle-work.)

In respectful attendance,
Under the window, I'll ply the needle, weave the threads.

(*Closing poem*)
MISTRESS NIU:

Don't listen to the cuckoo crying in the tree.

Within me,
Deep in my heart, filial love—
Who can understand it?

CHANG TA-KUNG (*played by the* mo *actor, enters and sings to the same tune):*

We are neighbors to each other,
Depend on each other,
And when anything happens, we come to report to each other.

TS'AI: Chang Ta-kung, how are you?
CHANG: Greetings!

Examination time is near;
Hurry, pack your bags and set out!

TS'AI: My parents are old; I mustn't leave.
CHANG *(laughs):*

Though the son worries over his parents, old and alone,
The parents' one wish is for their son to win glory.

Sir,

Seize this chance!
If you don't attend the examinations in your youth,
When can you ever attend?

If you're really unwilling to go, let's wait until your parents come out and see what they say. I'm sure they'll persuade you to go. Here's your father now!
FATHER TS'AI *(enters and sings to the same tune):*

My time is short,
My white hair hanging down.
Content in my poverty, there is nothing I seek to gain.
But I have a clever son,
And when he becomes an official, I'll be satisfied at last.

(He greets CHANG.*)* Son,

The emperor has summoned all wise scholars;
Every graduate seeks to pass his test.
Hurry to the spring examination,
Pack your bags without delay.

Son, the yellow placards are out, and the local officials have especially recommended you. Why won't you go?

CHANG: Ah, here comes Mrs. Ts'ai.

MOTHER TS'AI (*enters and sings to the tune* Wu Hsiao-ssu):

> My eyes are dim,
> My ears are deaf,
> Our family means—nothing and nothing again.
> All we own is the cleverness in our son's head.
> When he becomes an official,
> We won't fear poverty again!

I should never have married that woman to my son. It's only been two months, and already he's wasted away. I'm afraid three more years would make a skeleton out of him!

CHANG: It sounds like she'd rather they didn't get along so well!

FATHER TS'AI: The yellow placards are out and examination time draws near. How can a talented man like you fail to attend?

CHANG: Mr. and Mrs. Ts'ai, you must convince him to go.

TS'AI: Father, it's not that I don't want to go, but you and Mother are old, and there's no one at home to serve you.

MOTHER TS'AI: Listen, my husband, you don't have seven sons and eight sons-in-law. All you have is the one son. You old reprobate! Your eyes are dim, your ears deaf, and you can hardly move. What if our son goes off and there's trouble at home? Who would get us out of it? With no food, we'd die of hunger. With no clothes, we'd die from cold.

FATHER TS'AI: You don't understand anything. When our son becomes an official, our status will be raised. We must make him go.

TS'AI: It's hard for me to leave.

(*He sings to the tune* Hsiu-tai-erh):

> How much time is left to my old parents?
> Just now is the time to fulfill the filial way.
> Do you think for the sake of a blue official robe
> I would neglect to play in a son's motley clothes?
> I believe
> The honor that this trip could bring
> My parents may not live to see.

FATHER TS'AI (*continues the song*):

> Throngs of scholars always fill the examination hall—
> Surely it's not only orphans that go!

CHANG (*sings to the same tune with a modified opening*):

Don't be crazy!
A man should have ambition to climb to the clouds;
Why insist so on holding back?
You'll have wasted ten years of study by the lamp's blue flame
To make do with half a lifetime of meager meals of yellow leeks.
Surely you know,
To send you off is your parents' wish, and this you can't refuse.

Sir,

Where is your filial devotion to their wish?

MOTHER TS'AI (*continues the song*):

All we've gotten out of our long lives is this one son.

Old reprobate!

Do you think we've got a flourishing cassia tree outside our door?[3]

FATHER TS'AI (*sings to the tune* T'ai-shih yin):

What's on his mind I'd rather not say;
The truth of the matter I know well!

(CHANG: What do you mean?)

The love they share in bed holds him here;
He cannot bear to be a world apart from her.

Since you're a scholar, I'll give you a lesson from history.

The great Yü left his bride of four days,[4]
Yet my son can't face separation.

CHANG: That must be it. Sir,
(*he continues the song*):

If you love your mandarin duck mate and cling to the phoenix
   curtains,
You'll miss the chance to soar like a *p'eng* bird and be admired like
   the osprey.[5]

---

[3] Mother Ts'ai is referring to the fact that the couple has but one child from the symbolic significance of the cassia tree for children.

[4] The mythical emperor Yü (traditional dates 2205–2196 B.C.) left his bride after four days of marriage in order to subdue massive floods.

[5] K'ung Jung (153–208) recommended a scholar for an official appointment with the words, "Vultures by the hundreds can't match one osprey." The osprey is thus a symbol of a person eminently qualified for official service.

MOTHER TS'AI (*sings to the same tune*):

Concern for our care keeps him here;
How can you say it's for the sake of pleasure and passion?
Tseng Shen's filial piety has always been praised; [6]
He never took any examinations or tests.
Success, fame, wealth, and rank are gifts of Heaven;
If Heaven gives them, they come without effort.

TS'AI (*continues the song*):

Mother is right; Father, please believe her.

If it's desire for my wife that keeps me here,

Let Heaven punish such an unfilial crime!

Father, if you make me go and leave you and Mother alone, what if some trouble arises at home? People will say that I was unfilial to abandon my parents in pursuit of success and fame, and that you were unwise to send your only son far away. This is why I can't comply with your wish.

FATHER TS'AI: If you won't, that's up to you. But what is your idea of filial piety then?

MOTHER TS'AI: Old reprobate! You're seventy or eighty years old and still don't know what filial piety is. Filial piety is wearing hemp clothes and a rope belt. [7]

(CHANG *puts an end to the comedy.*) [8]

TS'AI: "Every son should warm his parents' bed in winter and cool it in summer, at evening settle them in bed and in the morning inquire after them." "He makes sure they're neither hot nor cold and soothes away their discomforts. Wherever they go, he assists their steps; whatever they want he respectfully brings." "As long as his parents are alive, he doesn't travel far away." "When he goes out, he goes only where he has told them and returns at the promised time." [9] Such was the great filial piety of the ancients.

[6] Tseng Shen, a disciple of Confucius, was most famous for his filial piety.

[7] This is a humorous play on words based on the fact that the word *hsiao* can mean both "filial piety" and "to be in mourning."

[8] The meaning of this stage action, frequently used in plays of the period, is not entirely clear. Apparently, there was a conventional gesture used by one of the actors (generally the *mo*) which signified an end to comic actions or speech and the return to the serious mode.

[9] The first, second, and fourth quotations are from the *Li Chi* (Book of Rites). The third is from the *Lun-yü* (Analects) of Confucius.

FATHER TS'AI: Son, what you speak of are minor rules. You haven't said a word about the great principles of filial piety.

MOTHER TS'AI: Old reprobate! You're not dead yet and you're already insisting on his going into deep mourning. He certainly wouldn't be able to go to the examinations after that![10]

CHANG: It's bad luck to talk that way.

FATHER TS'AI: Listen to me, son. "Filial piety begins in serving one's parents, progresses to service of the ruler, and culminates in establishing oneself in the world. Body, hair and skin are given us by our parents; never to venture to harm them is the beginning of filial piety. Establishing oneself in the world and practicing the way of right so that one's fame is known to later generations is the means of bringing glory to our parents; it is the culmination of filial piety."[11] Therefore, if one's parents are poor and old, to attain no official rank is unfilial. When you become an official, it will show to the world the virtues of your parents. What is this but the great principle of filial piety!

TS'AI: Father, what you say is true. But even if I go, how do I know I'll succeed in becoming an official? If I don't, then I won't be able to serve my ruler, nor will I be able to serve my parents—a double failure.

CHANG: Sir, you've spoken in error. I've often heard scholars say, "In youth, study; in maturity, put it into practice." "Possessing the precious gem of virtue, and yet watching the state go down to ruin is unbenevolent."[12] "Confucius never stayed home long enough for his mat to become warm, while Mo-tzu's chimney was never blackened with smoke."[13] I Yin carried the cooking pots for T'ang and Po Li-hsi sold himself for five goat-skins.[14] Their one wish was to bring order to the world and carry out the right way, aid society and make the

---

[10] The joke is again based on the double meaning of the word *hsiao* for both filial piety and mourning.

[11] The quotation is based on the opening passage of the *Hsiao Ching* (Classic of Filial Piety).

[12] The quotation is from the *Lun-yu* of Confucius (Legge, 1:17).

[13] The saying was common at the time; the two men's concern for humanity left them little time to remain at home.

[14] Legend tells that I Yin, who became the chief minister to the founder of the Shang dynasty, sought recognition by his cooking skills, while Po Li-hsi sold himself to a cattleman of Ch'in and tended his cattle in an attempt to meet Duke Mu of Ch'in, later becoming his chief minister.

people secure. Now you, sir, are just in the position of those who "having become master of all civil and military arts, should offer their knowledge for sale to the imperial ruler." Sir, how can a talented man like you fail to serve in the government, aid society, and make the people secure?

MOTHER TS'AI: The two of you have plenty to say to persuade my son to set out. Now I've got a story for you. In East Village there lived a young man, the son of a Master Li. Master Li was after him all the time to leave home and become an official. He couldn't take all the pressure, and finally went to Ch'ang-an. Once there, nobody helped him out and he ended up as a beggar. The prime minister was passing by one day, and the young man bowed down before him. Pitying him, the prime minister said, "I'll make you the chief of the poorhouse; go back and take care of your parents." The young man said, "If I become chief of the poorhouse, how can I look after my parents?" When he reached home, his parents were indeed in the poorhouse. His father said to his wife, "You see, I was right to send our son off. Now he's the chief here, and nobody will dare take advantage of us!" And now, son, if you go, please be sure to get an appointment as poorhouse chief or high official of the almshouse, so you can stop people from taking advantage of us there!

CHANG: She's got what it takes to be a beggar all right. She's kept our attention for hours.

FATHER TS'AI: Son, you'd better go.

TS'AI (with an action): I don't mind going, but who will look after you?

CHANG: Sir, from of old, it's been said, "A good neighbor is worth a thousand dollars, a house only eight hundred." Since it's my undeserved good fortune to be your neighbor, please go with an easy heart, for if your family should lack anything or become ill, I will personally be in constant attendance.

TS'AI: Well then . . . thank you very much! I will entrust everything to your care. Well then, I have no choice but to pack my bags and leave.

(He sings to the tune San hsüeh-shih):

I thank you sir—how kind your thought!
Everything I leave to your care.

Even if the day comes that with one exam I reach success,
It can't be said that it came before my parents grew old.
I only fear that when I come home in brocade clothes,
My parents will be unable to see their son.[15]

FATHER TS'AI *(sings to the same tune):*

Your mother and I are old!
We count on you to raise our family status high.

Don't worry about there being no one to take care of us.
When you become an official,

There will be the three meats and five tripods for our offerings
morning and night.[16]
How much better than drinking water and sipping pulse!
If you return home in brocade clothes,

Though I may be dead,

My spirit will still rejoice.

CHANG *(sings to the same tune):*

Trust everything to your neighbor's care;
I'll do all I can to be of service.

Sir,

What were they for, those ten years of obscurity in your study?
All for that one examination which will raise your name to the
world!
If you don't return home in brocade clothes,
Who's to know you've read ten thousand books?

MOTHER TS'AI *(sings to the same tune):*

Suddenly gone, the pearl in my hand,
My old age without a prop.
They'll let parents die of hunger and cold
In hopes of a son's triumphant return.
But though you return home in brocade clothes,
Never can you mend your ruined name.

[15] The lines are a variation of a popular rhyme:

The day that he passed with but one try
His parents were not yet old.
In brocade clothes, he returns to his hometown;
He is a son indeed!

[16] The line describes the type of sacrifice carried out by nobles or high officials.

(Closing poem)

FATHER TS'AI: My son,

Hurry, pack your bags and leave for the examination.

TS'AI:

My father's stern command I must obey.

TOGETHER:

One exam will place you first on the Tiger Dragon List;
Ten years' time will find you by the Phoenix Pond.[17]

(They exit.)

---

[17] The term Tiger Dragon List dates from the T'ang dynasty, when the list of successful candidates included an unusual number of brilliant men, referred to as tigers and dragons. The Phoenix Pond was located in the palace complex; its name symbolizes the prime minister.

SCENE FIVE

WU-NIANG (*enters and sings to the tune* Yeh chin-men):

My spring dream shattered,
I approach the mirror, black clouds of hair disheveled.
I've heard that young scholars are traveling to the capital;
More and more the sighs of parting.

TS'AI (*enters and continues the song*):

Alas, my father forces me to go.
No end to the turmoil in my heart!
Bones and flesh will suddenly be severed;
How pitiful the pain at parting!

WU-NIANG (*recites in parallel prose*):

Sir, perhaps you can bear to leave me, your bride of two
months, forsaking the pleasures of "cloud and rain" love.[1]
But how can you go without a thought for your eighty-
year-old parents, whose temples are covered with frost
and snow? As soon as you began to think about success
and fame, you suddenly forgot all desire to provide them
with comforts.

Why is that?

TS'AI: Wu-niang, don't say that. Although I must travel far
from my parents, it certainly is not from lack of devotion to
them. It's my parents who are determined on this trip and
won't listen to reason—what can I do?

WU-NIANG: I see through you.

(*She sings to the tune* T'e-t'e ling):

Through your studies you aim to become First Winner.
But I fear that your learning is superficial and your intelligence
lacking.

(TS'AI: I've never lacked intelligence.)

Of the Classic of Filial Piety and Book of Rites
You've forgotten already half.

---

[1] Clouds and rain are a common euphemism for sexual intercourse, after the poem
attributed to Sung Yü, probably of the third century B.C., in which a goddess told her
lover that she was manifested in the morning clouds and evening rain.

(TS'AI: I haven't forgotten.)

WU-NIANG: You have forgotten.

> Isn't it said, "In summer cool them, in winter warm them,
> At evening help them to bed,
> In the morning inquire after them?"
> "While parents still live, how can one travel far away?"

TS'AI (*sings to the same tune*):

> Wailing with sorrow, I gave excuses by the million.
> Arguing in a fever, they insisted with all their might.
> Then they accused me of a serious wrong,
> And there was no way I could argue back.

(WU-NIANG: What wrong?)

> They said that because of my attachment to my bride,
> I would disobey my parents.
> That desire for her
> Kept me from the examination.

WU-NIANG (*sings to the tune* Ch'en-tsui tung-feng):

> How biased is your father!
> An only son he doesn't keep at home.

(*With an action*) I'll go with you and try to dissuade him. No, wait!

> He'll think that out of wantonness,
> I seek to bind you to me.

Ah!

> Nothing but grief in all this!

(*They sing the chorus together*):

> It's for Father, our tears fall,
> For Mother, our tears fall.
> Never has our own love been in the way.

TS'AI (*sings to the same tune*):

> How can the son's filial piety be complete?
> The father won't yield to his "gentle remonstrance."[2]

Ah! A son shouldn't talk like this.

---

[2] In the *Lun-yü* (Analects) of Confucius it is said that a son has the responsibility to gently remonstrate with his parents when they are at fault (Legge, 1:170).

I don't mean to blame them,
But they'll be all alone;
When I'm gone, who will take care of them?

(They repeat the chorus above.)

TS'AI: Wu-niang, Mother and Father are coming. Please dry your eyes.

FATHER and MOTHER TS'AI *(enter and sing to the tune* La-mei hua*)*:

Today our son sets out;
We come to see him off.
Our only hope is that the fish will become a dragon,
Find a path to clouds above,
Pluck the highest branch in the cassia tree and reach the palace in the moon.[3]

FATHER TS'AI: Son, have you packed your bags yet?

TS'AI: Yes.

FATHER TS'AI: Since you're packed, why not set out?

MOTHER TS'AI: When he's gone, we won't have anybody here but a daughter-in-law; shouldn't you give her some instructions?

TS'AI: I'm just waiting for Chang Ta-kung to come to entrust you, Mother and Father, to his care. I'll tell him to wait on you day and night, so that I can leave with an easy heart.

WU-NIANG: Here comes Chang Ta-kung now.

CHANG *(enters and recites in* shih *form):*

Sword in hand, goblet before him,
Shame in his face to be a wandering son.
But his will is set on merit and fame;
So why all these sighs as he goes?

(CHANG and the Ts'ai family greet each other.)

TS'AI: I'm leaving today. We have no other relatives at home, and my parents are old and weak. Their daughter-in-law is, after all, just a woman. What can she know about anything? I depend upon you to take care of everything, to look after

[3] Because the cassia flower is a symbol of excellence, the phrase "to pluck the cassia" has, since T'ang times, indicated the passing of the imperial examinations. Legend says that a cassia tree grows on the moon; thus, such phrases as "reaching the palace in the moon" and "being blessed by the moon goddess" also represent success in the examinations.

them early and late, and if there's anything they need, I hope you'll take care of it. Yesterday you already promised me in person, and now I make a point of entreating you. If I have the slightest success, I'll certainly try with all my heart to repay you and never forget your kindness!

CHANG: When a man receives someone's trust, he must carry out his promise to the end. Besides, "once a word has been spoken, even a team of horses can't overtake it." I promised you yesterday, and after you've gone I certainly won't be negligent.

TS'AI: Thank you!

FATHER TS'AI: Go now, son.

TS'AI: I'll bow in parting to you, Mother and Father, and then I'll be off.

TS'AI (bows and sings to the tune Yüan-lin hao):

I'm leaving now—
Father and Mother, don't worry about me.
I'm leaving now, this same year will return,
And only hope to find my parents still in good health.

(They sing the chorus together):

Surely you'll be back to bow before us again,
Surely you'll be back to bow before us again.

FATHER TS'AI (sings to the same tune):

My son, you must not worry;
Your father only hopes you'll gain high honors.
If your name is placed high on the list,

(They sing the chorus together):

Be sure to send news right away,
Be sure to send news right away!

MOTHER TS'AI (sings to the tune Chiang-erh shui):

From his mother's knee, the tender child goes forth.
His old mother sits alone in the hall—
Nothing left for her but to sew with careful hands the traveler's
     clothes.
Her eyes will strain to gaze beyond the distant mountains and
     passes.
In chill loneliness, she'll lean constantly on the gate.
Tell me how to relieve that sorrow!

(They sing the chorus together):

> To dispel our anxious thoughts,
> Nothing can help but a letter from him.

WU-NIANG *(sings to the same tune):*

> These feelings in your wife's heart,
> Thousands upon thousands,
> To speak them would only add to these entanglements of sorrow.
> Severed the love between husband and wife after sixty days,
> No way to care for Father and Mother aged eighty years.
> Tell me, how can I help but grieve?

(They repeat the chorus above.)

CHANG *(sings to the tune* Wu kung-yang):

> Old and poor,
> I've received a neighbor's trust;
> The responsibility is mine.
> You must force yourself to make this trip,
> So don't hang back so.
> Your father and mother, night and day,
> Night and day, I'll stay near.
> Of course strong men too have tears,
> But they don't let them fall at leave-taking.

(They sing the chorus together):

> Bone severed from flesh,
> Deepest feelings slashed in pieces.

TS'AI *(kneels and sings to the same tune):*

> Have pity, sir!
> My father and mother,
> I beg you to protect.
> If I win any honor,
> I'll show my gratitude to you.

WU-NIANG *(continues the song):*

> They have a son, all in vain!
> Your parents you ask others to care for.
> Limitless my feelings now,
> Secretly my tears drop.

(They repeat the chorus above.)

FATHER TS'AI *(sings to the tune* Yü chiao-chih):

I won't sigh at this farewell—
Not because there's no pain in my heart,
Or because I find it easy to insist on this separation,
But only because I want glory for you.

MOTHER TS'AI (*continues the song*):

Hasten to pick the cassia in the moon palace;
Time is short for the day lily in the northern hall.[4]

(*They sing the chorus together*):

How can we know when we'll be together again?
How can we know when we'll be together again?

TS'AI (*sings to the same tune*):

My parents are weary and worn;
Give them support in their old age.
When they're hungry, urge them to eat,
When it's cold, bring them clothes.

WU-NIANG (*continues the song*):

As your wife, I need no reminder to serve your parents;
It's you, the son, who is leaving them—and when will you return?

(*They repeat the chorus above.*)

FATHER TS'AI (*sings to the tune* Ch'uan-po chao):

Don't let your return be late;
Don't make us watch for you with frozen gaze.

TS'AI (*continues the song*):

There'll be a day when I return to my old home;
I fear that on that day, my parents will be old.

(*They sing the chorus together*):

How can we put our minds at ease?
We can't stop our tears.

WU-NIANG (*sings to the same tune with a modified opening*):

How can I express my grievance in words?
Difficulties on difficulties lie upon me.

TS'AI: Wu-niang,
(*he continues the song*):

[4] The day lily is symbolic of mothers; see Scene Four, note 2.

Just let your grievance be toward me;
Don't let your affection for my parents cool.

(*They repeat the chorus above.*)

(*Closing poem*)
TS'AI:

I'm forced to make this journey to the spring examinations.

ALL BUT TS'AI:

We hope you'll return next year in brocade clothes.

ALL:

In this world a thousand things can break the heart;
Nothing is worse than separation through death and parting in
    life.

(MOTHER *and* FATHER TS'AI *and* CHANG *exit.* TS'AI *and* WU-NIANG
remain on stage.)

WU-NIANG: Sir, how can you bear to leave?
TS'AI: What would you have me do?
WU-NIANG (*sings to the tune* Wei fan):

No matter the sorrow I feel to see you go;
My grief is not over the severed string,
My pain is not because of the broken mirror.[5]
My anxiety is all for your parents,
Insecure as candles in the wind.

TS'AI (*continues the song*):

Already my heart is broken—about to leave yet unable to bear it;
My tears hard to dry, without bidding they fall.

(*They sing together*):

In vain this reluctance to leave;
We'll be a world apart
A moment from now.

    [5] "Broken string" and "divided mirror" are both common symbols of separation be-
tween husband and wife. Because the musical instruments *ch'in* and *se* were used in
the *Shih Ching* (Book of Poetry) to represent a harmonious couple, a broken string
came to symbolize the death of a wife or separation from her. A story about a couple
who were forced to separate during a time of turmoil, each taking half of a broken
mirror as a token, is the source of the second allusion.

WU-NIANG (*sings to the tune* Wei fan hsü):

Limitless, my feelings at parting!
Husband and wife of but two months,
Suddenly each alone.
After you've gone, year after year
I'll gaze toward the distant capital.
And yet I think,
I'm not anxious about the distance over mountains and roads,
I'm not anxious about the coldness of pillow and coverlet.
I'm only anxious
That your parents, without support, will suddenly feel alone.

TS'AI (*sings to the same tune*):

Never did I
Long for fame.
I wanted only to fulfill my filial love.
But my father's command is hard to oppose.
My old parents
I hope that you'll look after.
In the end,
Please don't brood over the loss of morning rains and evening
    clouds;
In my stead, just keep my parents warm in winter and cool in
    summer.
As I think of it,
How can I bear to leave with open eyes?

WU-NIANG (*sings to the same tune*):

As soon as you change your student robe to an official blue gown,[6]
Strike the whip to return
And hurry home!
From the ten miles of red pavilions[7]
Don't take a beautiful lady as your wife.
This I enjoin you:
Even if you have no care that it will be cold within my flowered
    bedcurtains,
Remember at least that dusk is falling in the mulberry trees.[8]
I tell him this now,
Never knowing if he'll remember or if my earnest words are all in
    vain.

TS'AI (*sings to the same tune*):

[6] Students wore white clothes; officials, blue.
[7] "Ten miles of red pavilions" is a set description of the homes of aristocrats in the
capital city.
[8] The line refers to the old age of Ts'ai's parents; see Scene Two, note 11.

Wait for me with calm heart;
How could I be detained by flowers and willows?[9]
Or become a drifting weed?
I only fear that over thousands of miles of mountains and passes,
It will be difficult to get letters through.
Listen!
I'm forced to let our love be broken;
But never could I be unfeeling or unfair to you.

(They sing together):

From today,
Longing for each other, though we'll dwell apart, our tears will
    overflow the same.

WU-NIANG: Go, sir. Please, please come back quickly.
TS'AI: My father and mother are still living. How could I ven-
ture to remain away from home long?
TS'AI *(sings to the tune* Che-ku t'ien):

A thousand miles of mountains and passes, a thousand miles of
    grief.

WU-NIANG *(continues the song):*

One feeling in our two hearts, one anxiety in our minds.

TS'AI *(continues the song):*

With the life of my aged parents uncertain,
How could I stay long in distant inns?

(TS'AI exits.)

WU-NIANG *(continues the song):*

There he goes,
Slowly, with frozen gaze.
Truly, "For every ten steps of the horse, nine times he turns his
    head."
I fear if I go back, his parents will feel my pain;
My tears are so boundless, I don't dare let them flow.

(She exits.)

[9] Flowers and willows are symbols of beautiful women, especially courtesans.

SCENE SIX

STEWARD (*enters and recites in* shih *form*):

> On a broad road east of the royal park, green towers rise,
> Jade pavilions with red doors, curtains tightly drawn.
> Golden-belled dogs bark at the moon in the *wu-t'ung* trees;
> Vermilion-maned horses neigh at the wind in the willows.

I am a steward in the mansion of Prime Minister Niu. For the past few days, the master has been detained on some business at court and still hasn't returned. I've heard that the maids and the old housekeeper have taken advantage of his absence to come out and play in the back garden every day. Today they must have found out that the master's about to return—that's why they're not around. I'd better sweep up the hall and tidy the study before he comes back. How strange! Here comes an old lady. What could she be doing here?

FIRST MATCHMAKER (*played by the* ching *actor, enters and sings to the tune* Tzu-tzu shuang):

> As a matchmaker, how seductive am I!
> With playful chatter,
> I talk them apart, talk them together, my mouth like a knife.
> So clever am I!
> If the marriage divinations turn out well,
> There'll be some cash for me!
> My only fear is that someone will report my faking of the proposal
>   notes
> And I'll get a flogging.

STEWARD: What are you doing here?

FIRST MATCHMAKER: Greetings, sir! I have come for the purpose of arranging a match for Master Chang.

STEWARD: This young lady of ours is no ordinary girl. The master won't betrothe her lightly. But wait a minute—here comes another matchmaker!

SECOND MATCHMAKER (*played by the* ch'ou *actor, enters and sings to the same tune*):

> As a matchmaker, how diligent am I!
> I seek every advantage.

When a young man desires an alliance
Most urgently,
I always rush forth with all speed
To get the reply.

(With an action)

When someone comes ahead of me,
I get upset!

STEWARD: What are you doing here?

SECOND MATCHMAKER: I have come for the purpose of proposing on behalf of Master Li.

STEWARD: I was just saying to this woman that I'm afraid it will be hard to make a match here.

SECOND MATCHMAKER: So this lady came to make a match too! Listen, I'm Mrs. Chang and I've lived across the street for years. And now you expect to make this match?

FIRST MATCHMAKER: So only you can set up a match? The necessary thing is to bring forward a suitable candidate. If you think just because you live across the street the match is yours to make, what if you brought forward a beggar—would the lady marry him?

STEWARD: Don't make such a fuss! Wait until the master comes back; he's the one to decide.

PRIME MINISTER NIU (*played by the* wai *actor, enters and sings to the tune* Ch'i-t'ien lo):

The sound of jade pendants from Phoenix Pond is gone,[1]
But still imperial fragrance lingers in my sleeves.
Passing by the halberd-lined gate
On highways of smooth sand,
On what business rush those rumbling chariots and crowds of
    horses?
My hair has changed to frost,
And I fear these "jade handles" are useless,
That these "red slippers" have no talent.[2]
And when I think of my own home,
I feel sad that but one cassia branch grows there.[3]

---

[1] The emperor is said to move with the sound of jade pendants; the line indicates that the emperor has returned to his palace from the Imperial Secretariat.

[2] Both "jade handles" and "red slippers" are traditional symbols for high ministers.

[3] The single cassia branch represents Mistress Niu, an only child. See Scene Two, note 11.

(The STEWARD *bows.)*

FIRST and SECOND MATCHMAKERS: Greetings, your excellency!

NIU: What are these two old ladies doing here?

FIRST MATCHMAKER: I've come to propose on behalf of Councilor Chang.

SECOND MATCHMAKER: I've been sent by Secretary Li to arrange a match.

NIU: No matter who he is, unless he's a genius among scholars, able to finish off a thousand pages in a single brushstroke, he won't even be considered.

FIRST MATCHMAKER: Your excellency, my young man can finish off fifteen hundred pages in a single brushstroke.

SECOND MATCHMAKER: What crap! *My* young man can finish off thirty-three thousand, three hundred and thirty-three pages with a single stroke.

STEWARD *(putting an end to the comedy):* You can't carry on like that around here!

NIU: Don't talk such nonsense. Only the First Winner in the examinations can marry my daughter. Others aren't even allowed to propose.

FIRST MATCHMAKER: Your excellency, the horoscope of my young man has been read, and it clearly says that he will be First Winner.

SECOND MATCHMAKER *(grabbing at her from behind):* Your excellency, hers can't be the first. The horoscope of my young man shows clearly that he will be first.

(The FIRST MATCHMAKER *grabs the* SECOND *and the two hit each other.)*

NIU *(expressing anger):* How dare these two come to my house and show such disrespect! Attendant, search them and tear all their marriage documents to shreds.

(The STEWARD *searches the two matchmakers and tears up their documents. They cry.)*

NIU: Hang the both of them up in front of the reception hall and beat them eighteen times.

STEWARD: Yes, sir.

(He performs an action.)

(Exit poem): [4]

NIU:

Get these women out of my reception hall!

STEWARD:

For only the First Winner is allowed to propose.

FIRST and SECOND MATCHMAKER:

Eighteen strokes of the prickly staff is all we got for our pains.

ALL:

Who says, "Whether successful or not, there will be some wine?"

(The STEWARD *and* MATCHMAKERS *exit.)*

NIU: "Time like an arrow speeds us to old age; days and nights like a shuttle rush us through youth." I've lost my wife and have only a daughter. I've suddenly realized that she's grown into a woman without ever being sought in marriage. One thing worries me. My daughter has a tender, sweet nature and is very capable, but I fear that if I marry her to the son of a rich man, he'll have a bad influence on her. If I marry her to a scholar, she can attain perfection as a virtuous wife. Wouldn't that be best? They say that while I was away the maids have been going out every day to play in the garden. My daughter is to blame for failing to discipline them. Today people came to ask for her hand in marriage; how could I let her become a wife without the proper instruction? Daughter, Hsi-ch'un, and Mu-mu, come here!

MISTRESS NIU *(enters and sings to the tune* Hua-hsin tung):

Shut within secluded chambers,
The fair lady is asked,
"Why so reluctant to blacken your eyebrows?"—
"Days spent with needle and thread are long;
A springtime of books and painting is aimless.
Who can understand these hours upon hours spent by a dress-
      ing-table?
A rare flower, protected in curtains of purple silk,
Never allowing bees and orioles to suspect its presence there."

[4] Sometimes characters who exit before the end of a scene recite poems identical in form to the final "closing poems"; these I have termed "exit poems."

HSI-CH'UN and MU-MU *(continue the song):*

> Laughing by latticed windows,
> How many beautiful ladies sit in boredom!

MISTRESS NIU: Greetings, Father!

NIU: Daughter, the virtue of women depends on never going outside their secluded quarters. How can you fail to be aware of that? I've heard that while I was away at court the maids have been playing in the back garden. This is because you failed to discipline them. You're grown up now, and though today you're just my daughter, someday you'll be another man's wife. If you don't discipline them now and something bad comes of it, your reputation will be ruined.

MISTRESS NIU: Thank you, Father, for your teaching. From now on I'll be sure to discipline them.

NIU: Mu-mu, you're an old woman and in charge of the household. What kind of behavior is it for you to tempt the maids into indulging in idle games?

MU-MU: It's nothing to do with me. It was all Hsi-ch'un's fault.

HSI-CH'UN: It was your fault!

(She performs an action.)

MU-MU: Yours!

(She performs an action.)

NIU: Come here, my daughter.
(He sings to the tune Hsi-nu chiao):

> Ladies with soft apricot faces and rosy peach cheeks
> Must also have virtue enduring as pine and bamboo,
> Sentiments pure as orchids.
> "What is said in secluded chambers
> Must not pass beyond the threshold."

Old Mu-mu,

> You were wrong in failing to guide my daughter.

Hsi-ch'un,

> From today this wildness must cease.

(They sing the chorus together):

Remember in the future:
To avoid saying things that shouldn't go beyond our threshold,
We must remind each other.

MISTRESS NIU (*sings to the same tune with a modified opening*):

How sad
I was left without a mother!
The art of womanly deportment
I had no way to learn.
But now I've received my father's stern command;
How could I fail to reform!

Mu-mu,

Night and day, I hope you'll admonish me.

Hsi-ch'un,

You must reform without delay.

(*They repeat the chorus above.*)

MU-MU (*sings to the tune* Hei-ma hsü):

Please listen!
A father and mother
Must see that their child's marriage not be delayed.
I urge you, sir,
Hurry and pay off this debt you owe your child!

NIU (*continues the song*):

Stop this foolishness!
In my daughter's presence,
How dare you speak so boldly!

(*They repeat the chorus above.*)

HSI-CH'UN (*sings to the same tune*):

I beg a favor!
Such lonely frustration;
How would you have me bear it?
Think of it!
Doesn't it make tears flood your cheeks?

MISTRESS NIU (*continues the song*):

We treat you well:
Warm clothes, fine food.
Why make yourself so blue?

(They repeat the chorus above.)

(Closing poem)
NIU:

Women must not go out of their chambers.[5]

MISTRESS NIU:

Thank you for the kindness of your teaching.

ALL:

"To mature you can't do as you please;
If you do as you please, you'll never mature."[6]

(They exit.)

[5] Throughout the scene, Prime Minister Niu admonishes his daughter and the servants with two tenets of traditional morality; the first is that women themselves should not leave the secluded quarters; the second is that private talk among women should not be made known to others.

[6] This proverb occurs often in *ch'uan-ch'i,* but it is generally used to mean that only disciplined hard work can lead to success for a young man.

SCENE SEVEN

TS'AI (*enters and sings to the tune* Man-t'ing fang):

The willow's drifting catkins stain my clothes;
A trail of broken petals follows my horse.
The spring air, gently warm, gently cool,
This world of mountain and stream,
Perversely affect the traveler.
I look back—how far the distance to my parents has grown!
I grieve over past love so lightly left behind.
What wound my heart
Are the occasional cries of cuckoos,[1]
And traveler's tears cover my collar.

(*The* mo *actor, playing a traveler, enters and sings to the same tune*):

Green, green the fragrant grass.
A lady gazes out from the garden back home,
But her young man's far from sight,[2]
Wasting away at roadside stations—
For who is there to offer him comfort?

(*Two travelers, played by the* ching *and* ch'ou *actors, enter and continue the song*):

They say Lo-yang is near,
But still several cities away.

(*They sing the chorus together*):

We'll wash away depression,
Unsaddle the horses, buy some wine,
And get drunk together in Apricot Blossom Town.[3]

(*They recite to the* tz'u Huan-ch'i sha.)

---

[1] The cry of the cuckoo evokes the traveler's sadness because it is said to sound like the words *pu ju kuei ch'ü* (Better go back home!).

[2] The three lines allude to the poem "Chao yin-shih" from the ancient collection of southern poems *Ch'u-tz'u,* two lines of which read:

The gentleman is on a journey and doesn't return.
The spring grass is growing oh so green!

[3] Apricot Blossom Town is a stereotypic name for a rustic village often used in poetry.

TS'AI:

"For a thousand miles the orioles sing amid the dazzle of red blossoms and green leaves."

CH'OU:

"A village by a stream, ramparts on the mountains, wine-flag blowing in the breeze."[4]

CHING:

The traveler feels he's moving in a painting.

MO:

Neither hot nor cold, how fine the weather!
In both directions, the travelers pass.

ALL:

At such times, who can hold back sighs over loved ones far away?

TS'AI (*sings to the tune* Kan-chou ko):

Grief breaks my heart.
I sigh at this thousand-mile road.
Day after day, thoughts of my family.
The green plums are already the size of beans;
No blossom-filled branch is left to send to them.[5]
The hair on my parents' temples has turned to frost,
While I on the road can do nothing but gaze at the clouds above.

(They sing the chorus together):

The taste of a journey,
The experiences of travel,
Can never compare to a simple life at home by a flowing stream.
Don't turn your head;
It will break your soul!
The sound of crying birds I cannot bear to hear.

(The mo *sings to the same tune):*

Amid this scenery of late spring,
Though we may grow weary,
Why must we grieve?

[4] The two lines are from the poem "Chiang-nan ch'un chüeh-chu shih" (Spring in Chiang-nan) by Tu Mu (803–852). (*CTS*, 522: 5964).
[5] The line alludes to a gift of a branch of plum blossoms, along with a poem, sent by Lu K'ai (198–269) to his friend Fan Yeh. Here, since the blossoms have already given way to green plums, Ts'ai cannot send such a gift to his family.

From green trees, showers of red petals
Stain the traveler's robes with fragrant dust.
On a ladder of clouds to the moon palace, we aim to win glory,
And don't begrudge sleeping by streams and eating only wind.

(They sing the chorus together):

We'll mount the peach waves,
Leap across brocade scales,
With a sound like thunder, pass through Dragon Gate!
When we return in glory,
Our green sashes of office new,
There will be no laughing at Su Ch'in![6]

(The ching *sings to the same tune):*

Whose home is that on the river bank,
Past a painted bridge and misty willows,
Its red door lost in shade?
A swing casts a shadow over the wall
And tops of lovely faces appear for but an instant.
Their heartless laughter and talk gradually grow faint.
Never will they know how it has pained the heartstricken one
    outside their wall.

(They sing the chorus together):

How far our homes!
How hard the road!
We'll refuse "to pay ten visits to the nobleman's gate without
    success."[7]
From this journey we'll be sure
To pay court at the Purple Palace,
By Phoenix Pond, in Hanlin Academy, we'll hear the imperial
    voice.

(The ch'ou *sings to the same tune):*

Far off in mists and clouds,
Are those the palace gates of Lo-yang?
Step by step, we draw near,
Exhausted by the journey.
I wish to drink some cups of wine,
But must not yet halt my weary horse by hanging willows.

---

[6] The famous strategist of the Warring States period, Su Ch'in, was unable to find employment the first time he left home. When he returned, his relatives laughed at him for his failure.

[7] Variations of this phrase are common in Yüan-Ming drama as an indication of a rebuff.

Already in ancient trees, the twilight crows have all returned to
    roost.

(They sing the chorus together):

The sky grows dark,
The sun has set,
From the watch tower the evening horn sounds no more.
Seeking an inn,
We hasten our pace.
In the village ahead lights appear, and now it's dusk.

(They sing the coda together):

Toward dwellings ahead
We hasten to seek refuge.
We'll unsaddle, buy wine, and talk of literature.
Tonight while rain beats on pear blossoms, we'll be safe inside.

(Closing poem)
TS'AI:

The world of mountain and stream wounds my heart.

ALL:

From north, south, east, and west in search of wealth and fame.
As long as we find flowers and wine on our way,
We'll lengthen each day's journey to two.

(All exit.)

SCENE EIGHT

WU-NIANG (*enters and sings to the tune* P'o ch'i-chen):

Faded the blue of my lucky phoenix curtains,
And vapid the fragrance from the jeweled duck incense burner.
Melancholy clouds hang over the inns of Ch'u,
A chill moon rises above the pavilions of Ch'in.[1]
Everything provokes the sadness of separation.
My gaze cut off from the distant horizon past clouds and
   mountains,
While the snowy hair of his parents grows sparse.
Why is there no letter?

(She recites in the ku-feng *form):*

Bright, bright my boxed mirror,
And fine, fine was my morning adornment.
I remember when I served you;
At cock-crow I'd leave your bed,
Approach the mirror, pin up my hair,
Go with you to your parents' room for the morning greeting.
Suddenly you're far away from me,
My mirror's brightness hidden in its box,
My fine clothes darkened by dust.
Moss grows in our wedding chamber,
Scattered, my gold hairpins,
Faded, my gauze robes—
And my own haggard form
Will never regain its orchid freshness.
My feelings are bitter and cold;
His road is long and difficult.
But my sighs are not for this;
I grieve only for his mother.
I think of the little monkey so far away,[2]
And pity the mulberry tree at fall of dusk.
I vowed to follow the correct way of the wife,

[1] Although "inns of Ch'u" and "pavilions of Ch'in" often denote courtesans' houses (as in Scene Twenty-nine of this play), here the phrases are used to describe lodging places for travelers. Wu-niang is imagining the desolation of her husband on the road.

[2] The *yüan-nao* monkey specified in the text is said to be especially loving toward its offspring; a story in the *Sou shen chi* (c. 300) tells of a mother monkey who committed suicide when a hunter killed her son.

But I can't expect the return of that wanderer.
Don't play the green-embroidered *ch'in;*
It's broken string brings on sorrow.[3]
Don't listen to the "Song of White Hair";
Its grieving tone breaks one's heart.[4]
How confused are human affairs!
Pairs of mandarin ducks make me blush.

Po-chieh and I had been married only two months. I hoped then that the two of us would grow old together in service to his parents. But instead his father commanded him to attend the official examinations. Since he left, there hasn't been a single letter from him. He's abandoned his parents, and left me to care for them alone; I must both uphold his good name as a filial son and carry out my own responsibilities as a good daughter-in-law. With all my heart, with all my strength, I serve them day and night. How true that "The vast world of sea and sky may someday reach an end; what will never be exhausted are these feelings in my heart."
(*She sings to the tune* Feng-yün hui ssu ch'ao yüan):

He was forced to go to the spring examination;
Our love knot had just been tied.[5]
Alas, the sounds of "Yang-kuan" died away,
And I saw you off from Nan-p'u.[6]
How long since we parted!
Nothing left but tears which soak my jacket!
Nothing left but tears which soak my jacket!
Our *ch'in* and *se* are covered with dust,
Our embroidered coverlet I'm ashamed to unroll.
At lonely window,
By deserted door,
Year after year I'll pass in vain.

Ah!

---

[3] The poet Ssu-ma Hsiang-ju (179–117 B.C.) played a green-embroidered *ch'in;* the broken string is a symbol of separation between husband and wife.
[4] "Song of White Hair" was composed by Ssu-ma Hsiang-ju's wife, Cho Wen-chün, when she learned he was planning to take a concubine. In the song she expressed her pain that they will be unable to grow old together.
[5] The sash is tied in a special way to indicate love.
[6] The famous parting song "Wei-ch'eng ch'ü" (Song of Wei-ch'eng) by Wang Wei (699–759) concludes with the line, "When you go west from Yang-kuan, there will be no more old friends." Nan-p'u is used as a traditional place of parting, after a line in the "Li-sao" of Ch'ü Yüan (fourth century B.C.).

From somewhere comes the thought
That the feelings between us
Suddenly became transitory as the morning dew.
The road you travel is a thousand miles;
My heart is filled with a thousand sorrows.
If you remember me,
From far, far away, you'll long to come home.

(She sings to the same tune):

Gone, the pink of my cheeks,
My black clouds of hair I'm reluctant to comb.
He who painted my eyebrows is far away.
My lover with powdered cheeks is gone.[7]
Like the phoenix, I blush at my solitary form in the mirror.[8]
Secretly, I count the days till he returns.
Secretly, I count the days till he returns.
Lost are the fish and goose that carry his letters,[9]
Each alone, phoenix husband, phoenix wife.
Green covers our river island,
And the fragrant pollia tree blossoms once more.[10]

Ah!

Day by day he draws near the imperial city.
Fragrant grass in the light of the setting sun
Leads my gaze toward the road to Ch'ang-an.
How could you stay long a wanderer?
I am not meant to be a wanderer's wife.
This situation I'm in—
Out of millions of people, not one could I tell it to.

(She sings to the same tune):

Softly I walk on delicate feet
Toward his parents' room to ask what they need.
If they're short of food, I must offer more;
Torn clothes I must mend,

[7] Chang Ch'ang (d. 51 B.C.) of the Han dynasty was such a devoted husband that he used to paint his wife's eyebrows for her. Ho Yen (190–249) of the Wei dynasty was an exceptionally handsome young man who decorated his face with powder. The two phrases here describe a romantic young husband.

[8] A story tells of the King of Cashmere who captured a phoenix. When the bird refused to sing for three years, a mirror was placed before it in the hope it would think its reflection to be a mate and thus sing. The bird was so moved by the reflection that it burst into mournful cries and died.

[9] The goose and fish are traditional symbols of carriers of letters.

[10] The two lines may be an allusion to the poem "Hsiang chün," one of the Nine Songs in the Ch'u-tz'u, which treats of a broken rendezvous between goddess and man.

Feeble limbs I'll support.
Alas, the sun has set over western hills.
Alas, the sun has set over western hills.
And whom can I hire
To carry word to my husband?
You may ascend to the high clouds;
I only fear your parents are returning to the yellow earth.
As you left, how I entreated you!

Ah!

Are you really such a dedicated scholar?
I only fear that in ten miles of red pavilions,
Power and wealth you'll covet.
But though you may forget me,
Surely your parents will stay in your thoughts.
There's no one to whom I can speak of this—
This cold, cold loneliness—how can I bear it?

(She sings to the same tune):

Candidates fill the examination hall;
So many talented young gentlemen!
So many mirrors broken as pledges by loving couples!
They all seek to climb high on the examination list;
But it is he alone who does me wrong.
Still I mustn't be bitter.
Still I mustn't be bitter.
Since he entrusted me with the family altars,
How can I shirk my duty?
Why not become a filial daughter-in-law and virtuous wife,
And have my name recorded in history?
Then my loneliness won't be in vain.

Ah!

I'll carry on here as best I can,
So his reputation won't be harmed,
I'll cover up for him somehow.
When you have donned golden belt and purple robes,
Remember my thorn hairpin and cotton skirt.
My depression's a skein—
Such tangled piles even Sung Yü could never describe.[11]

---

[11]Sung Yü (third century B.C.) was most famous for his *fu*, a form of poetry that often consists of long, elaborate descriptions.

(Closing poem)

For my parents-in-law the sun is setting fast;
What keeps the wanderer at the ends of the earth?
"The lives of lovely ladies are more than others' harsh;
Don't blame the spring breeze; it's our own fault."[12]

(She exits.)

[12] The saying was common at the time. Because the spring breeze is associated with loss of youth and beauty, the line expresses the idea that it is the inevitable destiny of beautiful ladies to grow old and out of favor, rather than the fault of the spring breeze.

SCENE NINE

PREFECTURAL SUPERVISOR *(played by the* mo *actor, enters and recites in* shih *form):*

> In the morning he was a humble peasant;
> By evening he had climbed to the imperial hall.
> Generals and ministers are not born, but made;
> To be a success a man must give his all.

I am a supervisor in Honan prefecture. Every year the First Winner in the examinations is entertained at a feast in Ch'iung-lin Garden and paraded through the streets for three days. The governor of Honan directs all the preparations— saddling the horses, setting up the feast, arranging for musicians. This year the winner is Ts'ai Po-chieh, and the celebration is today. My chief is unable to attend and appointed me to supervise things. Yesterday I ordered the officer of imperial mounts in charge of attending to the horses and the officials of Lo-yang in charge of the feast to report here to get their instructions at the sound of three drumbeats. *(He beats the drum.)* Where is the groom in attendance?

THE GROOM *(played by the* ch'ou *actor, enters):* When there's a question, I answer. If there isn't a question, I give no reply.[1]

SUPERVISOR: Have you gotten the horses ready yet?

GROOM: We have plenty of horses—ten thousand fine ones!

SUPERVISOR: What does a good horse look like?

GROOM: *(recites in parallel prose):*

> His ears are like slices of twin bamboo, his mane a flow of
> multicolored flowers. He expands his phoenix chest
> under the dragon mane, and holds high that crowlike
> head with tiger jaws. Clip-clip-clop, on blue-black hooves
> of chiseled jade he runs. Drip-drip-drop, the crimson
> sweat like glowing pearls falls. Mirror-bright is the green
> glow in the corners of his eyes, and the mane at his neck

---

[1] Servants in *ch'uan-ch'i* plays generally enter with two formula phrases such as these.

ripples like a string of many-colored coins.[2] In one leap, his tail brushes the Milky Way, and he clears the highest peaks of K'un-lun. In an instant, he can traverse the whole world, overtaking falling stars and flashing lightning. He'd win the praise of Chiu-fang Kao, who'd gladly pay a thousand pieces of gold to acquire him.[3]

SUPERVISOR: What colors are these horses?

GROOM: Date bay, chestnut, swallow, rabbit yellow, true white, jade face, silver mane, flowered shoulders, blue flower.[4]

SUPERVISOR: What names do they have?

GROOM: Flying Dragon, Crimson Rabbit, Yao-niao, Hua-liu, Purple Swallow, Su-shuang, Nieh-hsi, Exceeding Brightness, Unicorn, Son of the Mountains, White Mist, Renouncer, Floating Cloud, Red Lightning, Hermit, Easy Rider, Lu-li, Little Dragon, Little Unicorn, Mounting Frost, Glistening Snow, Frosty Dew, Hanging Light, Bursting Waves, Flying Rosy Cloud, Lightning Red, Flowing Gold, Soaring Unicorn Purple, Speeding Crimson, Night Shining White, Ten-Foot Crow, Nine-Flowered Dragon Boy, Cloud-Bound, Sudden Thunder, Fist of Hair, Lion Blossom, Jade Rover, Red Ch'ih-po, Purple Ch'ih-po, Gold Ch'ih-po.[5] In Kokonor and Yüeh-chih they're born; from Ferghana and Yüeh-t'an they come.[6]

SUPERVISOR: What famous stables are there?

GROOM: Flying Dragons, Soaring Unicorn, Lucky Omen, Dragon Mates, T'ao-t'u, Spirited Racers, Fabulous Phoenix, Six Herds, Garden of Heaven, Pasture of Phoenix, Flying Stars, Colt Corral, Fliers of the Left, Fliers of the Right, Left Quarter, Right Quarter, Southeast Corral, Southwest Corral.[7] They're branded with "three flowers" and "flying phoenix" characters;[8] within these stables are kept ten thousand steeds of heaven.

SUPERVISOR: How are they adorned?

GROOM (recites in parallel prose):

[2] The passage consists of a number of descriptions of fine horses from various sources.

[3] Chiu-fang Kao of the Ch'un-ch'iu period was a famous expert on horses.

[4] Seventeen colors are listed in the text, eight of which defy even literal translation.

[5] The forty horses named are all famous horses from ancient times.

[6] All are regions to the west of China noted for producing fine horses.

[7] All are names of historical stables, although a number of the names are written incorrectly in the text.

[8] The line refers to an ornamental style of calligraphy used in brands.

Their embroidered saddlecloths are like glittering clouds, their golden stirrups brilliant as the sun. Perfumed gauze covers protect their golden saddles, and gossamer purple reins move the jade bridles. Halters are studded with agate, saddles inlaid with coral.

SUPERVISOR: How many have you chosen for today?
GROOM: Sir, today I don't have any. We have only ten thousand horses.

(He continues in parallel prose):

Of these, one thousand and three hundred have broken shoes, two thousand and seven hundred have "smeared jaw,"[9] three thousand and eight hundred are lame, and two thousand and two hundred are blind. The saddles are broken, the seats askew. We've nothing but hemp ropes for bridles and bramble sticks for whips. The "hungry-owls" are drooping, and the "geese-wings" are all in pieces.[10] Not one of the bridle and saddle sets is complete, nor is there a single pair of intact reins.

ctually none of the horses is fit for use.
RVISOR: Don't talk like a fool. If you don't get them ready, I'll speak to the governor and you'll get a real beating.
GROOM: Please have mercy! I'll take care of everything.
SUPERVISOR: When the horses are ready, lead them outside the fifth gate. When the First Winner comes out from thanking his majesty, he'll mount and parade through the city.
GROOM: No problem. It will be just as they say—"In spring, he reached his goal—how fast his horse's hooves! In one day he'll see all the flowers in Ch'ang-an."[11]

(The GROOM exits.)

SUPERVISOR: Arrangements officer of Lo-yang, come here!
OFFICER *(played by the* ching *actor, enters):* "From the top of the hall, one summons; from below the steps, a hundred assents."

[9] The *Morohashi Dictionary* defines this term as a sickness of a horse's face, but cites only this passage from *The Lute* as an example.
[10] I have not found definitions for these two terms; *Morohashi,* again citing this passage only, defines "hungry owls" as a device for a horse.
[11] The lines are from the poem "Teng-k'o hou shih" (After passing the examinations) by Meng Chiao (751–814), which describes the parade of the successful First Winner through the streets of the capital city (*CTS,* 374: 4205).

SUPERVISOR: Are the arrangements completed?
OFFICER: Everything is completed.

(He continues in parallel prose):

 The pearl screens are rolled up high, the kingfisher curtains hanging low. Coral mats are arranged to perfection, tortoise-shell mats ingeniously spread. Smoke of jade camphor drifts up from golden burners, and enchanting rare blossoms fill the jade vases. Everything is encircled by painted screens, every space covered by embroidered mattresses. Mingled brilliance of gold plates and horn chopsticks illumines the rare fruits and sweets, and amid the shimmering light of "silver seas and vermilion boats,"[12] the wine nectar ripples. We've sprinkled and swept it so clean not a half speck of dust remains. We've set everything in perfect order—it's really a marvelous sight! It's truly like the saying, "Transported here are the splendors of Valley of Gold,[13] to make a Heaven of riches in Ch'iung-lin."

SUPERVISOR: All right, go there and wait in attendance. If everything isn't ready immediately, you'll be severely punished.
OFFICER: Deep within Ch'iung-lin, how beautiful the scene! In the world of man, a heavenly paradise!

(The OFFICER exits.)

SUPERVISOR *(recites to the* tz'u Lin-chiang hsien):

Sun shines on palace flowers, a screen of bright blue.
Newly made are his verdant robes of tender green,
Just posted the list of winners outside the flower gate.
He rides on golden saddle and noble steed,
His privilege to climb the steps to Heaven.
In ten miles of red pavilions, every screen is rolled high,
As beautiful ladies struggle for a glimpse of the famous winner.
Yellow banners flying, a hubbub everywhere—
Everyone suddenly falls silent
As the First Winner comes in view.

(He exits.)

---

[12] A frequently used poetic description of wine cups.
[13] Valley of Gold was a sumptuous park built by Shih Ch'ung (249–300) of the Tsin dynasty.

(TS'AI *and two successful candidates, played by the* ching *and* chou *actors, all on horseback, enter and sing to the tune* Su-ti chin-tang):

> Sewn by the Moon Lady, his robe of green clouds;
> In Toad Hall he plucked the highest branch.[14]
> Palace flowers hang from his hat.
> One examination made his name known to the whole world.

(*They sing to the tune* K'u ch'i p'o):

> In the splendor of Lo-yang,
> Flowers are like brocade.
> In miles of red pavilions,
> Every woman is divine.
> "In spring he reached his goal—how fast his horse's hooves!"
> He'll parade all through the streets of Heaven, and only then
>   return.

(TS'AI *and the* ching *exit.*)

CH'OU (*falls from his horse and cries out*): Help! Help! Father! Mother! Wife! Son! Big Brother! Sister-in-law! Little Brothers! Uncles! Everybody, come save me!

OFFICIAL (*in charge of escorting the winners to the feast, played by the* mo *actor, on horseback, enters and sings to the tune* Shui-ti yü-erh):

> While attending court at the Secretariat,
> Yesterday I received an imperial command.
> The winner in the examinations has been chosen
> And I must accompany him to the feast.

(*His horse stumbles over the* ch'ou.)

CH'OU (*calls out*): You've kicked me so hard I feel like a woman having a miscarriage!
(*The* OFFICIAL'S *horse balks.*)

OFFICIAL (*continues the song*):

> The more I whip, the more he balks.
> What could be the matter?
> I turn my head to look—

(*The* ch'ou *calls out.*)

> Who's that calling me?

[14] Legend tells of a toad that lives on the moon; Toad Hall thus represents the moon, while "the highest branch" refers to the cassia, symbol of success in the examinations.

(The OFFICIAL *dismounts and looks around.)*

OFFICIAL: Who are you, man?
CH'OU: I'm the First Winner—at falling off horses.[15]

(The OFFICIAL *helps him up.)*

CH'OU: Who are you?
OFFICIAL: I'm the official from the Secretariat assigned to escort the First Winner to the feast. How did you happen to fall off your horse?
CH'OU *(sings to the tune* Pei tao-tao ling):

Such hubbub in the streets as revelers swarmed!

(OFFICIAL: Your horse was startled?)

That devil with all his might tried to turn around.

(OFFICIAL: Why didn't you hold him in?)

I trembled, I shook, in fear the reins would break.

(OFFICIAL: Why didn't you beat him?)

My spirits had long since fled from fright.

(OFFICIAL: Are you hurt?)
(The ch'ou *groans):*

My thigh's close to broken,
My head nearly smashed,
Just like the young Prince of Ch'in after leaping thrice over the mountain gorge.[16]

OFFICIAL: I wonder where your horse has gone off to.
CH'OU: Who cares where he's gone? "Was anybody hurt? He didn't ask about the horses."[17]

---

[15] This phrase is one source of humor throughout the scene. In the original, the *ch'ou's* statement could also be understood as "I am the First Winner, fallen from my horse." The official mistakes him for the First Winner.

[16] T'ai Tsung, second emperor of the T'ang dynasty (r. 1123–1134) was called Prince of Ch'in before his ascent to the throne. This episode, not included in official histories, is recounted in the historical romance *Ta T'ang Ch'in wang tz'u-hua* (Tale of Prince of Ch'in of the T'ang Dynasty).

[17] The quotation is from the *Lun-yu* of Confucius. Legge (1:234) translates it as follows: "The stable being burned down when [Confucius] was at court, on his return he said, 'Has any man been hurt?' He did not ask about the horses." *Ch'uan-ch'i* plays often put quotations from the classics into the mouths of clowns as a comic device, though generally the humor lies in misinterpretation, either deliberate or accidental, as in the next quotation.

OFFICIAL: What a fine, learned scholar! I'll borrow a horse for you.

CH'OU: Take it easy! If you borrow a horse for me to ride, it will be the death of me.

OFFICIAL: Why would it be the death of you?

CH'OU: Haven't you heard what Confucius said: "A man who owned a horse lent it to someone to ride. Now he's dead!"[18]

OFFICIAL: What garbage he talks! Here come two men. You wait here—maybe they'll have a horse to lend you.

TS'AI and the CHING (*enter on horseback and sing to the tune* Su-ti chin-tang):

> Lotus robes freshly imbued with imperial incense, I return,
> Leading the crowd of immortals out of Ts'ui-wei.
> In the Apricot Garden, my poem will be the first;
> Today is the day I've reached my goal.[19]

CH'OU (*calls out*): You can go on together. I've been knocked to pieces. You two go on!

CHING: It looks like you fell off your horse.

CH'OU: Isn't that obvious?

OFFICIAL: If I hadn't come along to help, he'd be dead now.

TS'AI and CHING: So he's indebted to your help![20]

CHOU: You two go ahead to the feast. I'm going to Doctor Li's place in T'ai-p'ing district and will meet you later.

OTHERS: Why go there?

CH'OU: To get my wounds healed![21]

OTHERS: Come with us. We'll get a horse from our attendants for you.

---

[18] The passage from the *Lun-yü,* as translated by Legge (1:301), is as follows: "Even in my early days, a historiographer would leave a blank in his text, and he who had a horse would lend him to another to ride. Now, alas! There are no such things!" The misinterpretation is based on the dual meaning of *wang,* "to die" or "to exist no longer."

[19] The song is probably derived from a poem included in the early southern play *Chang Hsieh chuang-yüan* (First Winner Chang Hsieh). Lotus clothes refer to the green clothing presented to new *chin-shih,* those who successfully passed the final examinations. Ts'ui-wei was the name of an imperial palace during T'ang times, and the Apricot Garden was the place where new *chin-shih* were feted. The First Winner rides at the head of the successful candidates and is the first to compose a poem during the celebration in the garden.

[20] There seems to be a joke intended here, perhaps on the basis that *lai,* "to depend on," can also have the meaning of "repudiate," so that the line would read, "He'll repudiate your help."

[21] Here I have been unable to determine the nature of the joke.

CH'OU: Please excuse me. You three go on.

OFFICIAL: But you said you were the First Winner. How can you miss the feast?

CH'OU: I wouldn't mind going to the feast—it's just that I refuse to get on a horse again. I've got it! You three go on ahead on horseback, and I'll follow you carrying a camp chair.

OFFICIAL: How odd that would look!

CH'OU: There are two ways you can explain it. If people on the road ask about it, just say that I'm a servant. If people at the feast ask, say I'm your assistant.

OFFICIAL: Not much of an answer!

ALL (sing to the tune K'u ch'i p'o):

Jade whips curling,
Like dragons our noble horses.
Amid the yellow flags,
Music and song bubble.
Today he's become a man indeed;
He'll be able to "return home in brocade clothes."

OFFICIAL: This is the Apricot Garden. Please wait a minute.

CH'OU: Let's lead the horses over there out of the way. If people see there are four gentlemen and only three horses, won't they find it ludicrous?

OFFICIAL: Who's going to lead the horses there?

CH'OU: I'll do it myself.

OFFICIAL: Wouldn't that be beneath your dignity? Gentlemen, now that you're here, the annual custom is for each of you to write a poem.

TS'AI: Let me think.

(With an action): I have a poem.

CHING and CH'OU: Please recite it for us.

TS'AI (recites in shih form):

Out of five hundred, his genius is the first.
Flowers are like embroidery, willows like mist.
His green robe's newly donned, the emperor's favor great;
The yellow list was just posted, the imperial ink still fresh.
Three thousand songs resound as he enters the Forbidden City,
And through ninety thousand miles of clouds and wind ascends to
    the blue sky.
Everyone marvels at how quickly he passed the test,
Scarcely believing that the Moon Lady would favor one so young.

OTHERS: A great poem!

CHING: I have a poem too.

OTHERS: Please let us hear it.

CHING (*recites in* shih *form*):

> In lingering sunlight, the mountain and streams are lovely;
> In spring wind, the flowers and grass are fragrant.
> From melting mud, swallows take off;
> In warm sand, mandarin ducks sleep.

OTHERS: That won't do; somebody else wrote it![22]

CHING: Scoundrels! I used other people's stuff for all three exams and passed every one. Do you mean to say I can't get away with borrowing a little poem?

OFFICIAL: No wonder he can "make a poem in seven steps."[23]

CHING: You think I really can't do it, but I'll put one together somehow! It goes like this:

> To take the exams there's no need to enter the hall!
> I never thought that I would don these lotus robes.
> Three exams—for each one I sent a substitute;
> For I'm a turtle whose sole skill is to fart.
> Now smiling to myself I sip this undeserved wine—
> But how can I ever write a poem?
> When people ask me for a sample of my work . . .

(OTHERS: What do you reply?)

> I'll ask my teacher and then let you know!

OFFICIAL: No doubt: "When it comes to goodness, he yields nothing to his teacher."[24]

CH'OU: All you gentlemen have been composing regulated verse, but I prefer old-style poems. Your poems are all about the exams, and I don't want to use a hackneyed theme like that. I have a new theme.

OTHERS: What is your theme?

CH'OU: I'll take my recent fall off my horse as a theme. It was an extraordinary event that should be commemorated in song. I've composed an old-style poem about it.

---

[22] The lines are from "Chüeh-chü erh-shou" (Two poems in the *chüeh-chu* form) by Tu Fu (712–770) (*CTS*, 228:2475).

[23] Ts'ao P'ei (187–226), first emperor of the Wei dynasty, once commanded his young brother Ts'ao Chih (192–232) to compose a complete poem in the time it took to take seven steps.

[24] The quotation is from the *Lun-yu* of Confucius (Legge, 1:304).

OTHERS: Let's hear it!
CH'OU: It goes like this:
(He recites in the ku-feng *form):*

> Didn't you see last year's First Winner Chang astride his horse?
> One stumble, and his left thigh was no longer attached.
> And didn't you see, the year before, Examiner Li in the saddle?
> One stumble, and his buttocks now lack one half.
> There are three things in the world in which one risks his life—
> Traveling by boat, riding a horse, and playing on swings.
> This year I risked my life indeed
> When I mounted on that golden saddle.
> Once I mounted a golden saddle,
> How could calamity be avoided?
> That detestable beast played tricks on me.
> Three cries I cried—he wouldn't go forward.
> Two urgings I urged—it was no joke.
> I grasped the reins—tight, tight, I held them.
> I had a long whip, but how could I dare strike?
> In a moment I'd tumbled down,
> Like a piece of tile blown by a fierce wind.
> Yesterday as I passed by the Office of State,
> Three soldiers approached and bowed down to me.
> All in a flurry, off I ran.

(OTHERS: Why?)

> For fear they'd ask me to become a horse trainer!

OFFICIAL: This is a dream that bears no repeating!
(He takes a drink of wine and sings to the tune Wu kung-yang):

> His writings excel those of the masters Ch'ao and Tung.[25]
> Presented at the Red Stairs, he was blessed with imperial favor.

(All continue the song):

> We go to celebrate at Ch'iung-lin,
> Our winners' decorations all atremble, we're led slowly forward by
>   bridles of gold.

(The ching *and* ch'ou *continue the song):*

> His fame has resounded to the Ninth Heaven
> And red phoenixes brought down a purple-sealed message from
>   the emperor.[26]

[25] Ch'ao Ts'o (d. 154 B.C.) and Tung Chung-shu (176–104 B.C.) were famous writers of the Han period.
[26] A red phoenix is said to carry decrees from the emperor; imperial letters and decrees are traditionally sealed with purple wax.

(All continue the song):

Though he is urged to return home, his services are required at
    the emperor's side;
The day will come when gold lotus lanterns light his way home.

OFFICIAL *(sings to the tune* Shan-hua-tzu):

Revelers crowd around tortoise-shell mats,
Struggling for a glimpse of the heroic Five Hundred.

TS'AI *(continues the song):*

I rejoice that in my first trial I found success,
By imperial favor I'm victor in the battle of pens.

(They sing the chorus together):

The world's at peace, chariots and scripts everywhere the same;[27]
Shields and battle-axes are put away, civil arts honored above all.
At such a time fish can change into dragons.
We're urged to linger in Ch'iung-lin—
Scenery of infinite beauty!

CHING *(sings to the same tune):*

Three thousand songs bubble up like springs;
His one pen's like a rainbow a hundred thousand feet high.
See how light from K'uei flies to the Purple Palace;
Its brilliance outdazzles the ten thousand pieces of jade.[28]

(They repeat the chorus above.)

TS'AI *(sings to the previous tune with a modified opening):*

Breaking through high clouds, I found a path,
With one try reached the heights.
Over three thousand miles, the water flies up in turmoil.[29]
What need to hang my bow on the Fu-sang tree,
Or lean my sword on K'ung-t'ung Mountain?[30]

[27] The standardization of axle-widths of the wheels of chariots so that they could fit
in the same tracks and of scripts is a common indication of unity of the empire.

[28] The star K'uei rules literary endeavors, while the star Purple Palace represents
the imperial palace; the phrase thus symbolizes Ts'ai's success. The ten thousand
pieces of jade are the court officials who are all less brilliant than Ts'ai.

[29] When the giant *p'eng* bird described by the philosopher Chuang-tzu soars up, the
force of its wings roils the water of the sea for three thousand miles.

[30] Jüan Chi (210–263) of the Three Kingdoms period wrote a poem containing the
lines, "My bent bow I hang on the Fu-sang Tree / My long bow I lean beyond the
sky." The Fu-sang tree is, according to legend, a huge tree in which the sun rests at
night. The meaning of the two lines is that Ts'ai need not take a heroic stance, as he
has already achieved success.

(They repeat the chorus above.)

CH'OU *(sings to the previous tune with a modified opening):*

How great the kindness of the emperor!
Eight delicacies in a stream he sends to us;
Nothing less than camel humps in kingfisher pots.

OFFICIAL *(continues the song):*

Our emperor treats scholars with such great esteem;
Not in vain are ten years of solitary study.

(They repeat the chorus above.)

TS'AI *(sings to the tune* Ta ho fu):

Billows of fragrance pour from precious burners,
Enveloping the clusters of embroidered coats in thick clouds.

CH'OU and CHING *(continue the song):*

As "jasper boats and silver seas" are moved, wine ripples red.
In one drink, each cup's emptied.

TS'AI *(continues the song):*

As cups are passed, my heart's stricken by its old pain.
The wine may be sweet—but how hard to swallow!
They—all alone with no one to offer even pulse and water;
I—here amid the clamor of passing cups.

(They sing the chorus together):

You mustn't
At such a revel let your thoughts be sad.

(They sing to the tune Wu ni-shang):

We hope the assembled worthies will be loyal and true,
Loyal and true.
In the Cloud Palace Gallery of Worthies, their portraits will hang,
Portraits will hang.[31]
In such untroubled times, the emperor's kindness is hard to
    repay;
We can only compose petitions urging the East Sacrifice,[32]

---

[31] The Cloud Palace of Worthies was a hall in the imperial palace of the Han dynasty in which portraits of meritorious officials were hung.

[32] The East Sacrifice on T'ai-shan was a major ceremony performed by the emperor; to urge that the sacrifice be carried out indicates respect for the ruling emperor.

And write hymns of praise to such virtue and peace.
The essences of heaven and earth are in perfect accord;
No jade pillar is needed to support the sky.[33]

ALL (*sing together to the tune* Hung hsiu-hsieh):

We get wildly drunk with the east wind,
East wind.
Servants help us mount our fine steeds,
Fine steeds.
As we return,
We gaze back to the east of the painted bridge—
Over blossoms blurred by darkness,
The sun bursts forth.
Amid bubbling of flute and song, flicker silk lanterns,
Silk lanterns.

(*They sing together to the tune* I pu-chin):

Tonight pomp and glory will fill our dreams;
Tomorrow morning we'll hear the distant palace bells.
Having thanked the emperor, the attendants depart, rows of leopard tails.

(*Closing poem*)
TS'AI:

My fame's risen to the gold hall, my robes changed to green.

CHING and CH'OU:

Our spirits soar from the wine we drank at Ch'iung-lin.

OFFICIAL:

"The world's ten thousand affairs are all low class;

ALL:

Scholarship is higher than them all."

(*All exit.*)

[33] Early mythology spoke of eight mountains like "jade pillars that hold up the sky." In later times, the term came to describe ministers of special importance to the emperor.

SCENE TEN

WU-NIANG (*enters and sings to the tune* I Ch'in-o):

> Deeply I sigh,
> Pity myself for this hard life that is my fate.
> My fate it is to have
> Parents-in-law grown old,
> And a husband with a shallow heart.

(*She recites to the* tz'u Ch'ing-p'ing yüeh):

> Husband and wife for but two months,
> Suddenly we were separated.
> With no protector, my parents-in-law lack all comforts.
> Boundless grief in my every thought!
> Our family's poor—we've always suffered;
> But how much worse in this year of bad harvests!
> So many difficulties, so much suffering!
> And even Heaven won't take pity on us.

Ever since my husband left, we've been suffering in this famine. With my parents-in-law so old, each morning I fear they can't last until evening. How can I take care of everything all by myself? Day and night, Mother curses Father. She says he should never have sent their son away, that in a famine like this it's impossible for me to manage all alone. Father won't give in, and just mutters and fusses around the house all day. The only thing I can do is wait for them to come out and try to make peace between them.

FATHER TS'AI (*enters and sings to the same tune*):

> Since he left, there's been not one word from our son;
> In our old age we're left in insecurity.

MOTHER TS'AI (*enters, grabs* FATHER TS'AI *by the ear, and continues the song*):

> Insecurity!
> Why don't you reflect how on that day
> It was you who forced our son to leave?

(WU-NIANG *attempts to placate her.*)

MOTHER TS'AI: Old reprobate! How you insisted on sending our son off to the examinations! Now we have nothing to eat, and even if he becomes the First Winner, how is it going to help you? If our son was here now, how hard he'd work to support us! We'd never have come to this hopeless situation. Old reprobate! Just go ahead and die!

FATHER TS'AI: Am I a magician that can predict famines? What family isn't suffering now? But who else complains like you? Never mind! I'll die, I'll die! If I don't die today from hunger, I'll be talked to death by your complaints.

WU-NIANG *(restrains him):* Father, Mother, please don't be angry any more. Just listen to me a minute. Mother, when Father sent your son away, no one could have known that today there'd be such a famine. You mustn't hold it against him. And Father, when Mother suffers through this terrible famine with no son by her side, it's only natural that she's distraught. You shouldn't blame her for holding it against you. Please calm yourselves. I'll pawn some of my hair ornaments and jewelry for rice so that you can have a few mouthsful of food. Better that I die of starvation myself than ever fall behind in my duties to you!

MOTHER TS'AI: Very well, daughter. It's just this old reprobate I hate!

(She sings to the tune Chin-so kua wu-t'ung):

> Our fine attentive son
> Was the support of both our lives.
> You had no cause to think of fame,
> And give up the comforts he gave to us.
> You sent him off to become an official
> And raise our family status high;
> Now if he becomes an official, you'll already be a ghost!

Old reprobate!

> You planned that the three sacred meats and five tripods we'd be
>   offering day and night:
> And now who will bring you a single sip of rice soup?
> Instead you've brought it about
> That our son will never be known as a true Confucian.

(They sing the chorus together):

How senseless disputing who's right and who's wrong!
How senseless disputing who's right and who's wrong!
Nothing for us now but streams of tears.

FATHER TS'AI (*sings to the same tune*):

Sons are always taught to study,
All in the hope of a glorious career.
When yellow placards summon scholars,
Don't they all go to try the test?
When Fan Ch'i-liang
Was sent to work on the Wall,
Against whom did his wife complain? [1]
The time to live, the time to die, are both decreed by fate.
Even families with sons and grandsons all around still suffer in
    famine.
Don't grumble and fuss so!
After all, at least we suffer together.

(*They repeat the chorus above.*)

WU-NIANG (*sings to the same tune*):

Though your son has left for a while,
Surely the day will come when he returns.
My gold and pearls
I'll pawn for food.

Mother, Father, please don't fight.

The neighbors will think that your daughter-in-law
Has proved a disappointment,
And that's why you two quarrel so.

Mother,

He loved his son, his one wish was that he win some fame.

Father,

She sees no son by her side and can't hold back her complaints.
No way to flee!
It must be Heaven that sent this calamity down upon us.

(*They repeat the chorus above.*)

FATHER TS'AI (*sings to the tune* Liu p'o-mao):

[1] Popular stories told of the young man Fan Ch'i-liang, who died while on corvèe service at the Great Wall, and his wife Meng Chiang-nü, who went to seek for him.

Before long we're sure to meet our end;
How sad that it was all through my own mistake!

Alas!

Better to be dead and let all these anxious cares cease.

(They sing the chorus together):

With each thought,
Our hearts are shattered.

MOTHER TS'AI *(sings to the same tune):*

We had a son, but you sent him away;
How can you expect our daughter-in-law to provide for us alone?

Daughter-in-law,

How pitiful that your years of youth will be spoiled!

(They repeat the chorus above.)

WU-NIANG *(sings to the same tune):*

I am the wife of your own son;
To toil for you is but my duty.
My one hope is that the two of you from today
Will live in peace.

(They repeat the chorus above.)

(Closing poem)
FATHER TS'AI:

Our bodies weak, our strength exhausted—how can we go on?

WU-NIANG:

Whatever you need—food and clothes—just ask it of me.

MOTHER TS'AI:

"Don't complain that our arguments last all day;

ALL:

For if one turns a deaf ear, the arguments will cease."

(They exit.)

SCENE ELEVEN

STEWARD (*enters and recites in* shih *form*):

Dimly through clouds of mist there gleams a silken window screen
Where deep within a golden chamber, a beautiful lady is locked
   away.
The peacocks in her screen are difficult to hit;
Who dares pull forth from behind her curtains the red thread?[1]

I'm the steward in the mansion of Prime Minister Niu. For the past few days, I've been hearing rumors that the master is going to take in a son-in-law. This young lady of ours can't be compared to ordinary young ladies. Not only is she the daughter of the prime minister, but she's also as accomplished as she is beautiful. The husband for her must be a learned official who is destined for good fortune. It won't be easy to find such a man. I don't know who the master is planning to take as a son-in-law. I'll just wait until he comes out, and then I'll find out what's going on. Here he comes now.

PRIME MINISTER NIU (*enters and sings to the tune* Ssu-niang-erh):

As my gray hair becomes starred with white,
I worry about making a marriage for my darling daughter.
But only the genius that wins the highest honors is a worthy
   match.
In the red pavilion on this day,
The red thread awaits his pull.
I must find a red leaf to carry my message.[2]

[1] The two lines allude to stories that concern the choosing of sons-in-law. Tou I (519–582) chose a son-in-law by asking prospective candidates to shoot arrows at the eyes of a pair of peacocks painted on a screen. The man who succeeded in hitting the eyes, thus winning Tou's daughter in marriage, later became the first emperor of the T'ang dynasty. Prime Minister Chang Chia-chen (667–729) could not determine which of his five daughters to marry to an eligible young man. He hid the five behind a screen, each holding a red thread, the bride to be determined by which thread the young man selected.

[2] The phrase "red leaf" is commonly used to symbolize a matchmaker. A number of stories tell of love messages that lead to marriage being written on red leaves. The most popular tells of a young man who found a red leaf floating in a ditch leading out of the imperial compound. The poem written on it expressed the loneliness of a young palace lady; the two were eventually married.

(The STEWARD *announces himself.)*

NIU: "The parents of a boy wish him to make a family; the parents of a girl wish to find her a home." My wife died many years ago and I'm left with only a daughter—a real beauty! Yesterday I had an audience with the emperor, and he asked me, "Is your daughter married yet?" I replied, "Not yet." He said, "Ts'ao Po-chieh is a fine, talented man. Why not take him in as your son-in-law?" After I had thanked him, he said, "I'll be the marriage sponsor for you." So now I want to send an official matchmaker to propose the match to Ts'ai Po-chieh. What do you think?

STEWARD: Sir,

(He continues in parallel prose):

 "When boys grow up, they ought to take wives; when girls are matured, they ought to be given in marriage." Your daughter is like a goddess from Paradise, and Ts'ai Po-chieh is an honored resident in the imperial offices. Moreover, the emperor himself suggested this marriage and wants to act as marriage sponsor. Let them become a happy couple together for a hundred years and not waste their destiny as husband and wife!

Sir!

(He recites in shih *form):*

How lovely to see a beautiful woman and brilliant man unite!
A marriage made in Heaven can't go wrong.
I'm sure that their marriage is preordained on the moon;
The cassia tree will approach the Moon Goddess.[3]

NIU: Well then, call the matchmaker from across the way, Old Lady Chang, and we'll have her go propose the match.

STEWARD: Yes, sir.

(He calls out.)

MATCHMAKER *(played by the* ch'ou *actor, carrying shoes, scales, and other things, enters and sings to the tune* Tsui t'ai-p'ing):

Everyone from Chang to Li
Calls on me,
For I'm the best matchmaker of them all!

---

[3]"The cassia tree" represents the talented Ts'ai; "the Moon Goddess," the beautiful Mistress Niu.

(STEWARD: Why?)

Just see how many tools I have!

STEWARD: Let me ask you, Granny, why are you carrying so many shoes?

MATCHMAKER: You have no idea how desperately the young ladies in mansions want to get married these days! It's the matchmaker who sets things in motion so they can be on their way, so when they're about to leave, they always make a pair of shoes to express their thanks to me. I can't count the number of marriages I've stirred up this year, and now I have so many shoes I can't begin to wear them all. The extras I sell.

STEWARD: Who buys them?

MATCHMAKER: The young ladies in the mansions!

STEWARD: The young ladies in mansions have tiny, tiny feet. What would they want with those shoes?

MATCHMAKER: You devil! They're so desperate to get married they buy these to give to the matchmaker and save the trouble of making them themselves.

(The STEWARD *stops the comedy.)*

NIU: Steward, where is the matchmaker?

STEWARD: Here!

(The STEWARD *leads the* MATCHMAKER *to meet* NIU.*)*

NIU: Matchmaker, why are you carrying so many things?

MATCHMAKER: Sir, these are the trademarks of a matchmaker.

NIU: Ask her what the axe is for.

STEWARD: The master asks you—what is the purpose of that axe?

MATCHMAKER: In the Book of Poetry, there's a good saying:

"When we cut firewood, how do we do it?
Without an axe it would not be possible.
When one takes a wife, how is it done?
Without a matchmaker he cannot get her." [4]

That's why I carry an axe as a trademark.

STEWARD: Don't wave an axe in front of Lu Pan! [5]

[4] Legge, 4:157.
[5] Lu Pan was a legendary skilled workman to whom Mencius referred. The popular saying means that one should not overrate one's own abilities before an expert.

NIU: Ask her what the sacks are for.

STEWARD: Matchmaker, the master wants to know what you do with the sacks.

MATCHMAKER: They're a trademark too. Everybody always talks about the matchmaker's sacks.[6]

NIU: Ask her what the scales are for.

STEWARD: The master asks what the scales are for.

MATCHMAKER: These are very important. They're called "mate-weighing scales." Whenever I arrange a match, first I weigh the prospective bride and groom; only if they're similar in weight do I complete the match. Then the husband and wife will be sure to get along without any hostility. But if one is heavier than the other, then as husband and wife they'll have nothing but strife. The other day I was passing by the Chang house and saw a young girl crying. I asked her why, and she said: "My husband's no good." I weighed them both and it was obvious they weren't a match.

NIU: Why?

MATCHMAKER: The groom weighed twenty-eight and a half catties, the bride only twenty-three.

STEWARD: You're not quite balanced yourself!

NIU: Ask her what she uses the rope for.

MATCHMAKER: This is the red rope. People who get married must have their feet tied together with rope; otherwise they shouldn't marry.[7]

STEWARD: How do you tie them?

MATCHMAKER: I'll show you!

(She ties the STEWARD's feet, then starts to tie her own, tripping the STEWARD.)

(The STEWARD cries out.)

MATCHMAKER: It's obvious that we're not meant for each other—I can't tie the knot.

NIU: Enough of this nonsense. Come here! I've received the emperor's command to marry my daughter to First Winner

---

[6] The pun "("matchmaker's sacks" for "matchmaker's axe") is similar to that in the original text, though it is actually socks the matchmaker is carrying.

[7] Popular legend tells of an old man seen checking over a book by moonlight. The book is a list of all future marriages, and those who are destined to marry must be tied together by the feet with the red rope he carries.

Ts'ai Po-chieh. I want you to go speak to Ts'ai. If you arrange this marriage properly, I'll reward you richly.

MATCHMAKER: What could be the difficulty? First, it's the imperial will. Second, there's the mighty reputation of your excellency. Finally, everyone knows that your daughter is as accomplished as she is beautiful. What objections could Ts'ai have?

STEWARD: Well spoken!

NIU: Come here and listen to me.

(*He sings to the tune* So-ch'uang lang):

> In my family I've one daughter, a beautiful girl!
> I've betrothed her to no minister, no duke.
> Yesterday I received the imperial command
> To select for her a scholar.

Matchmaker, say to him,

> He need not use white jade,
> Nor yellow gold as betrothal gift.

(*They sing the chorus together*):

> If their former lives have destined this marriage,
> Then on this day,
> Together we'll celebrate!

MATCHMAKER (*sings to the same tune*):

> My reputation in the Eastern Capital's supreme;
> When I speak of myself I don't need to boast!
> Today this affair
> I will complete.
> If one's too heavy, one too light,
> The official scales will tell it true.

(*They repeat the chorus above.*)

STEWARD (*sings to the same tune*):

> Though in the exams his name was first,
> How honored is he to receive the minister's summons!
> True glory lies within the embroidered curtains,
> Awaits his successful shot at the peacock in the screen.

Matchmaker,

> When you go to him,
> Surely he'll accept what has been decreed.

(*They repeat the chorus above.*)

(Closing poem)

MATCHMAKER:

I'll bring the famous genius to your home.

NIU:

To carry the perfumed letter only a good matchmaker will do.

STEWARD:

A marriage to last a hundred years will be made today.

ALL:

That they were meant for each other is Heaven's decree.

(All exit.)

SCENE TWELVE

TS'AI (*enters and sings to the tune* Kao-yang t'ai):

In dreams I journey to my distant family home,
But my grief remains locked within a traveler's lodge,
And distance keeps all news cut off.
My feelings already lonely and cold;
How fearful are these cold nights!
Through half-open doors I hear the twilight rain,
My feelings twisted into a thousand knots.
I keep watch at my cold window,
Where one lonely lamp
Flickers, grows dim.

(*He sings to the same tune with a modified opening*):

So lightly I left her, so lightly went away;
Now I mourn as the sound of her jade panpipe dies.[1]
A bright moon rises over my small pavilion—
Such anxiety and grief
Makes of us both bitter mourners.
On my bed fall ten thousand homesick tears,
Accompanying the sound of the water clock on and on till dawn.
Eyebrows locked in sorrow,
I avoid my reflection in the bright mirror,
For my hair is suddenly turning gray.

(*He recites to the* tz'u Mu-lan hua):

Everyone longs to be first in the examinations,
But wealth and position were never my desire.
With no courier to whom I can entrust my message,
I have no way to send my feelings there.
My fields and gardens must be choked with weeds;
Are the pine and chrysanthemums still there?[2]
Life is so short,
And I so helpless as my parents grow old!

[1] The line alludes to a famous couple of the Chou dynasty, Nung-yü (daughter of Duke Mu of Ch'in) and Hsiao Shih. Both were excellent players of the panpipes. Legend states that they became immortals and disappeared in the sky—she seated on a phoenix, he on a dragon.

[2] The two lines allude to a poem by T'ao Yüan-ming (365–427), "Kuei-ch'u-lai tz'u" (Returning Home). See *Chien-chu T'ai Yuan-ming chi* (The annotated collected works of T'ai Yüan-ming), in *Ssu-pu ts'ung-k'an,* 94, *chuan* 5, pp 5–7.

My father forced me to come to the examinations, but who
would have expected that my return would be delayed so
long? Now the emperor has graciously appointed me to the
position of counselor. Though it's an honorable post, how can
I remain in a distant city when my parents are so old? Heaven!
How can I know if my parents are safe? How can I know if my
wife is taking good care of them? I want to petition to leave
my post, but I don't know how the emperor will respond. Just
like the old saying, "I feel I've swallowed needle and thread;
they pierce my bowels and stomach, tie my heart in knots."
STEWARD and MATCHMAKER (*enter and sing to the tune* Sheng hu-
lu):

> By special favor of the emperor, he offers a marriage alliance;
> We come to transmit the news.
> If the young genius consents to unite in love,
> A happy affair will be completed on this very day.

TS'AI: "The doors of my home were layer on layer locked; how
could spring have found its way in?" Who's there?
STEWARD and MATCHMAKER: We carry the bountiful kindness
of the emperor and the stern command of Prime Minister
Niu. They want to present you with a lovely bride.
TS'AI (*sings to the tune* Kao-yang t'ai):

> My body is sunk in the sea of officialdom,
> My eyes blinded by the dust of the capital.
> Fame's a bridle, profit a lock I can't cast off.
> My gaze is cut off from my distant hometown,
> Where my spirit strains to fly in dreams.
> With empty babble,
> Don't entangle me with worthless vines and wild creepers,
> For I am already entwined with dodder and familial vines.[3]
> Who is it
> Who with no cause incites me to wrong,
> Wastes his breath in vain?

STEWARD (*sings to the same tune with a modified opening*):

> His rank's exalted;
> A famous lord in a purple pavilion,
> The prime minister behind a yellow door,

[3] From a line in one of the "Nineteen Old Poems," probably of the Han dynasty,
"dodder" has come to mean a wife.

He stands among the three noble locust trees.[4]
And she's a beauty in a golden chamber,
Bewitchingly charming, upright and pure.

MATCHMAKER *(continues the song):*

Great happiness!
In the red chamber on this day they summon a phoenix mate.
They sent me to come and make the match.
I hope that you
Will be quick to nod your head,
Won't delay to knot your hair with hers.[5]

TS'AI *(sings to the same tune with a modified opening):*

I'm held by one thing;
Over a thousand miles of passes and mountains
Awaits my own flesh and blood family.
How would you have me abandon them?
My wife is in her youth,
My parents' hair like drooping snow.
Mistaken, this proposal!
Surely you know that when a young man has once loved,
Even your moon goddess mustn't bother to summon him.
Filling the capital
Are powerful families without number;
Why must you choose the most humble?

STEWARD *(sings to the same tune with a modified opening):*

It's you who are wrong.
The prime minister seeks this marriage;
A noble family offers you betrothal gifts.
As if they're beneath you, you refuse.
The rare flower behind embroidered curtains
Is in her springtime, just eighteen.

MATCHMAKER *(continues the song):*

Don't refuse!
We know you've just plucked the cassia branch,
But now this flower awaits your hand.
Besides, he's personally received
A command from the emperor;
It's not just we who promote this match.

---

[4] The line indicates that Niu is one of the three highest officers of the empire.
[5] The traditional marriage ceremony included the knotting together of locks of hair from bride and groom.

TS'AI (*sings to the same tune with a modified opening*):

My heart's in a fever!
Since childhood I attacked the books,
Always I have understood right and wrong.
Could I bear to do what's wrong and ruin my good name?
My father and mother are still alive;
Surely to marry without telling them would be wrong.
I choke with grief—
Though I've been selected by the prime minister,
I think of the lovely lady who stood beside me in poverty.
Though the other has a flower face and beauty like the moon,
How can she compare to my own flesh and blood?

STEWARD (*sings to the same tune with a modified opening*):

How foolish you are!
His power subdues the officials of the court;
His authority could topple cities and states.
Now you oppose him,
And I fear that if he chooses to turn around the sun and sky,
The catastrophe will fall on you.

MATCHMAKER (*continues the song*):

We prepared this feast in vain!
"In empty stream, the water cold, fish wouldn't bite.
How laughable that our boat returns carrying nothing but bright
    moonlight." [6]
For dropping the silken line,
Fear not, there are other places!
How I laugh at this peasant!

TS'AI: Don't carry on like this. If I've really received such
imperial kindness, tomorrow I'll petition to leave office and at
the same time decline the marriage.

(*Closing poem*)
STEWARD and MATCHMAKER:

It is the imperial will; yet you will not accept.

[6] The lines are attributed to Monk Hua-t'ing chuan-tzu of the Sung dynasty; see
Shih Hui-hung, *Leng-chai yeh-hua* (Night talk in the cold studio), in *Pi-chi hsiao-shuo ta-
kuan* (Notes on Fiction), 6 vols. (Taipei: Hsin-hsing shu-chü, 1962), 1:903a. They are
common in *ch'uan-ch'i* plays to express disappointed hopes.

TS'AI:

Tomorrow I'll send a letter to the emperor.

ALL:

"If it's destined, they'll meet though a thousand miles apart.
If it's not, though face to face, they'll never meet."

(All exit.)

SCENE THIRTEEN

PRIME MINISTER NIU (*enters and sings to the tune* Ch'u tui-tzu):

Anxious morning and night,
I worry about nothing but my child.
How fares the Old Man of the Moon?
Why does the Iceman send no news?[1]
All day I stare off into space;
Deeper and deeper twist the strands of care.

My eyes strain through green mists, watching for the blue phoenix with a message; I scan the golden ditch for a red leaf with his answer.[2] Yesterday I sent the steward and a matchmaker to Ts'ai Po-chieh to arrange a match. Why haven't they returned? All I can do is wait and watch for them.

MATCHMAKER and STEWARD (*enter and sing to the same tune*):

That ridiculous phony!
He made all sorts of excuses to refuse our proposal.
How could we lack for fine bridegrooms who want to mount the
   dragon?
Is his fate so fine he's destined for a phoenix mount?[3]
It must be that all scholars
Are fated to be poor all their lives.

NIU: Matchmaker, you've returned! How did it come out? Is he willing?

MATCHMAKER: He's a thousand times unwilling, ten thousand times unwilling, both unwilling and unwilling, determinedly unwilling, firmly unwilling, just unwilling, unwilling.

STEWARD: Stop that! Let me tell you, sir. Ts'ai Po-chieh said that he already has a wife and that his parents are old. He

---

[1] Both the Old Man of the Moon and the Iceman are conventional terms for matchmakers.

[2] The red leaf symbolizes a matchmaker; see Scene Eleven, note 2.

[3] "To mount the dragon" is a conventional term for the marriage of a man; it derives from stories concerning the couple Nung-yü and Hsiao Shih (Scene Twelve, note 1). Although the phrase "phoenix mount" is more properly applied to a woman's marriage, the author uses it here again to symbolize Ts'ai's marriage.

shouldn't marry again without telling them, and therefore it would be hard to carry out your command.

NIU (*showing anger, sings to the tune* Shuang hsi-ch'ih):

> As I listen, my anger rises.
> In the court I am honored above all.
> I have a daughter;
> Could he think there are no mighty families to take her in marriage?
> I received an imperial command
> To take the First Winner as son-in-law.

Matchmaker,

> In his reply,
> What did he say?

MATCHMAKER (*sings to the same tune with a modified opening*):

> Let me tell you, sir,
> That man was most strange!
> He said that since he had passed the examinations,
> There is no point in offering even a flowerlike beauty to him.
> He insulted you,
> Insulted your daughter.

(NIU: How did he insult my daughter?)

> He said her feet were over a foot long!

STEWARD (*stops the comedy, then finishes the song*):

> There's no reason to tell such lies!

(*He sings to the same tune with a modified opening*):

> Sir, just listen to my report:
> As Ts'ai listened, his eyebrows knotted in sorrow.
> Loyal and filial,
> Virtuous and kind,
> He thinks of his eighty-year-old parents.
> Even more, since he's already married,
> To take another wife can't be right.
> He intends in early court
> To send up a petition
> For permission to give up his post and return home,
> And he asks that you choose another son-in-law.

NIU (*laughs and sings to the same tune with a modified opening*):

> So he really wants to petition the emperor
> And dares to contend with me!

(They continue the song together):

> These scholars
> Won't listen to reason!
> Without a thought he disobeys the emperor's will.
> I'll never let him leave his post or reject this marriage.

NIU: The two of you must go back to speak to Ts'ai again and find out what he's planning. I'm going to court to request the emperor to refuse his petition to leave office.

(Closing poem)
NIU:

> His petition to the emperor will be in vain.

MATCHMAKER and STEWARD:

> He'd best make haste to accept the command.

ALL:

> We'll make a green silk net to trap the phoenix mate,
> A jade cage to capture the mandarin duck.

(All exit.)

SCENE FOURTEEN

MISTRESS NIU (*enters and sings to the tune* T'i yin-teng):

My father really goes too far!
With no regard for others' feelings, he forces his own will.
Though the birds fly in opposite directions, he insists upon joining
    their wings;
Though the flowering trees are separated by a wall, he forces
    them to link branches.[1]
A destined marriage—
Could it be like that?

I want to speak to him,

  But how can young ladies talk about the marriage state?

Destined marriages, destined marriages—they're in no way accidental. It's ridiculous how my father keeps inviting the First Winner to be my husband. Since he won't accept, we ought to let the matter drop. Who would have thought that my father would refuse to give up the idea and insists on making him his son-in-law? If the man is unwilling, then we could never live in harmony as husband and wife. I want to speak to my father, but this is something a girl can never mention. Ah, what unhappiness!

(*She performs an action.*)

(MU-MU *comes in secretly and spies on* MISTRESS NIU.)

MU-MU: Aha! I've finally caught the young lady in a sad mood. Miss, what are you thinking about?
MISTRESS NIU: I'm not thinking about anything.
MU-MU: Then why are you sitting here leaning your sweet cheek on your hand? Are you unhappy about something? Let me ask you, nothing has ever upset or moved you, but now I begin to suspect that was all show. Is it the scenery outside that's bringing on sentimental thoughts?

[1] Pairs of birds with joined wings and trees with branches grown together are traditional symbols of true lovers.

MISTRESS NIU: What are you saying? It's because my father is acting inappropriately that I'm unhappy.

MU-MU: What is he doing?

MISTRESS NIU: The other day he decided to give me in marriage to Ts'ai Po-chieh, the First Winner, and sent a matchmaker to speak to him. The First Winner declined to accept. Since he's unwilling, we ought to let the matter drop. But now Father has sent the matchmaker there again. I don't dare speak to him about this—I wish you'd speak to him for me.

MU-MU: If such is your father's wish, why would he listen to me?

(*She sings to the tune* Kuei-chih hsiang):

> That scholar's low opinions
> Are really too stupid!
> He won't lie down on his eastern couch[2]
> And goes in vain to plead his case in the imperial hall.
> I think the truth must be
> He holds you in contempt.
> Your father is not upset for nothing;
> He's afraid you would be talked about.
> People would say that you, the daughter of a noble lord,
> Couldn't even get the First Winner for a mate.

MISTRESS NIU (*sings to the same tune*):

> A loving marriage to last a hundred years
> Surely starts from mutual consent.
> He declines with all his strength,
> So we must not persist.
> I think the truth must be
> There's something that holds him back.
> When a favor is too insistently bestowed, it may lead only to resentment.
> With no lack of noble gentlemen in the capital,
> Why must it be the First Winner I marry?

MU-MU (*sings to the tune* Ta ya-ku):

> It's not that your father is stubborn;
> He only fears that as spring flowers and autumn moons pass by,

---

[2] Wang Hsi-chih (276–339), a famous calligrapher, was chosen as a son-in-law because he continued to relax on a couch in the eastern section of his home in the presence of a servant sent to propose, while his brothers all put on airs. "To lie down on the eastern couch" thus means to become a son-in-law.

Your youth will slip away.
And how fine that man's talent and form!
First genius among the Five Hundred.
Your father wishes to take the goddess of the moon
And entrust her to this young man.

MISTRESS NIU (*sings to the same tune*):

Destined marriages are surely made in Heaven.
If the desire's not there,
Husband and wife will blame each other to the end.
I think that the red rope has not been tied,
That he has no jade to plant at Lan-t'ien.[3]
Don't force the goddess of the moon
Upon this young man!

(*Both exit.*)

---

[3] A story in the collection *Sou shen chi* tells of a retired scholar given some stones and
told that if he planted them, they would produce jade which he could use to betrothe
a wife; the prophecy was fulfilled. Lan-t'ien is an area famous for its fine jade.

SCENE FIFTEEN

EUNUCH (*played by the* mo *actor, enters and sings to the tune* Pei tien chiang-ch'un):

Night's darkness fades;
Dawn's brightness grows.
I roll up the pearl screen,
Pass through the red courtyard,
To set out the Gold Dragon's desk.

(*He sings to the tune* Pei hun-chiang lung):

I live in the palace park;
For all it's worth, I'm inches away from Heaven's majesty and right next to the Dragon Face.
Every day I follow behind the imperial carriage
And hear the sound of the marshal's whip.
I kneel where the dragon's head is carved
And follow wherever the panther tails lead.
Day after day, I dwell in the barracks,
Morning after morning, follow the ranks.
I'll never get to be a cabinet minister of the first rank,
But I've had plenty of experience watching the water clock in the chill of dawn.
Don't sigh in envy over my life!
In mountain monasteries when the sun is high, the monks sleep on;
And I reflect that wealth and fame can never compare to their tranquil life.

I am an insignificant eunuch of the imperial court.

(*He continues in parallel prose*):

 I come and go in the forbidden chambers and stand in attendance at the red court. I receive the reports of the hundred officials, carry down the orders of the One Man. Indeed it's true, "If the virtue of the lord is without blemish, it is due to the good work of his attendants. When the heavenly countenance is pleased, his close officials know it first."[1]

[1] The second line is from the poem "Tzu-ch'en-tien t'ui ch'ao k'ou-hao" by Tu Fu (712–770) (*CTS*, 225:2409).

Now the sky is gradually brightening, and it's time for early court. The emperor ascends the hall, and I must wait here in case officials come to present petitions. How does this early court look?

 Just see the Milky Way grow pale, the Big Dipper glimmer. Sounds from a trumpet bring down the dim stars; three rolls of the drum announce the clear light of dawn. The water clocks with their silver arrows continue their cold dripping at the nine gates of the palace. Through carnelian towers and jade halls can be heard the muted sound of morning bells in the myriad courtyards. Softly, gradually, spreading over all, the first rays of the sun illuminate the towers. Along with the soft whisper of breezes, billowing mists drift through the imperial park. Vapors curl up from the jade hand towering in the air, where drops of luxuriant dew are not yet dry.[2] In the clear deep arch of jade above, a perfectly full moon begins to set. A few calls of the regal cock—*i-i-wo-wo*— announce to the imperial streets that the watches of the night have ended. A hundred warblings from soaring orioles—*chieh-chien-kuan-kuan*—proclaim to the royal park the dawn of a spring day. Chariots roll outside the five gates with a clatter, making dust fly. Music strikes up within the six palaces like a bubbling caldron. Just see in Chien-chang Palace, Five Oaks Palace, Tall Catalpa Palace, Eternal Good Faith Palace, and Eternal Pleasure Palace, the opening of golden locks on jade gates—doors within doors, by the thousands and ten thousands; in Shining Bright Hall, Golden Splendor Hall, Eternal Life Hall, P'i-hsiang Hall, Ch'ang-men Hall, Unicorn Hall, Yuan-luan Hall, T'ai-chi Hall, and White Tiger Hall, the rolling up of embroidered door screens and pearl curtains, in the hazy dawn, one after the other.
   Suddenly in the stillness—*hung-hung-hua-hua*—like thunder the sound of the watchman's rattle crashes on the ears. Throughout every hall, one smells, pervasive and enshrouding as fog and yet not fog, the pungent fragrance of incense from imperial burners. Behind the misty red clouds, pheasant-tail fans screen the emperor in his yellow ochre robes. At the deeply sheltered red stairs, the dragon-scale throne is protected by a red "iris" umbrella. To the left—so numerous, so imposing—are arranged in perfect order the Yu-lin Corps, Ch'i-men

---

[2] Emperor Wu of the Han dynasty (r. 140–87 B.C.) had a statue of an immortal in his courtyard. Dew was collected in its hand to be used for elixirs.

Corps, K'ung-ho Corps, Shen-ts'e Corps, and Hu-pen
Corps. "Flowers touch the swords which hang from their
waists as the last stars disappear from the sky." To the
right—so many, so dignified—are ranked in precise order
the Chin-wu Guard, Lung-hu Guard, Kung-jih Guard,
Ch'ien-niu Guard, and P'iao-ch'i Guard. "The willows
which brush against their banners and flags are still wet
with dew."[3] Jade and gold ornaments reflecting back and
forth, how bright and splendid are the divine attendants!
Kingfisher blue and purple decorations shining together,
in such perfect order are the rows upon rows of civil and
military officials! At the foot of the dragon steps stand a
pair of bewitching lady attendants, faces as beautiful as
flowers or the moon, wearing robes and slippers
embroidered with phoenix patterns. Amid the ranks of
those adorned with leopard tails are set a pair of dignified
censors, with hearts of iron and courage like steel, holding
white ivory tablets and wearing unicorn hats.

Some bow, some kneel—who would dare push and
shove or make a disturbance? Some move forward, some
retreat to the back—who could fail respectfully to follow
the set ritual? Their only desire is always to gaze in
reverence at the imperial regalia and see the Sage's virtue
each day reborn—day after day reborn! And with their
fellow officials bow to the heavenly countenance, hoping
that the emperor's long life will last for ten thousand
years—ten thousand times ten thousand years! Never
before could one believe that the perfect ritual of Shu-sun
T'ung could exist; only today is the honor of being
emperor demonstrated.[4]

Here comes a petitioner already!

TS'AI (*in formal attire, enters and sings to the tune* Tien chiang-
ch'un):

As the moon pales and stars disappear,
In Chien-chang Palace[5]
Dawn breaks at a thousand doors,

[3] This line, along with the line beginning "Flowers . . ." is from the poem "Feng-
ho chung-shu she-jen Chia Chih tsao-ch'ao Ta-ming kung" by Ts'en Shen (715–770)
(*CTS*, 201:2096).

[4] Shu-sun T'ung (third to second century B.C.) was responsible for establishing the
ritual to be used in the Han court. The first emperor of the dynasty was so pleased
with the conduct of his court that he said, "Only now do I understand the honor of
being emperor."

[5] Chien-chang Palace was an imperial palace of Han times. It was said to have one
thousand doors and ten thousand windows.

Smoke curls up from imperial braziers,
And the distant sound of marshal's whip fades.
Suddenly I recall past times
When I'd go at dawn to greet my parents in their room.
The cock has crowed;
Depression winds round my feelings.
At these times, how great my grief!

(*He recites in* shih *form*):

Unable to sleep, I hear the sound of golden keys;
Imagine jade pendants on windblown reins.
Tomorrow I go to petition at court;
Again and again I ask, when will this night end?[6]

Because my parents are still alive, I am going to petition today
to leave my official post and go back to care for them. The sky
is already brightening, and here is the gatehouse outside the
fifth gate. I'll go on in.

(*He enters, then sings to the tune* Shen chang-erh):

Clouds of dust as I kneel,
Clouds of dust as I kneel.
I gaze up at the lofty firmament,
Glimpse the dragon scales glinting in the sunlight.

EUNUCH: You can't go up to the court.
TS'AI (*continues his song*):

Inches away from the double pupils shining on high.[7]

EUNUCH (*continues the song*):

All communications
Must be here
One by one explained.

TS'AI (*continues the song*):

I bow to the distant emperor,
I bow to the distant emperor.

(*He sings to the tune* Ti-liu-tzu):

[6] The lines are by Tu Fu (712–770) from the poem "Ch'un su tso-sheng" (Spring
night in the chancellery) (*CTS*, 225:2411). The poet describes a night waiting to appear in court. Because of his anxiety, he imagines the sound of keys unlocking palace
doors and the bells of courtiers' horses on their way to court.
[7] Legend states that Emperor Shun (trad. dates 2255–2205 B.C.) had double pupils,
and the term is often used to describe a wise emperor.

This minister Yung,
This minister Yung
Was received at the emperor's court.
This minister Yung,
This minister Yung
Begs to return the notice of appointment.
Not because I consider the post too low,
But because my home is ten thousand miles away,
My parents both old.
For thus annoying his imperial majesty,
I beg to be forgiven.

EUNUCH: I am a eunuch in charge of receiving petitions. If you
have a communication, it must now be divulged.

TS'AI (*kneels and sings to the tune of* Ju-p'o ti-i):

Your subject Counselor Ts'ai Yung reports:
I was by imperial decree
Appointed to the position of counselor.
I was further favored by the offer of Mistress Niu in marriage.
For thus annoying his imperial majesty,
I'm deeply upset, deeply fearful,
Bow my head, bow my head!
I humbly submit that this obscure official
In youth held high resolves:
Reciting poetry and history,
I put my strength into study and self-cultivation,
With never a desire for glory or wealth.
To serve my parents,
Enjoy a rustic life—
From the beginning my heart's desire was this and nothing more.
I never thought the local authorities
Would promote my attendance at the examinations.
In the capital,
How could I expect that my stupidity would be favored
With first place?

(*He sings to the tune* P'o ti-erh):

Again I received an imperial invitation
To marry the daughter of Lord Niu.
Humble and worthless,
How could I deserve such favor?
But my parents are old,
And since I went away,
Time's passed on and on.
My cottage and fields
Left untended so long!

(*He sings to the tune* Kun ti-san):

My old parents,
Their hair hanging white,
Their strength worn away,
Are all alone.
I have no brothers;
Who will care for them?
Separated from me by thousands of mountains and streams,
Are they dead, are they alive?
Letters bearing news are hard to send.
What grieves me most:
When I can offer no comfort to them,
I feel shame at my official wages.

(*He sings to the tune* Hsieh-p'ai):

Without informing my parents,
How can I take a wife?
Further, I have heard
That in my hometown
Disaster's descended,
Famine has struck.
So often I feel that my parents
May fall into the ditches and become ghosts;
It could have happened.
Then tell me, can I stop
These tears that fall in pain?

EUNUCH: This is not a place for crying. You mustn't alarm his majesty.

TS'AI (*sings to the tune* Chung-kun ti-ssu):

Paid a handsome salary,
Girdled in vermilion and purple,
I come and go in the imperial palace.
But I think of my parents—
Cold without clothing,
Hungry without food,
Falling in the ditches to die.
I recall that in former dynasties
Chu Mai-ch'en set out from his home
And became governor of K'uai-chi.
Ssu-ma Hsiang-ju,
Tally in hand, returned in brocade.[8]

[8] Chu Mai-ch'en (d. 115 B.C.) came from a poor family in K'uai-chi, but rose to become governor of the area. Ssu-ma Hsiang-ju (179–117 B.C.) was sent as an envoy by the emperor to his native region of Shu and was received with great respect by the

(*He sings to the tune* Sha-wei):

When they lived, sages reigned;
Both were able to return to their family home.
Why is it I must be
Separated from Father and Mother,
Far away from my ancestral home,
Receiving no news of them,
All my heart's wishes denied?
I humbly hope that your majesty
Will be moved by my resolve,
And send me home
So I can serve my parents.
What could compare to such bounty!

(*He sings to the tune* Ch'u-p'o):

If still you feel that I have some small ability,
I would like to be appointed to a local post at home.
In this way,
Loyal heart and filial intent
Can be together fulfilled.
Unworthy as I am to gaze at the Sage in Heaven,
How my anxiety grows!

EUNUCH: I see. I'll transmit your petition to the emperor. You wait here for his reply. As they say, "Eyes search for the battle flag; ears strain for the good news."[9]

(*He exits.*)

TS'AI (*sings to the tune* Shen chang-erh):

Clouds of dust as I kneel,
Clouds of dust as I kneel.
I see far off, misty and vague, auspicious clouds,
And think that the eunuch must have arrived.
I expect that when the emperor has read it all,
It's most likely
He'll feel compassion for this filial crow.[10]
My straining eyes cannot penetrate those nine layers of clouds.
My straining eyes cannot penetrate those nine layers of clouds.

governor and other prominent men, including his father-in-law, who had earlier treated him with contempt. Both were able to return in glory to their native regions, while Ts'ai is kept in the capital.

[9] This saying is common in Yüan-Ming drama and fiction to express the feeling of one waiting for the reply to a message or the solution of a problem.

[10] Baby crows are said to disgorge their food to feed their parents and are often used as a symbol of filial children.

(*He sings to the tune* Ti-liu-tzu):

Let Heaven consider,
Let Heaven consider
The prayer of Ts'ai Yung!
Both my parents,
Both my parents
Are in a crisis of life or death.
How sad that their loving care of me is still unrepaid!
A single petition rises through nine layers of clouds;
Will it be heard?
Shall we come together or remain apart?
All will be decided now.

Why hasn't the eunuch returned yet? Surely the emperor has granted my petition! Heaven! If only I'm able to return and serve my parents, what need have I to be an official?

EUNUCH (*bearing the emperor's reply, enters and sings to the previous tune*):

On this day,
On this day,
The counselor brought a petition.
I carried it up,
I carried it up.
The Sage's eyes have read it.
He said that yesterday a petition came from the grand tutor;
He wants to take Ts'ai in as son-in-law.
What can be done?
The Jade Tones are manifest;
Approach and hear his decision.

The Sage's reply is here. Kneel while I read it.

(TS'AI *kneels*.)

EUNUCH (*reads*): "Though the filial way is great, it culminates in serving one's ruler."[11] "The ruler's affairs are so taxing, what time is left to repay one's father?"[12] With my trifling virtue, I have inherited the Great Enterprise. I worry at the winds of turmoil; the transformation to harmony and peace is not yet completed. I summon wise scholars to make up for my own deficiencies. It is reported that you are talented and learned and are widely respected by the populace. I have chosen you

[11] *Hsiao Ching* (Classic of Filial Piety), p. 2a.
[12] The quotation is from the *Shih Ching* (Book of Poetry) (Legge, 4:248).

to fill an advisor's position and serve as a rectifier. You ought
to observe these duties and cease this determined refusal. As
for the matter of the marriage, you should accept the grand
tutor's invitation and thereby form a perfect union. By special
decree of the emperor. Give thanks for his bounty!

TS'AI (*bows, then rises*): Brother eunuch, please go and petition
the emperor for me again. I really don't wish to be an official.

EUNUCH: This scholar knows nothing of the ways of the world!
Who dares to disagree with the wish of the emperor? This is
really no place to make a scene.

TS'AI (*in a panic*): I'll go myself and beg to return the letter of
appointment—how would that be?

EUNUCH (*restrains him*): Do what? This scholar is really weird!
You can't go there!

TS'AI (weeps): Alas!

(*He sings to the tune* Cho-mu-erh):

> My parents are old and worn,
> My wife young and delicate.
> Over thousands of miles of mountains, all news of them is lost.
> There they raise their eyes to nothing but loneliness;
> Here I turn my head to nothing but distance.
> There they strain their eyes in search of a son who never returns;
> Here I cry till my tears run dry over parents whose fate I cannot
>   know.
> Cut off from each other by a red phoenix edict!

EUNUCH (*sings to the same tune*):

> Why feel so anxious?
> You need not be upset!
> Life is always so—partings many, reunions few.
> A bold young man should become lord over ten thousand miles;
> How could he be content to waste his life growing old in native
>   fields?
> After all, service to rulers and service to parents are alike noble;
> How can a man be perfect in both filial service to parents and loy-
>   alty to ruler?
> Haven't you heard how Wang Ling's mother died to ensure his
>   allegiance to the court?[13]

---

[13] Wang Ling (d. 181 B.C.) was a supporter of Liu Pang (256–195 B.C.), founder of
the Han dynasty. Hsiang Yü (232–202 B.C.), a rival, captured Wang Ling's mother in
order to prevent his assisting Liu Pang. The mother committed suicide so that he
would not let worry for her interfere with his support of Liu Pang.

TS'AI (*sings to the tune* San tuan-tzu):

> How can I make known what's in my heart?
> The emperor's ear's as inaccessible as Heaven.
> How can I flee from this pain?
> So long the road where white clouds pass to my home!

EUNUCH (*continues the song*):

> Your official post brings glory to your parents;
> A title of nobility will grace their hall.
> How could you object to raising them to new status?

TS'AI (*sings to the tune* Kuei-ch'ao huan):

> A new lover,
> A new lover—
> How harshly they summon me to her!
> My wife's resentment will last forever.
> A year of famine,
> A year of famine—
> How can they endure it?
> My parents will die in ditches, become hungry ghosts.

EUNUCH (*continues the song*):

> When troops are dispatched to the four quarters of the world,
> The soldier standing guard in desert wilds
> Puts aside all thoughts of family and sacrifices himself for the sake
>   of the empire.

(*Closing poem*)
TS'AI:

> So far my home, news so hard to send!

EUNUCH:

> But what can you do if the ruler denies your request?

TOGETHER:

> When thoughts of the past become too painful to bear,
> Just cast all regrets to the east wind.

(*They exit.*)

SCENE SIXTEEN

VILLAGE HEAD (*played by the* ch'ou *actor, enters and sings to the tune* P'u-hsien ko):

I'm the village head—a hard job to fill!
All sorts of duties keep me busy day and night.
When officials come to check the granary stores,
And find all the grain is gone,
It will be a beating for me, upside-down!

(*He recites*):[1]

I'm the local chief, in charge of the village folk;
This job is something else!
Raggedy shoes, raggedy hat, raggedy clothes—
For one should really dress the part.
Up at the village seat, I flatter and pay court,
But when I return to the village, my spirit soars.
When I ask for official rations, the standard measure I make big;
But when I sell the public salt, I weight the scale a bit.
When I choose tax collectors, I let off the rich and appoint the poor.[2]
In determining the high brackets, I impose on the weak and cringe before the strong.[3]
Without a care I've thrown my weight around,
For the job must end in the end.
I forgot that Heaven doesn't give as man desires,
That everything in life is preordained.
I squeeze out five or ten ounces of gold,
Then five or ten ingots I'm forced to spend.
Officials leave and demand their farewell gifts;
Roll calls are ordered and I must hire extra men.[4]

[1] The passage is in a form of simple poetry; lines are of unequal length but are rhymed.
[2] Tax collectors were responsible for submitting to the authorities the amount due from citizens of the area. Because they were required to make up any deficiency in this amount from their own pockets, the job was an undesirable one to be avoided.
[3] Wealthy families in the high brackets had to provide more laborers for convoy duty, taxes, and horses. The village head was responsible for determining into which bracket a family fit, and could be bribed into listing the family at a lower financial level than it actually was.
[4] A corrupt village head would overstate the number of militia in his jurisdiction in order to appropriate the extra provisions and money for his own use. If a roll call was ordered, he would have to hire extra men to fulfill the number of men listed in his roster.

My fields are all in mortgage;
Not an inch of land remains.
How I hate the runners from the district seat!
How I hate the scribes in the central office!
They oppress me in a thousand ways,
So many ordeals they put me through.
For nothing they rip off my raggedy hat,
Beat me till I'm sick with yellow sores.
I'll jump in the river or hang myself, I often think—
Who needs this life I've got?
And now again they come to check the granary stores,
And I haven't the grain to meet their demands.
But if they turn me upside-down,
I'll call out for justice,
"I am not the village head!
I am not the local chief!
Don't beat a law-abiding citizen for no cause!"
"Then who might you be?"
"I'm the *fu-ching* in an acting troupe!"[5]

Alas! I've been taking grain home from the official granary to feed my wife and children. And now the authorities are coming today to inventory the stores and distribute grain to the poor people. How can I get some grain? I haven't got any money to buy it. There's no other way—I'll have to sell my wife! That way I can get enough money to buy some grain to make up the shortage. Old lady, come on out!

(His wife, played by the ching *actor, enters.)*

WIFE: Alas, alas, old man! How can you get the grain? You're in for another beating!

VILLAGE HEAD: There's no other way! "One night as husband and wife grows to a hundred nights of love."[6] I'm sure you don't want to see me get a beating, and in a year of famine like this, there's no way I can provide for you in comfort anyway. I'm going to have to sell you for a little cash, so I can buy the grain.

WIFE: My god! For fear of a beating, you'd sell your own wife! What's more valuable—your own buttocks or your wife?

VILLAGE HEAD: I've no other way!

[5] The *fu-ching* is one of the role titles in Chinese drama. The joke is a characteristic example of the *ch'uan-ch'i* author's playing with stage conventions.

[6] This proverb is common in Yüan-Ming drama. The meaning here is that a woman and man who have shared love should be willing to sacrifice for each other.

(He grabs his wife and calls out): You in the streets and in the markets, all you high-class people, your village head offers his wife for sale! Who will buy?

WIFE: You can't sell me!

(She knocks him down and runs off.)

VILLAGE HEAD *(after getting up):* Great! What a fine wife I married myself! I've no other way! All I've got now is a son—I'll have to sell him. Son, come here!

(His son, played by the ching *actor, enters.)*

SON: Daddy, if you're in for a beating, that's your problem—don't sell me!

VILLAGE HEAD: Come here. You, my son, have always been filial and obedient. As your daddy, I raised you up—you know I cherish you! But this is a crisis; the authorities will be here soon, and I brought home all that grain from the granary for the family to eat. I didn't eat it all myself—you had your share! My son, when I've sold you, I'll have some money to buy grain.

SON: Damn! Out of fear of a beating you'd sell your own son! Which is more valuable—your buttocks or a son?

VILLAGE HEAD: You won't do as I say?

(He grabs the son and calls out): You in the streets and in the markets, all you high-class people, your village head offers his son for sale! Who will buy?

(The son knocks him down and runs off.)

VILLAGE HEAD *(after getting up):* Great! What a fine wife I've got, what a fine child I raised! This is retribution for the mischief I've done all my life. There's no other way! I'll have to talk it over with the citizen chief Li. I pass the bend, turn the corner, and here's his house. Citizen chief Li, citizen chief Li!

LI *(played by the* ching *actor, enters and sings to the previous tune):*

I'm the citizen chief in charge of the public stores.
My whole family, old and young, live off the granary.
And if anything goes wrong, I needn't fear,
For the village head is the first one they'll beat.

Elder brother,

Only after they finish with the village head
Will they start on the citizen chief!

You're in big trouble! The authorities will be here soon, and if you don't find a way to refill the granary, you're in for a beating!

VILLAGE HEAD: What would you suggest? You're the one who ate all the grain; you think of something.

LI: You wait here. I'll go to my friend clerk Chang and borrow some grain from him that we can use to trick them.

VILLAGE HEAD: Go on, and hurry back! I'll be waiting in the granary.

LI: I'm off. My only fear is that "It's easier to climb a mountain and catch a tiger than to open one's mouth and ask a favor of others."

(LI *exits.*)

(*The* VILLAGE HEAD *opens up the granary.*)

VILLAGE HEAD: It's a fine public granary—except that there isn't any grain inside. I wonder whether the citizen chief has been able to borrow some.

(*He looks off.*) It's a miracle! A miracle! He's really borrowed some grain!

LI (*enters*): "When you ask a favor, you've got to go to a big man; when you help someone out, you've got to help when their need is most urgent." Okay! I was able to borrow two polesful, three piculs, seven pecks, four pints, eight tenths, and two hundred and fifteen grains. You go on up in the granary and I'll pass it up to you.

(*They perform actions.*)

VILLAGE HEAD: It's a miracle! The granary is full! You go see if the officials are coming yet. I'll seal up the granary.

LI: I'm off. As they say, "Our eyes stare out to glimpse the victory banners; our ears strain to hear the good news."

(LI *exits.*)

OFFICIAL and ATTENDANT (*played by the* ching *and* mo *actors, enter and sing to the previous tune*):

Commanded by the emperor to relieve the starving masses,
We leapt to the saddle, raised our whips, and set forth.

Where is the village head?

Make haste to open the public stores
To apportion grain to the populace.

Ah!

Be truthful in your accounts—tell no lie!

Village head, bring the account book here and let me have a look.

(The VILLAGE HEAD *performs an action.)*

OFFICIAL *(reads):* "Originally in receipt of twenty-nine piculs. Recently supplied thirty-six piculs. Disbursed nineteen piculs. Balance forty-six piculs." Open the granary!

(The ATTENDANT *and the* VILLAGE HEAD *open the granary.)*

OFFICIAL *(looking in):* Nonsense! How could that be forty-six piculs?
VILLAGE HEAD: Sir, it is, it is!

OFFICIAL: Get a statement from him.

(The ATTENDANT *performs an action.)*

OFFICIAL: Village head, go and tell all the villagers to come here and make their requests for grain.
VILLAGE HEAD: I'm off! "My heart speeds like an arrow, my feet move as if on wings."

(He exits.)

OFFICIAL: That scoundrel is lying. How could this pile of grain be forty-six piculs?
ATTENDANT: That's his problem. If there's grain missing, he'll have to pay it back, that's all.
OFFICIAL: Right!
VILLAGE HEAD *(disguised as a beggar, enters and sings to the tune* Wu chih chi):

My stomach's starving,
My eyesight blurred,

Not a penny is left in my home.
My children's screams and wails I can't bear to hear.
I've heard that his excellency has come to provide relief,
So I come to request grain to save us from distress.

ATTENDANT: What is your name, old fellow? How many people in your family?

VILLAGE HEAD: My name is Confucius. I live in the big village. I have three thousand and seventy mouths to feed.

OFFICIAL: What nonsense!

VILLAGE HEAD: Let me explain, sir. "The great man Confucius converted three thousand and seventy people."[7]

ATTENDANT: A mouthful of nonsense!

OFFICIAL: How many are really in your family?

VILLAGE HEAD: Myself, my wife, and two children.

OFFICIAL: Give him his allotment.

(The ATTENDANT *performs an action.)*

ATTENDANT: Allotted four portions of grain.

VILLAGE HEAD: Thank you very much, sir. As they say, "If you can forget shame for one day, your stomach will be full for three days."

(He exits.)

OFFICIAL: Check him off the list. Well, we've already distributed to one. I wonder why the village head isn't back yet.

ATTENDANT: Sir, "Better to look after the thousand troops than to worry about one fellow." There are so many people here; how could he call them together all at once? He'll be along.

VILLAGE HEAD *(in a different disguise, enters and sings to the previous tune):*

Day after day,
How can I bear this hunger?
And my family numbers eight or nine.
The day before yesterday my wife pawned her skirt;
Today we've had to pawn her pants.
Just in time, the officials come to relieve the poor!

[7] The sentence, in the original divided into three-character phrases, was a copybook exercise used by children learning to write characters.

OFFICIAL: Ask him his name and the number of people in his family.

ATTENDANT: What's your name? How many people?

VILLAGE HEAD: My name is Great Bhikshu.

ATTENDANT: Where do you live?

VILLAGE HEAD: I live in the Jetavana Park. We have one thousand two hundred and fifty people.

OFFICIAL and ATTENDANT: Nonsense!

VILLAGE HEAD: Your excellency, it's said in the Amitabha Sutra, "In the Jetavana Park, one thousand two hundred and fifty monks were provided the Great Bhikshu."[8]

ATTENDANT: "A snake in monk's clothing!"

OFFICIAL: How many are there actually in your family?

VILLAGE HEAD: I have two wives, three children, and myself makes six.

OFFICIAL: Give him his allotment.

ATTENDANT: Allotted six portions of grain.

VILLAGE HEAD: There are seven of us.

ATTENDANT: You said six—how do you get to seven?

VILLAGE HEAD: My old lady is pregnant—that child has to eat too!

ATTENDANT: Begone with you! Only a beggar born would live off the unborn![9]

VILLAGE HEAD: As they say, "Today I received the support of your helping hand; you saved me from sinking into the muddy ditch."

(He exits.)

WU-NIANG (enters and sings to the tune Tao-lien-tzu):

My fate, alas, is mean!
The year, alas, is rough!
Holding back my blushes and my tears, I must stand before others,
Yet what I fear most is the thought of my parents-in-law staring out to see me return.

"You can't turn back when you run into danger on the road; you can't do as you please when a crisis comes." I grew up in

---

[8] The sutra quoted is the Amitabha Vyuha Sutra, translated into Chinese in the third century. A great bhikshu is a monk of extraordinary virtue and old age.

[9] The line contains a pun difficult to translate. The phrase ch'ih-t'ai (to eat the womb) is similar in sound to ch'i-t'ai (a congenital beggar).

secluded chambers and know nothing of the outside world. Today I heard that the officials are distributing grain to relieve the poor, so I had to come to request some to save the lives of my parents.

(*She greets the* OFFICIAL.)

OFFICIAL: Lady, your name?
WU-NIANG: My name is Chao Wu-niang, wife of Ts'ai Po-chieh.
OFFICIAL: Where has your husband gone?
WU-NIANG (*sings to the tune* P'u-t'ien lo):

My husband's long been away in the capital.

(OFFICIAL: Who is in your family?)

I have only an aged mother- and father-in-law.

(OFFICIAL: Who else is there?)

Neither elder nor younger brother is there one.

(OFFICIAL: Then who takes care of your parents-in-law?)

I must perform all services myself.

(OFFICIAL: Why didn't you send somebody here to request the grain? Women shouldn't come out like this!)

(WU-NIANG *expresses grief.*)

So many difficulties I've been through, and who has shown me
    pity?

Your honor,

The rule of seclusion is for ordinary times—what point to speak of
    it now?

OFFICIAL: Give her an allotment.
ATTENDANT: There's no grain left.
WU-NIANG (*crying*): Alas!
(*She continues her song*):

Without grain I dare not return;
How could I bear to face my parents' pain?
Alas, how poor my fate
To suffer such oppression!

OFFICIAL: Attendant, go and get that village head. The scoundrel's going to have to make up for the grain that's missing.

ATTENDANT: I'm off. "Even if he's escaped to the Third Heaven, I'll mount on the clouds and catch him for sure."

(He exits.)

WU-NIANG: I look to you for support. Please use your authority to help me!

OFFICIAL: Certainly, certainly!

(The ATTENDANT *enters with the* VILLAGE HEAD *in custody.)*

ATTENDANT: "As easy as grabbing a turtle in a jug, I got hold of him."

OFFICIAL *(curses the* VILLAGE HEAD): This treacherous thief! What did you do with the grain? Confess immediately!

VILLAGE HEAD: I won't confess.

(The OFFICIAL *and the* ATTENDANT *perform actions.)*

VILLAGE HEAD: I confess!

(The OFFICIAL *supervises the* VILLAGE HEAD *in reading out the following confession):* [10]

> The guilty party's surname is Cat, his first name Wild;
> His age is about thirty or more.
> His body shows no marks of illness,
> Save for vaginitis.
> Now he confesses, in the abridged form,
> To a deficiency in the imperial storehouse.
> The confession goes: As for irregularities in the granary,
> There is nothing suspicious there at all.
> When the rice is harvested, I collect from each farm a share;
> When it's all collected, everybody takes some home.
> It's true the granary is not overflowing,
> Nor have I kept any record of receipts and disbursements.
> If there should be a little left,
> I just store it in our citizens' homes.
> When officials are sent to inventory the stores,
> I buy some grain to protect myself.
> When everybody, high and low, gets a little cash, it's all okay;
> They ask no questions about the empty stores.
> And if one of those pure incorruptibles comes by,
> I can fool him for a while with substitute grain.
> I just go and borrow ten poles from here,

---

[10] The passage is in a simple form of poetry, most lines being rhymed and of six characters each.

And five baskets from there.
As long as he sees that there's grain in the storehouse,
He'll never know what's going on!
I follow this custom every year;
Time after time I play the same trick.
Never did I think there'd be famine this year,
That there'd be starvation of the masses.
If officials hadn't come to relieve the needy with grain,
No one would have discovered this clever scheme of mine.
And now if we were to rise to Heaven to ask a judgment on my
    case,
I know I'd be declared innocent there!

OFFICIAL and ATTENDANT: Why?

VILLAGE HEAD: Everything I did was only because of those inspectors who come riding on horses and mules to extort some money for themselves. I swear my confession is true; now I humbly beg your excellency's decision.

OFFICIAL: Beat that scoundrel! He'll have to make up for the grain that's missing.

(The ATTENDANT takes the VILLAGE HEAD off in custody.)

ATTENDANT: "A man who respects the law will live day after day in happiness; those who cheat the state will grieve day after day."

(The OFFICIAL and WU-NIANG perform some actions.)

(The ATTENDANT, with the VILLAGE HEAD in custody, enters.)

ATTENDANT: "Even if a man's heart be as hard as steel, how can he escape the red-hot furnace of official law?"

ATTENDANT and VILLAGE HEAD: Here's the grain.

OFFICIAL: Give it to this young lady.

WU-NIANG: Thank you, sir!

VILLAGE HEAD (acting as if desperately coveting the grain): Wait till you leave—somehow I'll get it back from you!

(Exit poem)

WU-NIANG:

I thank the kind official for his judgment!

VILLAGE HEAD (with an action):

Just wait till she's on the road; calamity awaits her!

OFFICIAL and ATTENDANT: Truly it's said,

> "If you're in a position of power and don't use it to give help,
> It's like going up a treasure-filled mountain and returning with
>   empty hands."

(All but WU-NIANG *exit.)*

WU-NIANG: "The smallest event in life is determined by destiny." I came today to the official granary to request a share of grain. I never imagined that the village head had been so corrupt and that all the grain would be gone. If his excellency hadn't stood up for me and made the village head pay back the grain he took, how could I have gotten any grain to bring home to relieve my parents' hunger? How true what they say—"The mouthful you get when you're hungry is better than the peck you get when you're full."

(She starts to exit.)

(The VILLAGE HEAD *enters and blocks her way.)*

VILLAGE HEAD: "When you come face to face with a benefactor, your eyes grow extra bright; when you come face to face with an enemy, your eyes open up in rage." Now I come face to face with you! If you hadn't made such a point of complaining just now, his excellency would never have made me pay back the grain. I got this grain by selling my family, old and young, and all my possessions. How can you take it?
(He grabs the grain.)

WU-NIANG *(sings to the tune* So nan chih*)*:

> My husband went away;
> He has never returned.
> My parents are both old.
> From yesterday to today,
> We've been unable to find food.
> I ask for grain,
> While they at home stare out for my return.
> Think of my old parents;
> Do a good deed for us!

(The VILLAGE HEAD *performs an action.)*

WU-NIANG (*sings to the same tune with a modified opening*):

> Official of our village, please take pity;
> My parents' lives depend on you!
> If you insist on taking something from me,
> I'd rather strip off my clothes,
> And ask you to give me that grain in exchange.

(VILLAGE HEAD: Don't do that! You'll be cold!)

> Better that I
> Should suffer the cold!
> For I must help my parents,
> Must save them before they breathe their last.

(*The* VILLAGE HEAD *grabs the grain and exits.*)

WU-NIANG (*with an action, sings to the same tune*):

> You snatched it away—
> Pitiful, my plight!
> My parents will be watching for me, and I won't be there.
> And even though they may not blame me,
> They'll feel that as a daughter-in-law I've been of no use.
> When they suffer hunger,
> My husband's guilt grows greater.
> How then will I be able
> To face my husband?

All that's left for me is death. Here's a well—best now to jump in and die.

(*As she starts to jump in the well*): Aiiii!

(*She sings to the same tune with a modified opening*):

> To the springs beneath, I cast my body.
> Whatever I do now, my problems can't be solved.
> When my husband and I were separated,
> He bade me take good care of his mother and father,
> Enjoined me to look after them well.
> If I die,
> They'll be all alone.
> My husband, my parents-in-law—both sides will blame me.

FATHER TS'AI (*enters and sings to the same tune*):

> My daughter-in-law went out;
> Still she hasn't returned.
> We've been waiting at home, staring out looking for her.

(He trips. WU-NIANG *helps him up. He makes as if to beat her.)*

Here you are, strolling about at leisure,
While we've been waiting, our hearts about to break!

WU-NIANG *(continues the song):*
Father,

I asked for some grain
To supply your noon meal;
Who would have known somebody would come and cheat me?

FATHER TS'AI: You were cheated!
(He sings to the same tune with a modified opening):
Alas!

When I think of how perverse is our fate,
I can't stop the flow of tears from my eyes.
In the end, most likely I'll starve to death.
Better that I be on my way soon to the Yellow Springs,
And be a burden to you no more.

My daughter,

My wife is old
And can't last for long.
You must
Look after her well!

WU-NIANG *(sings to the same tune):*
Father,

If you cast away your life,
Unspeakable grief I'd feel.
And if you die, Mother could not live on.
If suddenly both of you were here no more,
How could I go on all alone?
I think of all our suffering and pain;
How hard it is to bear!
And in all this pain and grief,
We can do nothing but urge each other to be strong.

FATHER TS'AI *(sings to the same tune with a modified opening):*

Your clothes are all pawned,
Our coffers are all empty.
Though we're able to survive at present,
As time goes on and on,
Our attachment to each other will be hard to maintain.
When clothes and food are lacking,

Even to carry out mourning for me will be hard.
As if we were enemies, the best thing
Is to make a break right away.

(He jumps into the well. WU-NIANG *rescues him.)*

CHANG *(carrying grain on a pole, enters and sings to the same tune):*

A bad harvest year,
Filled with famine and want;
How pitiful to see the people parted in life, separated through
    death!
Even large families with many hands to help
Find it hard to escape starvation.
Hungry the children,
Cold the wives.
The sound of tormented cries—
How full of pain!
Everywhere I go I see only the hungry and the cold;
Not one person have I found who's well and content!

Ah! Could that be Mr. Ts'ai and their young lady? Sir! Miss!
What are you doing here?
WU-NIANG: It's a long story, sir. When I heard that they were
giving out grain today, I came to request some, so that my
parents-in-law could have a mouthful to eat. Who could have
imagined that the village head was a crook and that all the
grain was gone! Fortunately, his excellency made the village
head pay back the grain he'd taken and gave a portion to me.
But when I got halfway home, the village head snatched it
away and knocked me down. When I told my father-in-law
what had happened, he wanted to end his life by jumping in
this well. I was just trying to reason with him.
CHANG: I see! Let me curse that blackguard for you!
Hey!

(He recites): [11]

The authorities appointed you as our village head;
Your duty was to take care of the village people.
In prosperous years to store up grain in the public granary,
As preparation for the lean.
Instead, you and the citizen chief stole the grain,
So now there isn't enough for relief.
This young lady arrived

[11] The passage is rhymed, but the lines are of unequal length.

And found the granary empty!
His excellency ordered you to restore the grain;
Wasn't that the right thing to do?
Yet you turned around and snatched it from her,
Even knocked her down on the road.
Haven't you heard that "To save another's life
Is better than building a pagoda seven stories tall?"
When her father-in-law heard her story he was about to cast him-
    self in the well;
If I'd come just a moment later,
He'd now be a corpse in the ditch!
When you totally lack kindness and principles,
The plenty that fills your home is of no avail.
Why should you eat the food that man eats,
And possess a skull like human beings have?
Though the clothes you wear are those of a man,
It's just as if a horse or ox were dressed in trousers!
When I count up the crimes you've committed,
Death is too good for you!
At every chance, you act the tyrant and do your evil work;
What do you understand of pity for the lonely and orphaned?
If I'd gotten here one moment sooner,
Barbarian donkey headed for a violent end, I'd never have let you
    escape!
Though seventy years old, I'd risk my own life
To fight a struggle to the death with you!

(With an action): But enough of this! People who know me well would understand that I mean only to fight for the right. But those who don't know me would consider me a shifty old fool, presuming on my age. Young lady, when your husband left, he entrusted your parents-in-law to my care. But in this year of famine you've had to carry on all alone. Do you think that I could be content to be warm, my stomach full, while you suffer starvation and toil? The old saying goes, "When you save people from distress and take pity on your neighbors, you must do it when their need is most urgent." I got some grain from them too. Young lady, please take half of it to help your parents-in-law a little.

(He gives WU-NIANG *some grain.)*

· WU-NIANG: Thank you, sir!
(She sings to the tune Tung-hsien ko):
Alas!

We've nothing left of our property,
And I must provide everything myself.
My only wish is to save Mother and Father;
How could I shirk pain and toil?

(They sing the chorus together):

All we can do is wipe the tears from our eyes.
Who pities the starving, the poor?
Our suffering no words can describe.

FATHER TS'AI *(sings to the same tune):*

I was on the road to death;
Thank you for saving my life!
My only regret is that soon I'll be dead
And have no way to repay the love of my daughter-in-law.

(They repeat the chorus above.)

CHANG *(sings to the same tune):*

I can't bear to hear your words!
All the worse to hear because I am your neighbor.
How could I be content in my safety and prosperity
And bear to see you suffering so?

(They repeat the chorus above.)

(Closing poem)
WU-NIANG:

How mean is our fate to suffer all this pain!

FATHER TS'AI:

Better that I should die, and remain with you no more.

TOGETHER:

"It's only the feelings of gratitude and hate
That through thousands of years remain forever fresh."

(All exit.)

SCENE SEVENTEEN

MATCHMAKER (*played by the* ch'ou *actor, enters and sings to the tune*
Man p'ai ling):

> From dawn to dusk back and forth a thousand times I go;
> From my feet every hair's been worn away.
> A bowl of soup do I ever get to see?
> Not half a drop do I get!
> Better to be the madame in a whorehouse;
> At least my stomach would be filled with duck soup![1]
> What a prig of a sour scholar!
> When I offer him a mate, why does he play games?

(She recites):[2]

> I've been a matchmaker for a long, long time,
> But never have I seen anything as ridiculous as this!
> Such an insufferable scholar—
> I offer him a wife, and he won't accept!
> Other people are thrilled when they're offered a mate;
> Yet he starts a fight with me.
> His excellency won't give up,
> But waits at home, boiling mad.
> They've put me in the midst of it all,
> Turned me round in somersaults.
> I've walked holes in my shoes, rips in my socks.
> I've talked till my lips are dry, my mouth parched.
> But never mind!
> I have no doubt that this marriage will take place,
> That the fate which brings them together won't be in vain.
> I'll never accept the man's refusal,
> Nor believe that the lady doesn't want the match.
> My only fear is that in their ecstasy behind embroidered curtains,
> They'll forget to say "Thank you" to me!

Ah! Here comes the First Winner.

TS'AI (*enters and sings to the tune* Chin chiao-yeh):

> My heart's filled with resentment and regret;
> How can I know whether my parents are safe?

[1] The word "duck" was used to mean "cuckold" in Che-chiang, Kao Ming's native province.

[2] The passage is done in rhymed lines, most of which are six characters each.

How can I cast off fortune and fame?
How can I escape the lover they offer me?

(TS'AI *and the* MATCHMAKER *greet each other.*)

MATCHMAKER: Greetings and congratulations! Prime Minister
Niu has chosen today as your wedding day. The party is all set
up. Hurry on your way to the joyful meeting!
TS'AI (*sings to the tune* San huan-t'ou):

The bridle of fame, the locks of profit
Have already bound me down;
Now comes a phoenix to entrap me in chains.
When can I ever reach my home?
But they are not to blame.
The truth is,
It's only I
Who was wrong to come
To view the flowers in the capital.
How unhappy must my parents be!
Their tears in silence flow.

(*They sing the chorus together*):

This marriage fate
I'm helpless to escape.

MATCHMAKER (*sings to the same tune*):

By the mirror stand, her makeup completed,
She prepares to journey across the magpie bridge.[3]
The happy day has come;
We invite the young genius to hasten there,
Though we know his heart is in turmoil.
The truth is,
You must take
That other one
And cast her off forever.
He bears the ruler's command;
How can you oppose his will?

(*They repeat the chorus above.*)

[3] Popular legend says that on the one night of the year the two constellations,
Spinning Maid and Cowherd, are allowed to spend together, magpies form a bridge
on which the former crosses over.

(Closing poem)

MATCHMAKER:

Hasten forth to this happy meeting!

TS'AI:

That happiness will turn to grief and blame.

TOGETHER:

"It's true they're not meant for each other,
But crisis has brought them together."

(All exit.)

SCENE EIGHTEEN

PRIME MINISTER NIU (*enters and sings to the tune* Ch'uan-yen yü-nü):

In the pulsing red of candlelight,
Incense smoke floats up from behind gauze curtains.
The painted hall's massed with kingfisher feathers and pearls.
To the lady's moonlit dressing table
Descend ethereal attendants like divine phoenixes and cranes.
Blending with the music of jade panpipes,
The phoenix couple's song.

Where are the attendants?

STEWARD (*enters*): Deep within painted halls, how beautiful the scene! Truly in the world of man a paradise of Heaven!

NIU: Come here! Today I'm giving my daughter in marriage. Is the party all set up?

STEWARD: It's all set up.

NIU: How does it look?

STEWARD (*recites to the* tz'u Shui-tiao ko-t'ou):

Where screens are opened, designs of golden peacocks unfold.
As mats are laid, embroidered hibiscus are revealed.
From animal-shaped burners, incense smoke curls up;
On lotus platforms, vermilion candles burn with the red of spring
    blossoms.
Coral mats cover the floor,
Pearl screens are rolled up high.
Kingfisher screens surround the hall.
The prime minister's mansion in the mortal world
Is the equal of Blossom Pearl Palace in the world of the gods.
Brocade drapes it all,
Bright flowers make it radiant,
Tinkling jade pendants fill it with sound.
From blended strings and clear flutes,
Joyful sounds bubble within the painted hall.
Twelve rows of gold hairpins—lovely ladies fill the hall;
Three thousand pearl slippers—courtiers take their seats.
Laughing and chatting, the guests are all dukes and princes.
Truly, "From behind the door, sounds of joy;
The son-in-law approaches to mount the dragon."

NIU: Has the First Winner arrived?

STEWARD: Far off I see a throng of men and horses. It must be the First Winner.

TS'AI (*enters and sings to the tune* Nü-kuan-tzu):

> *Du-su,* the sound of horses' hooves;
> Shouts and cries press round the carved wheels.

NIU (*continues the song*):

> Palace flowers cluster on his hat;
> Heavenly incense lingers in his robe.
> The young man has achieved his ambition;
> A fine son-in-law comes to mount the dragon.

MISTRESS NIU (*enters and continues the song*):

> My adornment completed, they won't let me pause.
> I cover my delicate face,
> My eyebrows knitted, my cheeks ablush.

(*The* ching *and* ch'ou,[1] *with fans in hand, enter and continue the song*):

> No ordinary marriage this!

ALL (*continue the song*):

> His name tops the golden list;
> Flowered candles fill the bridal chamber.

CH'OU: Bride and groom, please make your bows.

(TS'AI *and* MISTRESS NIU *perform actions.*)

TS'AI (*sings to the tune* Hua-mei hsü):

> To pluck the cassia I climbed to the Moon Palace,
> Never knowing that vines would wind round the tall tree.[2]
> They rejoice that on this day I have found in books
> A woman with face like jade.[3]

---

[1] The roles played by the *ching* and *ch'ou* are not specified in the text. The *ch'ou* is probably playing the matchmaker or the maid Hsi-ch'un, while the *ching* may be the housekeeper Mu-mu.

[2] From lines in the *Shih Ching* (Book of Poetry) (Legge, 4:389–390), sturdy trees with clinging vines have come to symbolize the relationship of woman and man in marriage.

[3] A popular saying of the time, attributed to Emperor Chen-tsung (968–1022) of the Sung dynasty, exhorted young men to study with the promise that they would thus gain riches and a beautiful woman in marriage. The lines are quoted several times in this play, often with ironic force.

From behind a silk curtain I pulled the red thread
Just after I'd first donned robes of lotus green.

(They sing the chorus together):

And now this dashing young bridegroom
Is truly worthy to enter the bridal chamber of flowered candles.

NIU *(sings to the previous tune):*

Your talent surpasses that of the scholars of T'ien-lü Ko; [4]
My daughter is virtuous and pure.
See the radiance of our mingled lights—
Father-in-law pure as ice, son-in-law true as jade. [5]
In brilliance the peacock screens open;
Brightly glow the hibiscus mats.

(They repeat the chorus above.)

MISTRESS NIU *(sings to the same tune):*

Rouge and powder I'm urged to complete.
A golden phoenix hairpin slants through my hair.
I've found a husband the equal of Hsiao Shih,
But feel shame that I can never be his Nung-yü. [6]
Jade ornaments sounding in a cool breeze, from fairyland I
    descend
To a golden chamber bathed in moonlight.

(They repeat the chorus above.)

CHING, CH'OU, and STEWARD *(sing to the same tune):*

Her sixfold skirts swaying,
Like the goddess of the moon, she descends to the mortal world.
We rejoice that on this day in Lan-t'ien,
The planted seeds have grown to double jadestones.
A scene more beautiful than Paradise;
Passion that puts Wu-shan to shame. [7]

(They repeat the chorus above.)

---

[4] T'ien-lü ko was an imperial library during Han times where celebrated scholars were retained to collate the collection.

[5] In the biography of Wei Chieh (286–312) in the *Tsin Shu* (History of the Tsin Dynasty), Wei Chieh is described as outstanding and his father-in-law as world famous; thus the two were like sparkling ice and lustrous jade.

[6] Hsiao Shih and Nung-yü, the famous couple of the Chou dynasty. See Scene Three, note 4.

[7] Wu-shan was the site of the meeting between king and goddess in Sung Yü's famous poem; see Scene Five, note 1.

TS'AI (*sings to the tune* Ti-liu-tzu):

They talk in vain of destined marriages
And divination of blissful unions.
But I only think,
How was this ever my desire?
For my parents are all alone.
How sad that surrounded by laughter and talk, the bridegroom
Is unable to see his loved one's tears!
On this eastern couch
I can't nonchalantly rest.

ALL (*sing together to the tune* Pao-lao tsui):

No need to knit your handsome brows!
The marriage rope has already bound your feet together;
The marital register lists your names.
No use to sigh,
No need to grieve,
Decline no more!
This painted hall holds the wealth and pomp of the Valley of
Gold.
Don't let your thoughts dwell on the pleasures of your old
hometown
And the deep love you shared with your own wife there.

(*All sing together to the tune* Ti-ti chin):

From censers shaped like gold lions and ancient characters,
incense smoke drifts up;
In silver seas and carnelian boats, the rare wine ripples.
Kingfisher sleeves billow in a delicate dance;
Oriole throats warble in lovely song.
When one tune ceases, the next begins.
We raise our cups to one another, offer congratulations,
Offer congratulations,
That this perfect union of man and wife will last a hundred years.

(*All sing together to the tune* Pao-lao tsui):

Their feelings are deep, their love sincere.
His compositions are worth ten thousand pecks of pearls.
It is Heaven that confers this beauty upon him—
Like a butterfly lingering in blossoms,
A male phoenix roosting in a *wu-t'ung* tree,
Or its lady resting in a bamboo grove.[8]
Let all young men devote themselves to books;

[8] According to popular belief, the male phoenix roosts only in *wu-t'ung* trees, while
the female favors bamboo.

"In books are mansions of yellow gold,
Thousands of measures of grain."

(*All sing together to the tune* Shuang-sheng tzu):

The young man's fortune is great,
The young man's fortune is great!
See his purple ribbon tied to yellow gold.
How fortunate the bride,
How fortunate the bride!
See her noble title carved on striped rhinocerous horn.
Their feelings sincere,
Their feelings sincere!
Nothing but good fortune,
Nothing but good fortune!
A pair of bright phoenixes
They'll fly together forever.

(*Closing poem*)
ALL:

A clear breeze and bright moon are perfect together;
Such a lovely lady and brilliant man are rare in the world.
Truly "a night of flowered candles lighting the bridal room."
Indeed, "a time when the golden placard lists his name."

(*All exit.*)

SCENE NINETEEN

WU-NIANG (*enters and sings to the tune* Po-hsing):

Empty wilds, barren plain,
Men have all fled, their means of living in ruins.
With all my heart I try to carry on the filial way,
But my strength is used up, my body exhausted.
I'm relieved that his parents
And I are able to stay well,
But I am pained
By the cries of starving people that fill the streets.
And when I lift my eyes, I wonder who will offer us support.

(*She recites in* shih *form*):

Empty plain, still and bleak, no smoke rises from deserted homes.
Day after day, desolate clouds darken the village.
Parted by death, wives mourn their husbands on empty plains;
Scattered in life, sons worry over their mothers far away.
All this suffering so painful to see!
More and more difficult my own life!
With his parents grown old, their lives in danger,
The son stays on and on in the capital.
My strength is exhausted, my schemes all used up—even my tears
    have run dry.
Now in my weariness I wonder, when will this life too reach its
    end?
Though mounds of yellow earth fill the barren plain,
Who will scatter a single handful over my bones?

Ever since my husband went away we've endured endless famine. My clothes and ornaments have all been pawned; our
family coffers are empty. I don't know whether his parents
can hang on to life, and never can I offer them the comforts
they should have. I can only manage to serve them a bite or
two of plain rice. I eat only the husks to keep myself alive, but
don't tell them for fear they'd be upset. I always steal away
and eat by myself so they won't see.

(*She prepares the rice.*)

My parents-in-law are coming.

MOTHER and FATHER TS'AI (*enter and sing to the tune* Yü-ching lien hou):

> We manage to endure our hunger,
> But when will the end come?

WU-NIANG: Dinner is ready.

(*She performs an action.*)

MOTHER TS'AI (*with an action of disgust*): I know there's a famine, but how can you expect us to eat such stuff?
FATHER TS'AI: At times like this, you can't be choosy.
MOTHER TS'AI (*sings to the tune* Lo ku ling):

> I suffer from hunger all day,
> But how can I eat what you've brought?
> Take it away!
> I'm not ravenous enough for that!

FATHER TS'AI (*continues the song*):

> Don't forget that all her clothes are pawned;
> What's left to trade for better food?

Wife,

> This disaster was sent by Heaven;
> Our daughter has no way to manage.

WU-NIANG (*continues the song*):

> Mother, please don't blame me, hold back your anger!
> I'll try again to find something for you.

(*They sing the chorus together*):

> We think of this,
> And tears cover our cheeks.
> It won't be long before we become ghosts,
> Our bodies buried in ditches.
> And if we escape death, our suffering can't be borne.
> Resentment rises in our hearts toward Ts'ai Po-chieh.

MOTHER TS'AI (*sings to the same tune*):

> Today I begin to suspect you;
> It must be that you're a secret glutton,
> Buying for yourself vegetables and fish.
> Why does she never eat with us?
> She must have evil in her heart!

FATHER TS'AI (*continues the song*):
Wife,

> Such tender love she's shown toward you;
> She wouldn't so perversely turn against you.

WU-NIANG (*continues the song*):

So many hardships, so much pain I endure!
Don't you know the feelings in my heart?
Hasn't my face grown yellow, my bones thin as brushwood?

(*They repeat the chorus above.*)

MOTHER TS'AI: Take it away! Take it away!
FATHER TS'AI: Daughter, you'd better take it away.
WU-NIANG (*after removing the food*): Let me go buy some things and prepare you something else to eat.
MOTHER and FATHER TS'AI: Go then.
WU-NIANG: They say, "The mute that tastes a bitter nut has no way to tell others how bitter it is."

(*She exits.*)

MOTHER TS'AI: My husband, after all no one is really close but a blood relative. Instead of keeping our son at home, you have this daughter-in-law taking care of us. We always used to have fish and vegetables for dinner, and now all we get is plain rice. How can I stand it? Just wait—in a few more days we won't even have rice. Think what a point she's made in the past few days of keeping out of our sight when she eats. There's no doubt she's been buying special things for herself to enjoy in secret.
FATHER TS'AI: Wife, be careful not to accuse people wrongly. It seems to me our daughter-in-law has suffered greatly, and she's not that sort of person.
MOTHER TS'AI: All right then, we'll wait until she eats and take a peek at her. It's the only way to find out the truth.
FATHER TS'AI: Right!

(Closing poem)
TOGETHER:

"In muddy water, no way to tell bream from carp;
Only when the stream's cleared can you see which is which."

(Both exit.)

SCENE TWENTY

WU-NIANG (*enters and sings to the tune* Shan-p'o yang):

Dark, dark disorders—not good, the harvest this year.
Far, far away—not coming back, my husband.
Wild, wild distress—not patient his parents.
Weak, weak trembling—not able to last, my lonely self.
My clothing all pawned;
Not a thread to cover my body.
At times I think of selling myself,
But then who would take care of Mother and Father?

(She sings the chorus):

And I reflect:
Empty, shifting is this life—who can predict one's fate?
So hard to endure!
Real and present are these disasters and dangers.

(She sings to the same tune):

Drop, drop, they fall, tears hard to exhaust.
All, all chaotic, my skein of sorrow hard to untangle.
Sharp, sharp jagged bones, my sick body hard to hold up.
Harsh, harsh dangers, this year hard to get through.

These husks!

I don't want to eat you—
But how can I bear my hunger?
I want to eat you—
But how can you be eaten?

(With an action): Alas!

Thinking of it, better that I should die first
And not see the death of his parents.

(She repeats the chorus above.)

I set out some rice for my parents-in-law this morning not because I didn't want to buy them fish and vegetables, but because we've no money to pay for them. Now Mother is sure that I've been secretly eating something else, and resents it deeply. She doesn't know that I've been eating nothing but damaged grains and husks. I don't want them to know, so I always hide from them while I eat. No matter how harshly she blames me, I mustn't tell them the truth. Alas! Impossible to eat these husks!

(She eats.)

(She sings to the tune Hsiao-shun ko):

> I've vomited till my stomach aches,
> Tears fall,
> Throat chokes.

Husks!

> You were ground by the pestle;
> They sifted you, fanned you,
> Every harm that they could do.
> As I, wretched beyond hope,
> Have been through endless hardship and suffering.
> A person of bitter fate, your bitterness I taste.
> Both bitter, we meet.
> I want to swallow, and can't.

(She eats, then vomits.)

(She sings to the previous tune):

> Husks and rice
> At the beginning depend on each other.
> Who has sifted and fanned you to fly apart?
> One despised, one honored,
> Just like my husband and I,
> Never again to meet.

Husband, you are the rice,

> Rice somewhere I can't find you.

I am the husk.

> How can husks save the lives of starving men?
> Just as since my husband went away,
> How can I
> Provide his parents with comforts?

(Without eating, she sets down the bowl.)

(She sings to the previous tune):

My life is without value;
My death too would mean nothing!
Better to starve and become an angry ghost!
But my parents-in-law are old
And depend on me.
I must hang on to life a little longer.
To hang on a little longer is easy,
But as the days go on, it will be harder for us to stay together.
Senseless to compare husks with myself!

These husks, at least, are being eaten,

But my bones—
Where will they be buried?

(MOTHER *and* FATHER TS'AI *enter and spy on* WU-NIANG.)

MOTHER and FATHER TS'AI: Daughter-in-law, what are you talking about?

(WU-NIANG *covers the husks.* MOTHER TS'AI *finds them and strikes* WU-NIANG.)

MOTHER TS'AI: Husband, do you see? She really did sneak away and fix something of her own to eat. This wretch needs a good beating.
FATHER TS'AI: Taste some and see what it is.

(MOTHER TS'AI *grabs a bite, then spits it out.*)

FATHER TS'AI: Daughter, what is this you've prepared for yourself?
WU-NIANG *(with an action, sings to the previous tune):*

This is fibers of grain,
Skins on rice.
I fixed it to overcome my hunger.

(MOTHER and FATHER TS'AI: These are husks! How can you eat them?)

I've heard it's written by an ancient sage,
"The food of swine is eaten by men."[1]

Father, Mother,

---

[1] Wu-niang is misinterpreting a line from *Mencius* (Legge, 2:132). The meaning of the original is that swine were being fed provisions that people could have eaten, an extravagant practice. With a change in punctuation, Wu-niang can interpret the line as quoted.

Surely it's better than roots of grass and bark of trees.

(MOTHER and FATHER TS'AI: Doesn't it choke you?)

> Su Wu did well on felt and snow,
> And a diet of pine cones and cedar makes one immortal.[2]
> Why should you worry that I eat this?

Father, Mother, other people couldn't eat this, but I . . . I *must* eat it.

MOTHER and FATHER TS'AI: Nonsense! Why must you eat it?

WU-NIANG (*continues her song*):

> My parents, never question it—
> Surely I am the husk wife of your son![3]

MOTHER and FATHER TS'AI (*weeping*): So we were wrong to blame you! How terrible we feel!

(*They fall to the ground.*)

WU-NIANG (*calling them, sings to the tune* Yen kuo-sha):

> Deep, deep in a stupor they fall.
> My cries in their ears in vain!

Father, Mother,

> I couldn't serve you as my heart desired,
> And now because of me you go down to the yellow earth.

Father, Mother,

> People will ask for what reason you died.

Father, Mother,

> How can you abandon me?

Father, Mother!

FATHER TS'AI (*regains consciousness and sings to the same tune*): Daughter,

---

[2] Su Wu (140–60 B.C.), a Han general, was captured by the Hsiung-nu. When he refused to submit, they locked him up without food or water. He survived by eating snow and felt from the tent. Pine cones and cedar are eaten by those striving to become immortal.

[3] "Husk wife" means a wife who has lived in poverty with her husband. Sung Hung (first century) of the Latter Han, after becoming successful, was sought as a husband for a princess. He refused, saying, "I've heard that the friends of one's poor and humble days cannot be forgotten and that a husk wife cannot be divorced."

You went hungry to care for us.

Daughter,

> How could you bear that hunger?
> We blamed you for nothing and still you didn't explain.
> Today for the first time I believe that there really are "husk
> wives."

Daughter,

> Before long, I'll surely die.

Daughter,

> Don't let my death cause even more suffering to the living.

WU-NIANG (*calls out to* MOTHER TS'AI): Mother!
(*She sings to the previous tune*):

> If you die, how can I go on?
> If you die, how can I endure it?
> How I suffered to protect my husband's name!
> And now it's hard to protect.
> I fear if Mother dies, Father's life will be in danger.
> And all our clothes pawned!
> Our coffers empty!

FATHER TS'AI (*calls out to* MOTHER TS'AI): Wife!
(*He sings to the previous tune*):

> I didn't think things through at first,
> And sent our son to the capital.
> My daughter-in-law was abandoned to suffering and loneliness,
> My wife put on the road to the Yellow Springs.
> Only I am to blame for your injuries,
> And my bones—where will they be buried?

WU-NIANG: Mother is completely unconscious; we'd better carry her inside. Truly: "The green dragon and white tiger come forth side by side; whether luck will be good or bad is completely unpredictable."[4]

(*They exit.*)

CHANG TA-KUNG (*played by the* mo *actor, enters*): "That good fortune never comes in pairs may be hard to believe; that misfortunes never come alone is certainly true." Why do I say this?

---

[4] The green dragon is an omen of good luck, the white tiger of bad luck.

Because the wife of my neighbor Ts'ai Po-chieh, Chao Wu-niang, had been married to Po-chieh only two months when he went off to the examinations. Since he left there's been continuous drought and famine. In his family are only his parents, both over eighty. How much they owe to Chao Wu-niang's care! She pawned her clothes and hair ornaments to buy grain for them, while she herself ate husks and damaged grain in secret to overcome her hunger. Ah! In a year of famine like this, even families of four or five sons can't provide their parents with food. This young lady is truly one of whom it's said, "Few today, rare in antiquity." Her parents-in-law, not understanding, actually blamed her instead. Now I've heard that they've learned the truth and have become sick with grief. I'm going there now to ask after them.

(He acts as if seeing something): Here comes Mistress Ts'ai! Why does she seem so upset?

WU-NIANG *(in a state of agitation, enters):* "The winds and clouds from Heaven can't be fathomed; the fortune of man changes between morning and night."

(She greets CHANG): Sir, my mother-in-law has died!

CHANG: I was just coming over.

WU-NIANG: Sir, my clothes and ornaments are all pawned or sold; now, my mother-in-law has died, what can I do? Please take pity and help me!

CHANG: Of course I'll provide for the burial clothes and coffin. You must just devote yourself to the care of your father-in-law.

WU-NIANG *(weeps, then sings to the tune* Yü pao-tu):

> A thousand thanks to you!
> What would I have done?
> How could I take her bones
> And with no coffin, bury them in a deserted mound?

(They sing the chorus together):

> When we see what we have come to,
> There's no way to stop our tears.
> Truly, "It was fate that brought us all together."[5]

CHANG *(sings to the previous tune):*

---

[5] This phrase is generally used to describe the fated union of lovers, but here it must indicate the whole Ts'ai family, perhaps also including the neighbor Chang.

Don't worry so!
I'll take care of your mother-in-law's burial.
Just devote yourself to the care of your father-in-law,
And don't let him become, like her, beyond help.

(They repeat the chorus above.)

(Closing poem)
WU-NIANG:

Thank you, sir!
It's only because I have no money to bury my old mother-in-law.

CHANG:

Rest your mind,
And have no doubt that your problems can be solved.

TOGETHER:

Returning home I won't dare cry aloud;
If others hear, it would break their hearts.

(They exit.)

SCENE TWENTY-ONE

TS'AI (*enters and sings to the tune* I-chih hua):

Locust tree shadows move through the quiet courtyard;
Lotus fragrance fills the secluded garden.
Behind hanging screens, clear daylight lingers long.
How can I pass away the time?
Twelve railings—
With nothing to do, I lean on each one.
Tired, I unroll the smooth mat.
In dreams I've just reached my hometown;
The wind pounding on blue-green bamboo shakes me awake.

(*He recites to the* tz'u Nan-hsiang-tzu):

A myriad of bamboo leaves glimmer gold;
In the pool pavilion, lattice screens gleam in the dusky shade.
The world is at rest, days long with no affairs.
I recite poetry to myself,
Too weary to go pour precious wine into my golden cup.
In dark pain, I search my bitter thoughts;
Who could have known this separation would last for years with
    no news?
Summers and winters press on, so easily men grow old.
My heart moved,
I'll entrust my weary grief to the precious *ch'in.*

Come here, attendant!

STEWARD (*enters and recites in* shih *form*):

Reading yellow scrolls, he passes away the day.
As red strings are plucked, a cool breeze rises.
Heat cannot pass under the pearled screen.
He dwells in a divine paradise.

Here are the *ch'in* and books.

TS'AI: Call two boys to come out.

(*The* STEWARD *calls out.*)

(*The* ching, *holding a fan, and the* ch'ou, *holding an incense burner, enter and sing to the tune* Chin-ch'ien hua):

Since childhood, we've attended in the library,
Library.
Our happiness is hard to match,
Hard to match.
All we do is hold fans and burn incense,
Enjoy cool breezes by the lotus pavilion,
Then eat ourselves full and crawl into bed.

(They laugh.)

TS'AI: Steward, I carved this *ch'in* out of a log that was being burned as firewood in a stove; that's why it's called "scorched end."[1] Since I came here, I haven't played for a long time. Now it's so lovely and cool I'd like to try to play a little to calm my heart. Come here, boys! One of you must fan me and the other hold the book. Steward, you burn the incense. Don't let the incense go out, don't ruin the fan, and don't drop the book! The three of you keep an eye on each other—I'll punish anybody who disobeys!
STEWARD, CHING, and CH'OU: Yes, sir!

(The ch'ou *extinguishes the* STEWARD's *incense with his fan.)*

CHING: Sir, the steward has put out the incense embers!
TS'AI: One of you put him on your back—and the other give him a good thirteen-stroke beating!

(The ching *beats the* STEWARD.)

TS'AI: He won't do! He can't burn the incense—let him fan.
(He addresses the ching): You burn the incense.
CHING: Yes sir!

(The STEWARD *fans.)*

TS'AI *(playing the* ch'in, *sings to the tune* Lan hua-mei):

I try in the fragrant breeze from the south to play the strings of Yü,
But it seems that beneath my fingers the lingering tones are not as before.
Where are those flowing streams and high mountains?

Ah!

---

[1] The historical Ts'ai Yung had such a *ch'in*, which he had carved out of *wu-t'ung* wood being burned as cooking fuel. Because part of the wood was scorched, the *ch'in* was called "scorched end."

How is it that before my eyes are only desolate wind and waves,
Like "Memories of the Water Immortals" who disappeared long
    ago?[2]

(The STEWARD *falls asleep and the* ching *burns the fan.*)

TS'AI: Why aren't you fanning?

(The STEWARD *acts confused.*)

CHING and CH'OU: Sir, the steward has ruined the fan!
TS'AI: Hang him up and give him another beating!

(The ching *and* ch'ou *perform actions.*)

TS'AI: He won't do! He can't fan—let him hold the book. You
fan.
CH'OU: Yes sir!
TS'AI (*playing the* ch'in, *sings to the previous tune*):

Suddenly I feel the lingering tones have turned to grief,
Like the songs, "The drake is gone, the goose alone" and "The
    solitary gibbon,"
Or "The phoenix suddenly separated from his mate."[3]

Ah!

---

[2] The song contains a number of allusions to famous stories about the *ch'in*. The first line refers to the mythical Emperor Yü, credited in some traditional works as the inventor of the *ch'in*. He is said to have played a song called "Nan-feng" (South wind) in order to harmonize the empire.
   The third line alludes to one of the most famous *ch'in* players, Po Ya. The *Book of Lieh-tzu* relates how Po Ya's good friend Chung Tzu-ch'i could understand Po Ya's playing perfectly. When the latter played with the thought of flowing streams in mind, Chung exclaimed at the broad and flowing rivers and streams he could see in his mind; when he thought of mountains, Chung exclaimed that the music was as lofty as Mount T'ai. Later stories tell how Po Ya broke his *ch'in* when his friend died, for there was now no one to appreciate his music. The line here indicates that because of the distress in his heart, Ts'ai is unable to play pure and lofty music, and also suggests the absence of one who could understand him—his wife, mother, or father.
   The last two lines refer to another story about Po Ya. On a trip with his *ch'in* master, Po Ya was asked to wait while the man went ahead to visit his own teacher. The two never returned, and Po Ya could find no trace of them. Depressed in the midst of a lonely forest by crashing waves, he composed a song called "Water Immortals," referring to the two men who had disappeared. These two lines contrast the lonely situation of Po Ya to the time when he used to play music suggesting mountains and streams to his good friend, and thus describe Ts'ai's similar loneliness.
   [3] The three song titles mentioned do not appear as listed in extant collections of *ch'in* melodies, but there are titles similar to them. It is obvious that all are sad songs of loneliness and separation.

Why is it that a murderous tone has entered the string?
It must be the mantis about to seize the cicada.[4]

(The STEWARD *falls asleep again, and the two boys steal the book.)*

CHING and CH'OU: Sir, the steward's dropped the book!
TS'AI: Give him another beating.

(They act as before.)

TS'AI: You hold the book, and let him burn the incense again.

(The ch'ou *takes the book.)*

TS'AI *(sings to the previous tune):*

When sun warms Lan-t'ien, jade gives off smoke;
Wang-ti's spring heart was entrusted to the cuckoo.
Even the best marriage may turn out to be a mistake.
I fear there are few who know my music.
How can phoenix glue mend the broken string?[5]

(The ch'ou *falls asleep, and the* STEWARD *steals the book. The* ching
and ch'ou *perform some actions.)*

CHING and CH'OU: Sir, the steward stole the book.
TS'AI: He just won't do! He's put out the incense and ruined
the fan.
STEWARD: Sir, these two are playing games with me.

---

[4] The two lines refer to an incident in the life of the historical Ts'ai Yung. About to
visit a group of friends, he heard the sound of *ch'in* music from within the house.
Sensing a murderous quality to the tone, he returned home. It was later disclosed that
the man playing had at the same time been watching a mantis about to seize a cicada.
Because he hoped the mantis would capture its prey, this murderous feeling was
expressed in his music. The meaning of the allusion here is that Ts'ai's feelings of
resentment are being unconsciously expressed in his playing.

[5] The song is especially complex, and it is difficult to define strictly the meaning of
the images and allusions used. The first two lines are taken almost exactly from a
poem by Li Shang-yin (813–858), "Chin se" (The embroidered zither) (*CTS*,
539:6144). The first suggests something that can be seen briefly at a distance but cannot be grasped in reality, alluding to a statement by Tai Shu-lun (732–789): "The
world of poetry is like sun-warmed Lan-t'ien; smoke arises from the fine jade there,
which can be seen from a distance but not brought close to one's eyes." The second
line refers to Wang-ti, king of the state of Shu, who, legend tells, died of shame after
having an affair with his prime minister's wife. His soul was transferred to the body of
a cuckoo. The term "spring heart" symbolizes passion, and the two lines here may
express empty longing. The fourth lines refers again to Po Ya, who lost the one
friend who could understand his music. The final line alludes to Emperor Wu (r.
141–87 B.C.), who was presented with some phoenix glue in tribute. He used it to
mend the string of his bow and it proved to be exceptionally strong. To mend a string
on a musical instrument symbolizes reunion with a lost wife.

CHING: You almost stole the book from him.

CH'OU: It's a good thing I had it tied with a rope!

TS'AI: My wife is coming—go away.

STEWARD, CHING, and CH'OU: How true what they say: "If you're lucky, others serve you; if you're unlucky, you serve others."

(They exit, TS'AI remaining on stage.)

MISTRESS NIU *(enters and sings to the tune* Man chiang hung):

> Over the tender green pond,
> Plum rains have ceased, fragrant breezes rise.[6]
> See from bright new nests
> The young swallows already flying.
> Smooth mats unroll like waves, silken fans wave,
> The song of "Golden Threads" is heard amid the warmth of vermillion cups.[7]
> Heat can't penetrate to our water side pavilion.
> The pearl screens are rolled up.

Sir, you were playing the *ch'in.* I've heard for a long time that you're a superb musician. Why is it that since you came here I haven't heard you play a note? Sir, please play me a song now!

TS'AI: What shall I play?

MISTRESS NIU: "The Pheasant Flies in the Morning"[8] would be nice.

TS'AI: Why should I play that? That's a tune for the wifeless, and I'm not short of wives.

MISTRESS NIU: Nonsense! What do you mean by saying you're "not short of wives"?

TS'AI *(beginning to play):* Ah! I made a mistake! Since I do have a wife, I'll play "Lonely Phoenix" or "Solitary Goose."[9]

MISTRESS NIU: But we're a happy couple; what can you mean about lonely and solitary?

---

[6] "Plum rains" is the name given to rains that fall between the fourth and fifth months in Kao Ming's native province of Chekiang at the time when yellow plums are about to drop from the trees. "Fragrant breeze" is the name of one of the eight winds; the meaning of the line is that summer is just beginning.

[7] "Golden Threads," a famous song of the period that exhorted one to enjoy life while one can, was often sung on occasions of feasting and celebration.

[8] "The Pheasant Flies in the Morning" was composed by a hermit who, at the age of seventy, stil had no wife. One day, seeing a pair of pheasants flying together, he composed the song to express his loneliness.

[9] The two titles are known, but not the exact nature of the tunes.

TS'AI *(with an action):* What would you know about that?
MISTRESS NIU: Sir, in this summer weather, it would be nice to hear "Wind Entering Pines."
TS'AI: That would be fine!

(He plays the tune wrong.)

MISTRESS NIU: Sir, you played it wrong!
TS'AI: Ah! When I played, "Longing To Return"[10] came out instead.
MISTRESS NIU: Have you gone mad? I know that you're a good player. There's no need for you to show off your versatility.
TS'AI: I'm not! The problem is, I can't play this string.
MISTRESS NIU: What's wrong with the string?
TS'AI: I was used to playing the old one; this one is new, and I'm not used to it.[11]
MISTRESS NIU: Where is the old string?
TS'AI: I threw it away a long time ago.
MISTRESS NIU: Why did you throw it away?
TS'AI: I got this new string, so I threw away the old.

(He performs an action.)

MISTRESS NIU: Why not throw away the new string?
TS'AI: Because it's hard to throw away!
(With an action): All I can think about is that old string!
MISTRESS NIU: You can't even throw it away? Forget it!
TS'AI *(sings to the tune* Kuei-chih hsiang*)*:

> Already severed the old string,
> Not yet used to the new.
> No way ever again to mend the old string,
> Too hard to throw away the new!
> A few notes,
> And the melody falls into chaos.

(MISTRESS NIU: Perhaps your feelings towards me have changed?)

[10] This tune is listed in the *Ch'm-ts'ao* (Lute Melodies), a music book attributed to Ts'ai Yung. Commentary states that it was composed by a young woman whose royal fiancé died before she reached his palace. She wished to return home, but was retained by his son. Locked in her chambers, she composed the tune.
[11] The conversation between Ts'ai and Mistress Niu is based on the symbolism of "broken string" for a lost wife and "new string" for a second wife. While Ts'ai is expressing his marital dilemma, Mistress Niu thinks he is actually talking about the strings on the *ch'm*.

No, it's not that my feelings have changed.
It's just that in this lovely cool weather
When my tune began to come out right,
It was blown by the wind to another key.[12]

MISTRESS NIU (*sings to the same tune*):

It's not that broken string;
It's the indifference of your heart.

No!

You talked about "The Lonely Phoenix," "Solitary Goose,"
Of the "Palace Resentment of Chao-chün,"
"Longing To Return" and "The Goose Has Gone"[13]
All songs filled with grievous sighs.

Sir, are you perhaps longing for someone?
TS'AI: I'm not longing for anyone.
MISTRESS NIU (*continues her song*):

If that's not it—

I understand now—

You wish only those who appreciate your music to hear,
You feel I can't appreciate it, and so won't play for me.

It's just that you're in a sad mood and don't feel like playing.
Shall I have Hsi-ch'un and Mu-mu bring out some wine to
cheer you up?
TS'AI: No, I don't feel up to drinking—I'd rather go to sleep.
MISTRESS NIU: Mu-mu, Hsi-ch'un, bring some wine!

STEWARD, MU-MU, and HSI-CH'UN (*enter and sing to the tune
Shao yeh-hsiang*):

Reflections of towers upside-down in the pond,
Deep shade from green trees, summer at its height.
A single yellow rose bush, yet the yard is filled with fragrance.[14]

MISTRESS NIU (*continues the song*):

[12] The two lines are based on the poem "Feng-cheng" by Kao P'ien (d. 887) (*CTS*, 598:6923).
[13] "Palace Resentment of Chao-chün" is a title listed in the *Ch'in-ts'ao*, where it is attributed to Wang Chao-chün, a wronged palace lady of the Han dynasty. The tune "The Goose Has Gone" is attributed to a man whose parents planned to send his wife away because she had borne no children.
[14] The lines are based on the poem "Shan-t'ing hsia-jih" (A summer day in mountain pavilion) by Kao P'ien (d. 887) (*CTS*, 592:6921).

The yard is filled with fragrance!
I'll drink with you from rosy cups,
Toward evening we'll roll up the screens
Just as the moon is rising.

Bring on the wine!
(*She sings to the tune* Liang-chou hsü):

New bamboo surrounds our pond pavilion;
Locust trees shade the courtyard.
Days last long, sheltered from the red dust.
Beyond the jade railings,
A crystal waterfall flies through space, rinsing jade rocks.
Just see how my fragrant flesh is cool,
Breezes rising from my white skin.
Unroll the little mat with its precious ornaments;
With days so long, people grow sleepy!
What lovely leisure—
When suddenly the sounds of chess wake us from our nap.

(*They sing the chorus together*):

Sing "Golden Threads"!
Please drink the cool, pure wine!
Facing icy mountains, snowy rails, begin the feast!
How many people can see such carefree times?

TS'AI (*sings to the previous tune*):

By the rose trellises,
Pondhouse filled with lotus—
A light breeze, and fragrance is everywhere.
Before her dressing case, days are long.
Heavy smoke curls from precious incense burners.
No use to me these headrests of cool jade,
And fans of fine silk,
When I've no way to serve my parents as did Huang Hsiang.[15]

(*He cries.*)

MISTRESS NIU: What are you doing?
TS'AI (*with an action, continues his song*):

Suddenly my breast is on fire,
I'm soaked with perspiration.
I want to fall asleep, drunk, by the south window.

[15] Huang Hsiang (d. 122) of the Later Han period was famous for his filial conduct. In summer he fanned his father's bed to cool it; in winter he warmed it with his own body before his father retired.

(They repeat the chorus above.)

MISTRESS NIU *(sings to the previous tune with a modified opening):*

Toward evening, rain falls outside the southern pavilion.
See the blossom-covered pond like a lovely face with fading traces
    of rouge.
Gradually light thunder grows distant,
The rain stops, clouds disperse.[16]
Just see—lotus fragrance over ten miles,
One hook of a new moon,
A scene of boundless beauty!
Just risen from the orchid water of her bath,
At evening, her makeup faint,
Though dusk fills the secluded courtyard, the lady is reluctant to
    go sleep.

(They repeat the chorus above.)

TS'AI *(sings to the same tune with a modified opening):*

Amid willows' shade, suddenly the sound of new cicadas.
Fireflies stream into the pavilion.
Listen, the song of water-chestnut gatherers—from where?
Their painted boats return at evening.
See the Jade Rope hanging low.[17]
At red doors, not a sound.
How the scene charms us!
We rise, hand in hand,
Your cloudy hair disarrayed.
The moon shines through gauze windows, and still we don't sleep.

(They repeat the chorus above.)

STEWARD, MU-MU, and HSI-CH'UN *(sing to the tune* Chieh-chieh
kao):

On rippling water, the mandarin ducks play,
Overturning lotus blossoms;
Clear fragrance wafts over radiant ripples.
Sweet breezes fanning,
By the fragrant pond,
Beside the peaceful pavilion.
Seated here, our spirits freshened,
Why envy those who dwell in fairyland?

---

[16] The line uses the sexual symbolism of clouds and rain to indicate that the couple
has just made love.
[17] Jade Rope is a constellation.

(They sing the chorus together):

> Our only fear, that the west wind will startle us into autumn;
> Unobserved, silent, the flowing years pass.

(They sing to the previous tune):

> A pure evening; hearts are light.
> Lovely cool weather,
> Like in the Palace on the Moon or Paradise.
> Immortal lovers
> Unroll the tortoise mat
> For yet another revel.
> Let the water clock push on its silver arrow,
> And end the flute and songs in the Crystal Palace.[18]

(They repeat the chorus above.)

ALL *(sing together to the tune* Yü-wen*):*

> Time rushes on like flashing lightning;
> How sad that lovely evenings too grow late!
> Just seize the chance to sing and laugh!

TS'AI: How many drumbeats from the tower?
ALL: Three.

(Closing poem)
MISTRESS NIU: Sir,

> On nights of merriment, don't ask the time!
> Lovely evenings like this are all too rare.

ALL:

> When you find a time for drinking, you must drink!
> When there's a chance to raise your voice in song, be sure to sing!

(All exit.)

[18] A story quoted in the *T'ai-p'ing kuang-chi* tells of a man who was taken by a goddess to a fairyland, where the palace and towers were all constructed of crystal.

SCENE TWENTY-TWO

WU-NIANG (*enters and sings to the tune* Shuang-t'ien hsiao-chiao):

It can't be borne, yet where can one flee?
Disasters and trials one on the other fall.
First the grief of Mother's death—
Now Father's illness
Grows more and more severe.

"When the house leaks, rain falls night after night; when the dragon is exhausted, he encounters his nemesis, Hsü Chenchün."[1] Since my mother-in-law died, I've lived a life of desperation, and now my father-in-law has become critically ill. I managed to buy some medicine for him. I'll prepare it now, along with a few mouthsful of gruel.

(*She prepares the medicine.*)

(*She sings to the tune* Fan hu-ping):

To buy medicine not a cent remains;
How can I employ a good doctor?
Even if I can save him for the present,
How will I ever get food to serve him?
These hardships will never cease.
They say that for the sick, good doctors will be found,
But how can one be saved from famine?

(*She sings to the previous tune*):
This sickness of my father-in-law—

Endless grief, limitless suffering, and infinite hardship
Have brought on this disease.

Though he takes this medicine—

For the present it may save him,
But how can he escape his anxiety and grief?
It surely can't be for long!

[1] Hsü Hsün (fourth century) of the Tsin dynasty was said to be able to subjugate dragons and capture devils. This proverb, common in different forms, expresses the idea that pieces of bad luck tend to come one after the other.

It's all because his son's not by his side. The cure of his sickness—

Only the filial conduct of his son can ease the father's heart
And save his life.

The medicine is ready. I'll go bring my father-in-law in and see if it helps.

(*She exits and returns supporting* FATHER TS'AI.)

FATHER TS'AI (*sings to the tune* Shuang-t'ien hsiao-chiao):

My spirit drifts in darkness.
I know I can't last long.
I raise my head, try to stand,

(*With an action*)

But this body's too frail.
How can it carry on?

WU-NIANG: Father, take it easy. The medicine is ready. Take a little—please try!

FATHER TS'AI (*with an action*): I can't drink this medicine!

WU-NIANG (*with an action, sings to the tune* Hsiang pien-man):

They say of medicine
That only after the son tastes of it can it be offered to the father
  and mother.[2]

Father,

Is it because you're in pain that there's no son to taste it first?

FATHER TS'AI (*forces himself to take a drink of the medicine, then spits it out*): I can't get it down!

WU-NIANG (*continues the song*):

You must make an effort;
How can you cast off your life?

(*She urges him to take the medicine.*)

FATHER TS'AI: Daughter, while you eat husks, you give me medicine to drink. How unfair to you!

---

[2] In the *Li Chi* (Book of Rites), *chüan* 1, p. 17a, it states that a son must first taste medicine before giving it to his parents. Commentary explains that this is to ensure that its taste is not too bitter.

(He cries.)

WU-NIANG *(continues the song):*

> So the reason that you won't take this medicine
> Is because I am a poor "husk wife"!

Sir, you couldn't swallow the medicine, so how about trying a sip of gruel?

(FATHER TS'AI *starts to eat, then spits it out.)*

WU-NIANG *(sings to the same tune):*

> Infinite grief and suffering
> Piled up in his heart to form this stomach ailment.
> No wonder each time you try to swallow, instead you vomit!

FATHER TS'AI: Daughter, I'm afraid there's no hope for me; death is certain. If my son does not return, you'll be the one that's wronged.

WU-NIANG: Father, please don't worry.

(She turns her back to him and cries.)

(She continues the song):

> Lest I add to his bitter memories,
> I turn my back while tears flow.

Father, eat another mouthful of gruel.

FATHER TS'AI: Daughter, while you eat husks, you'd have me eat gruel. How can I get it down?

WU-NIANG: Alas!

(She continues her song)

> So the reason he won't eat this gruel
> Is also because I am a poor "husk wife"!

FATHER TS'AI: Daughter, it doesn't matter if I die. I grieve only at how my son's absence wrongs you. Come here, I have something to say to you.

WU-NIANG: What is it, Father?

FATHER TS'AI *(sings to the tune* Ko-erh):
Daughter,

> I thank you for your three years of service,
> And only regret that at the beginning

It was I who brought this injury to you.
I wish to repay your great kindness;
In my next life I will serve as your daughter-in-law.
My blame is only toward the unfilial son Ts'ai Po-chieh.
My pain is all for the toilworn wife Chao Wu-niang.

WU-NIANG (*sings to the same tune with a modified opening*):

Thinking of it—
The first wrong is that no one will offer sacrifices after your death.
The second wrong is that you have a son,
Yet never received his care.
The third wrong is that through three years
You haven't had one day of being full and warm.
For three years we cared for each other through good and bad;
Suddenly we'll be separated, unable to die together.

FATHER TS'AI (*sings to the same tune*):
Daughter, when I die,

Don't bury my bones beneath the ground.

WU-NIANG: I wish my father to live to be one hundred and twenty. I don't want this to come to him. But if something should happen, since you don't want me to bury you beneath the ground, where should I bury you?
FATHER TS'AI: It's all my fault you're in such straits.
(*He continues his song*):

I want to be punished for my crime;
Let my corpse lie exposed!

WU-NIANG: You mustn't speak like that—people would ridicule you.
FATHER TS'AI: Daughter, you don't understand.
(*He continues his song*):

When people hear of it,
They'll know it was Ts'ai Po-chieh who failed to bury his father,
Their blame only toward the unfilial son Ts'ai Po-chieh,
Their pain all for the toilworn wife Chao Wu-niang.

WU-NIANG (*sings to the previous tune with a modified opening*):

I think of it—

Father, if you die,

You and Mother will be in one dwelling place,
And I think that I too
Before long will pass to the underworld.

Alas!

How sad that from a single family,
Three resentful ghosts will travel the road below.
For three years we cared for each other through good and bad;
Suddenly we'll be separated, unable to die together.

CHANG TA-KUNG (*enters and says*): "When you're poor it's hard to find a philanthropist to help you out with gold; when you're sick, there are plenty of busybodies to give you recipes for drugs." Sir, how are you feeling today?

FATHER TS'AI: There's no hope for me; nothing but death is left now. Mr. Chang, you came at the right time. I need you to witness the testament I want to write for my daughter-in-law. After I die, I don't want her to observe the mourning period, but to marry again as soon as possible. Bring me paper and pen.

WU-NIANG: Father, you mustn't write that! From ancient times it's been said, "A loyal minister doesn't serve two rulers; a virtuous woman doesn't marry two men." Don't write, Father!

CHANG: You mustn't upset him. You'd better try and humor him.

(FATHER TS'AI *tries to write but can't.*)

(*He sings to the tune* Lo-chang-li tso):
Daughter,

Your endless hardships
All come from the wrong I did you.

If you don't marry again,

Clothing and food
How could you obtain?

But no! Already I've wronged you. Now I tell you to marry again, but what if your new husband is just as bad? Wouldn't you have even more cause to blame me then?

Should I tell you then
To stay in mourning by my spirit tent?

(He puts down the pen.)

> I know my death's but a moment away;
> What use is my advice to those who'll live on?

CHANG *(sings to the same tune):*

> The truth of this,
> How painful to speak!

Young lady,

> If you don't marry another,
> I fear you'll have no means of life.
> But if you don't observe the mourning period,
> Others will deride you.

(They sing the chorus together):

> How sad the family is broken, each person on his own.
> How can we hold back tears?

WU-NIANG *(sings to the same tune):*

> My father's stern command
> I wouldn't venture to oppose.
> My only fear is that I'd marry another Po-chieh;
> Wouldn't I suffer then my whole life through?

Father,

> I'm a one-saddle horse,
> And swear to have no other wish.

(They repeat the chorus above.)

CHANG: Sir, you ought to rest for the time being. We'll work it out later.

FATHER TS'AI: Mr. Chang, to you I bequeath my walking stick. If that wicked, unfilial son Ts'ai Yung ever comes back, use this stick to drive him out of my house!

(He falls down and WU-NIANG and CHANG assist him.)

(Closing poem)
CHANG:

> Never get angry when you're ill.

WU-NIANG:

To protect your weak body, please calm your mind.

TOGETHER:

"Only diseases that aren't critical can be cured by drugs;
Only those originally destined can be converted by Buddha."

(They exit.)

SCENE TWENTY-THREE

TS'AI (*enters and sings to the tune* Hsi ch'ien ying):

All day lost in thought,
Regret presses down my brows,
Thoughts of her fill my heart.
The new phoenix mate causes my pain to grow;
The fish that carry my messages are stopped midstream.
So far apart we gaze toward each other, all in vain!
My emaciated face reflected in a bright mirror makes me
    ashamed.
Clear tones of jeweled *ch'in* can sound no more.
In nebulous dreams I return,
Winding through towering mountains and misty trees—
But where is my home?

(*He recites to the* tz'u T'a-so hsing):

Filled with resentment and grief,
Dispirited my song, lifeless my laughter,
All because I was given a new phoenix mate.
The wandering son, far from home, is unable to return;
Father and mother are left without care.
The fish which carries messages has drowned;
The goose which bears letters was cut off in its flight.
I've no way to send news to them.
How short is man's life!
Already I've let slip by the one wish of my life.

(*He sings to the tune* Yen yü chin):

I think
Of that day I left my hometown,
Recall when we reached the point of parting, how sadly she saw
    me off;
Holding hands, how reluctant we were to let go of each other.
I told her to take good care
Of my parents;
Surely she did not forget!
I hear of famine there,
And fear they can't live through such years of hardship.
And when no letter comes from me, to whom can they turn?

(*He sings to the tune* Erh-fan yü-chia ao):

I think
Of the books I read in youth.
They said a son must become a model of filial service,
But never talked of the reality.
How could I have known that I would suffer so many troubles?
Forced by father to attend the examinations,
Forced by ruler to serve as counselor,
Forced by father-in-law to live in marriage—
Forced against my will three times, and now I must bear my pain
    in silence!
I can't escape blame from both sides.
Here, they call me naïve, bashful, and cold;
There, they call me shiftless, fickle, and untrue.

(*He sings to the tune* Yen yü hsü):

So painful
To march in the ranks of ducks and egrets![1]
How much better to be like a baby crow feeding its parents from
    its own mouth!
I have no need of the golden seal of office
Attached to the purple sash.
I only wonder, those motley clothes—
Where are they now?[2]
I mustn't think of motley clothes,
For even if I return,
I fear that I will have to put on hempen clothes and carry a
    mourning staff.
Only because I strove to climb a cloud ladder to the moon,
Their tears rain down, their temples grow frost.

(*He sings to the tune* Yü-chia hsi yen-teng):

Several times in dreams,
I've suddenly heard the cock crow.
I wake, startled, call to my former wife
To go together to bid good morning to my parents.
When I awake from my confusion,
There, as before, my new wife in phoenix coverlet and ivory bed,
And I can only resent her fragrance, be hurt by her beauty to
    which my heart's not joined.
I feel it's because of her I'm bound here.
Because of that,

---

[1] The phrase is used to describe the orderly ranks of officials walking in procession
to court.
[2] "Motley clothes" are a symbol of filial devotion. See Scene Two, note 8.

I can't control this anguish.
Here I spend nights of pleasure behind hibiscus curtains;
There in still loneliness she hates the length of the hours.

(*He sings to the tune* Chin ch'an yen):

And my anxious grief
Turns all pleasure to empty depression.
Pulse and water are pure;
What heart had I
To covet costly wine and plump lamb?
The wedding chamber of flowered candles grieves my heart;
The gold list that bears my name pains my soul.
And I think to myself,
Truly, in the house I dare not cry aloud,
For the sound would break a hearer's heart.

Steward, come here!

STEWARD (*enters and says*): When there's a question, I answer. When there's no question, I give no reply. Sir, what instructions do you have for me?

TS'AI: You're closer to me than anyone here, and I want to discuss something with you. You must keep this to yourself.

STEWARD: Whatever you tell me I wouldn't dare divulge to others.

TS'AI: When I left my parents and wife to come here for the examinations, it wasn't my wish at all. But I was forced by imperial command to accept an appointment, expecting after my three years were up to be able to return home. How could I know that I would be taken in by Prime Minister Niu as son-in-law, and that ever since I'd be detained here, unable to return to see my parents even once? I want to discuss a plan with you.

STEWARD: "Without drilling, no hole can be made; without speech, no one can know." I've seen all along that you were unhappy here, but I didn't know the reason. Why don't you discuss it with your wife?

TS'AI: Though my wife is a wise woman, her father's power burns everyone that touches him. If I tell the daughter, the father would learn of it in a minute. He would think that if I went home, I'd never return; how could he let me leave? The best way is to suffer in silence for the time being, hiding everything from my wife. When my appointment expires, then I'll think of a plan for returning.

STEWARD: That's right. If the master knew the truth, he'd never let you go!

TS'AI: Now I want to send a letter home, but I have no way to do it. If I send a servant, I'm afraid my wife will find out. You go out in the streets and look for a suitable person to take the letter for me.

STEWARD: I'll look everywhere for such a man!

(Closing poem)
TS'AI:

All day the painful memories never end.

STEWARD:

I'll find the means to send your letter.

TOGETHER:

"Eyes gaze for the sight of the battle flag;
Ears strain to hear the good news."

(They exit.)

SCENE TWENTY-FOUR

WU-NIANG (*enters and sings to the tune* Chin lung-ts'ung):

> First the famine struck,
> Then the loss of my parents, one after the other.
> How can I go on all alone?
> My clothing all pawned,
> Not the smallest hairpin left—
> There's no other way but to cut my clouds of fragrant hair.

(*She recites to the* tz'u Tieh lien-hua):

> No way to cast off this endless suffering and hardship,
> My strength's used up, my spirit exhausted; tears flow like blood
>   from my eyes.
> My cotton skirts and thorn hairpins have all been sold.
> My mother and father died one after the other.
> Metal scissors, bright as white snow,
> Reflect my black clouds of hair and grieving crescent brows.
> No words can express the filial love in my heart;
> I can only entrust it to this silken black hair.

When my mother-in-law died, Mr. Chang took care of all the arrangements. Now my father-in-law has also died, and I have no money for burial expenses. How hard to ask Mr. Chang again for help! I think of it, and there's no other way but to cut my silken black hair and sell it for a few strings of cash to use for the burial expenses. My hair, I know, isn't worth much—it's only a symbol, for what I'm really doing is begging in the streets. How true that . . .

(*She recites in* shih *form*):

> My two parents one after the other perished,
> Always to ask help from others can't be right.
> I'll use these locks of shining black
> To bury those with hair of white.

(*She sings to the tune* Hsiang-lo tai):

> Ever since my phoenix mate went far away,
> Who has combed these clouds of hair?

My makeup table I never approach; only dust grows there.
Everything I've pawned—combs, adornments, hairpins—not one
is left.

My hair!

Already I've ruined
Your years of spring,
And now I must cut you
So my old parents will have a burial place.
It wounds my heart to cut my hair,
Fills me with resentment toward the fickle man with whose locks it
was bound.

(She starts to cut, then puts down the scissors.)

(She sings to the same tune):

Thinking of that fickle man
And the wrong he's done me,
I try to cut, then pause as tears fall.
If only I'd first donned a cassock, shaved my head, and entered
Buddha's Gate,
If I were a nun,
Never would I have suffered this today!

And yet, my hair in it's beauty is worthy still to adorn a bride,

To be covered with pearl and feather ornaments, perfumed with
musk.

While I have come to the point that

When I die,
I'll have no burial place—
Why should I act the foolish woman lamenting over her hair?

(With an action, she sings to the same tune):

How pitiful, this foolish woman,
Destitute and alone!

I would not cut you, my hair,

But to ask help from others—how could I bear the shame?

I must cut,

But the stroke of metal blade is answered with pain in my heart.

Enough! Enough!

I'll use piles of raven tresses,
My dancing phoenix locks,
To repay, like the baby crow,
The love of white-haired parents.
Then people will say that the girl with cloudlike hair
Provided burial for those with hair of frost.

(She cuts.)

(Weeping, she sings to the tune Lin-chiang hsien):

Parents lost one after the other, no way is left to me
But to cut my fragrant clouds.
I care not for the filial fame I'll leave behind me,
But only that "it's easier to climb a high mountain and capture a
    fierce tiger
Than to open one's mouth and ask help from others."

My hair is cut. Now I must go out to the streets to sell it. As I
pass here and there, I call out, "Hair for sale!"

(She calls out.)

(She sings to the tune Mei-hua t'ang):

Hair for sale!
Buyer, don't argue about the price.
Think of the hunger I suffer—
Empty my coffers,
Husband far away,
Parents-in-law both lost.
No way is left to me now
But to sell this hair
To give them burial.

Why does nobody ask to buy?

(With an action, she sings to the tune Hsiang liu niang):

See my hair, like fine black silk—
How lovely it is!
How can no one offer to buy?
In such a year of famine and death,
How would you have a woman
Face such desperation?
Day after day, suffering from hunger,
How can I lift my feet?
It's too hard to bear!

(She falls down, then rises.)

(She sings to the same tune):

> Through front streets, back streets, I search;
> Not a person's in sight.

I try to cry out again,

> But the breath chokes in my throat
> And I can't make a sound.

Alas!

> If I die here now,
> My corpse would lie exposed,
> For who would cover it for me?

Heaven! Only death is left to me now!

> If only I can sell my hair,
> Bury my parents-in-law,
> What would my death matter?

CHANG TA-KUNG *(enters):* "An act of compassion is better than reciting Buddha's name a thousand times; the evildoer can't be helped by burning ten thousand sticks of incense." Hey! Isn't that young Mistress Ts'ai? Why does she lie fallen in the street?

WU-NIANG: Help me, sir!

CHANG *(helps her up):* Mistress Ts'ai, why are you carrying that hair?

WU-NIANG: My father-in-law has died, and I'm using this hair to provide for his burial.

CHANG *(weeps):* So your father-in-law has also died! Why didn't you tell me? How could you cut off your hair?

WU-NIANG: I've annoyed you too many times already; I didn't dare bother you again.

CHANG: What are you saying!

(He sings to the previous tune):

> Your husband entrusted you to my care;
> How could I go back on my word?
> If you have no money,
> It's my duty to lend it to you.
> You cut off your hair,
> Lie fallen in the street,
> And I alone am to blame.

(They sing the chorus together):

Lament the family in ruins!
Now that misfortune has reached its depth, why doesn't good fortune begin?
From both of us tears flow.

WU-NIANG (*sings to the same tune*):

I thank you for your compassion,
For the money you lend.
Under the ground my parents-in-law are grateful too.
I only fear that I myself
Will die, with no one to bury me.

Sir,

Then who will repay your kind loan?

(*They repeat the chorus above.*)

CHANG: Mistress Ts'ai, you go ahead home. I'll send a servant with cloth, money, rice, and other things you'll need.
WU-NIANG: Sir, please accept this hair.
CHANG: What would I do with it?

(*Closing poem*)
WU-NIANG:

Thank you, sir, you've saved my life!

CHANG:

Your husband put a neighbor's trust in me.

TOGETHER:

Truly, "Out of the blue there stretched a cloud-snatching hand
To raise up the prisoner caught in Heaven's nets and earth's traps."

SCENE TWENTY-FIVE

SWINDLER (*played by the* ching *actor, enters and sings to the tune* Ta-ch'iu ch'ang):

> For years and years
> I've been a swindler—
> I'm famous everywhere!
> No matter how clever you may be,
> I can catch you in my trap.

(He recites in parallel prose):

 Tricks are my trade, picking pockets my profession. With tongue like a sword, lips like a spear, I can bewilder the most clever. With false sympathy and sweet words, I can turn the stingiest man into a spendthrift. I change my address at will, never use my real name. When I make a trap, whoever comes along walks right in. When I pull my tricks, he'll never get out again! I've tricked the bat out of Chung K'uei's hand and the pill of immortality from the gourd of Lü Tung-pin.[1] I come without footprints, leave without a trace, cheat people face to face as easy as snapping my fingers. I'll walk with you, sit with you—but when you find you've been cheated, you'll never know who's to blame. In the army of swindlers, I'm the leader; in the division of cheaters, I'm the top general. Why bother to bore through walls? I'm superior to thieves who sneak through the darkness. I don't need to brandish staffs and knives, for I do my stealing in the light of day. As they say, "As the earth doesn't put forth grass without roots, so Heaven doesn't let people live without means."

I'm out of business right now, but I've heard that the official Ts'ai Po-chieh has a family in Ch'en-liu. His parents are still alive, but he's had no news of them. I've been to Ch'en-liu before and am familiar with the area. So now I'll make myself a native of Ch'en-liu and fake a letter from his parents to deliver to him. Of course he'll write a letter to send back to

---

[1] Chung K'uei, a spirit guard, first appeared in a dream of Emperor Ming Huang (r. 712–756) of the T'ang dynasty; he is traditionally portrayed with a bat in his hand. Lü Tung-pin was a scholar of the T'ang dynasty who, through spiritual cultivation, became immortal.

them—and, who knows—he might give me some money for traveling expenses along with it. There may be a real profit involved, but at least I can be sure of the money for traveling. Here's Ts'ai Po-chieh's house—I'll go on in. But why is there nobody around?

STEWARD *(enters):* "Behind our lord's gates, it's deep as the sea. No outsiders are allowed to knock."

(The two greet each other.)

STEWARD: Who are you? What's your business here?

SWINDLER: I've just come from Ch'en-liu with a letter from Ts'ai Po-chieh's parents.

STEWARD: He was just looking for a way to send a letter home—you've come at the right time! Let me call him out.

(He performs an action.)

TS'AI *(enters and sings to the tune* Feng-huang ko):

Searching everywhere for a courier,
I have no way to send a letter.
I turn my head to gaze toward my old home, but all in vain;
Even white clouds passing there can't be seen.
Like threads, the traces of my tears,
As I think of my phoenix wife casting her solitary shadow in the
    mirror.

Steward, where did this man come from?

STEWARD: He says he's come from Ch'en-liu.

SWINDLER: I have come from Ch'en-liu.

TS'AI: Do you bring a letter from my family?

SWINDLER: Yes, I have a letter.

TS'AI: Let me see it!

(The SWINDLER *hands the letter to* TS'AI.)

TS'AI *(reading the letter, sings to the tune* I-feng-shu):

Ever since you went away,
Constantly we think of you.

Yes, I also am constantly thinking of my family.

Have you achieved success and fame?
We think that surely you've plucked the cassia branch!

Success and fame, I've achieved.

By good fortune, father, mother, and wife
Are all in good health—no calamities have fallen.

I'm happy my family is doing well!

When you read this letter from home,
We know that you
Will hurry back—delay no more!

(With an action): How could I not want to go? Alas, it's not up to me! Steward, bring me paper and pen. I'll write a letter and give it to him. While you're at it, bring some gold and pearls too.

(The STEWARD *exits, then returns with the things.)*

STEWARD: Here are paper and pen, gold and pearls.
TS'AI *(writing, sings to the tune* Hsia-shan hu):

Ts'ai Yung bows a hundred times
To his honored parents.
Since the day I left your side,
Suddenly I realize several years have passed.
My gaze can't reach to my old home;
Constantly my eyes strain toward it.
And all this time I've been cut off from news.
The things of fame and profit, alas, have bound me.
To no avail, my tears flow.
I petitioned the emperor
To leave my official post,
But the ruler had no pity.

(He sings to the tune Man p'ai ling):

Suddenly your letter came—
How it comforts my anxious heart!
I rejoice that father, mother, and wife
Are all in good health.
For still your son is kept here,
And is unable to serve those loving faces.
In haste, this note was written;
I beg that you forgive its roughness.

Come here, man. Take this letter, gold and pearls to my home. Tell my family that someday I will return, that they must put their minds at rest and not be worried about me.
SWINDLER: I understand.
TS'AI: And here's some change for your traveling expenses.

SWINDLER: Thank you sir!
TS'AI (*sings to the tune* Chu-ma t'ing):

> I send a letter to my hometown.
> When I speak of it, my heart aches.
> Bring word to my old father and mother of eighty years,
> And explain to my bride of two months,
> Separated from me by thousands of mountains and streams.
> The blue silk's streaked where I've sealed the letter with tears.
> My soul in dreams winds round those silver screens that block the
>   way.

(They sing the chorus together):

> They tell me they're safe and comfortable;
> Our whole family surely has been blessed with good fortune!
> Just say that the day will come when we see each other again!

STEWARD (*sings to the same tune):*

> Thoughts of his distant hometown—
> His lady there stares out with frozen gaze.
> She sees the geese again and again fly by,
> But his returning boat never comes in sight,
> And still from high balcony she leans.
> When she sees the silver strokes flying across rainbow-cloud
>   paper,
> Then tears will fall in streams, her makeup ruined.

(They repeat the chorus above.)

SWINDLER (*sings to the same tune):*

> When I go westward out of Yang-kuan,
> I sigh that from today the road I travel will be hard.
> But I'll think how you've been separated so long,
> That I carry for you this slip of delicate paper.
> Crossing land and water,
> I'm only afraid of the robbers who swarm like wolves along the
>   road,
> And fear that the wild goose courier may never reach your home-
>   town.

(They repeat the chorus above.)

STEWARD (*sings to the same tune):*

> Your sweeping strokes cover the paper,
> Expressing all the pain of separation.
> I think that on those twelve high towers,

Someone stands,
Leaning from the high balconies.
She longs for the time of return,
Counts the flying geese,
All blocked by mountains and passes.
When she sees this letter, it will be like seeing that face of years
    ago.

(They repeat the chorus above.)

(Closing poem)
TS'AI:

I depend on you to carry good news over thousands of miles.

STEWARD:

All the pain of separation he's expressed to them.

TOGETHER:

Only after a separation lasting through the years,
Does one believe that "a letter from home is worth more than ten
    thousand pieces of gold."[2]

(They exit.)

[2] An allusion to the poem "Ch'un wang" (Spring vista) by Tu Fu (*CTS*, 224:2403).

SCENE TWENTY-SIX

WU-NIANG (*enters and sings to the tune* Kua chen-erh):

In the green mountain all is desolate and still.
As thoughts arise, my spirit melts.
The yellow earth wounds my heart,
And red maple leaves are stained with my tears,
As I make by myself the lonely tomb.

(*She recites to the* tz'u P'u-sa man):

Mournful wind blows through the desolate white poplars;
Cold the air, dim the light, on the empty mountain.
Tigers howl, monkeys cry,
And the mourner's loneliness grows.
Deep and dark the Springs below,
Eternal night that never ends in dawn.
Tears for my parents-in-law splash the ground;
I wonder—can they hear me?

Since I lost them, no one's here to give me help. Now I must
make this grave to bury my parents-in-law. I've no money to
hire somebody, no one to turn to for assistance. I must move
the mud and earth all by myself.

(*She carries earth in her skirt.*)

(*She sings to the tune* Wu-keng chuan):

All alone I carry the earth,
Wrapping it in my skirt—how hard to keep on!
Deserted the empty mountain, no others come to mourn.
My feelings alone are devoted and sincere,
Hard labor I won't shirk for them.

Alas!

Parents have never been buried without their son in attendance.
They write of funerals with "mourners three-deep around the
    grave,"
But his parents were buried without even a diviner for the burial
    site.
I think
How the two of them, one after the other, were struck down.

Father,

> You hoped that he would soon pluck cassia and see the capital's
>   flowers,
> Never knowing that you yourself
> Would be buried under white poplars and parched grass.
> Nothing but pain!

(She performs an action.)

> Pain which must be kept to myself, for there's no one to tell.

(With an action, she sings to the previous tune):

> With only my own ten fingernails,
> How can I build the mound up high?

(With an action)

> See the fresh blood soaking my clothes!

Alas!

> My body weak, my strength spent;
> Surely I'll die here!

But wait!

> Let the blood flow on their burial place,
> For they are parents-in-law, close as bones and blood,
> And people will give praise.
> People will say,
> Chao Wu-niang practiced the filial way alone.

Alas!

> Heart worn out, strength exhausted, body emaciated—
> Only this fresh blood
> Still pours forth.
> When this grave is completed,
> I only fear my own life will be in danger.

Ah! I haven't any strength left. I have to lie down and rest a
little.

(She sings to the tune Pu-suan hsien):

> The mound not yet high,
> Already my strength is gone.

(She sleeps.)

MOUNTAIN SPIRIT *(played by the* wai *actor, enters and sings to the
tune* Fen tieh-erh):

How pitiful this young lady Chao!
Heaven has sent me to help her.

Wonderful, wonderful! I am the local spirit of this mountain. The Jade Emperor, moved by the filial conduct of Chao Wu-niang, commanded me to lead spirit troops to help her build the grave. First I'll summon Commissioner White Monkey and General Black Tiger of South Mountain. Monkey and Tiger, where are you? Report here immediately!

(MONKEY, *played by the* ch'ou *actor and* TIGER, *played by the* ching *actor, enter and perform actions.*)

MOUNTAIN SPIRIT: His majesty has commanded me that because of Chao Wu-niang's filial conduct, we must help her build the grave. You two must change into human form and move earth and stones to make the grave.
MONKEY and TIGER: Yes, sir!
MOUNTAIN SPIRIT: Take care not to startle the filial lady!
MONKEY and TIGER (*after making the grave*): Sir, the grave is finished.
MOUNTAIN SPIRIT: Chao Wu-niang, raise your head and listen to me.
(*He sings to the tune* Hao chieh-chieh):

Wu-niang, listen to me:
I received a special command from the Jade Emperor.
Moved by your filial heart, he sent me to help you.

MONKEY and TIGER (*continue the song*):

The grave is completed.
When you've buried your parents, go seek your husband.
Change your style of dress and go to the capital.[1]

MOUNTAIN SPIRIT: Chao Wu-niang, do you understand? Truly is it said, "Sun and moon light the world . . .
MONKEY and TIGER (*joining in*): So that no one need travel through life in darkness."

(*The three spirits exit and* WU-NIANG *awakens.*)

WU-NIANG (*sings to the tune* Pu-suan hou):

---

[1] In one edition of the play (*Liu-shih chung-ch'u*), it is specified that Wu-niang should dress as a nun. In this version it only later becomes clear that she does so.

In my dream, I know that spirits came;
It must be that Heaven has taken pity on me.

How strange! While I was sleeping, confused and hazy, like a dream, yet not a dream, I heard somebody tell me that when the grave is completed I must go to the capital in search of my husband. But when will I ever be able to finish the grave by myself?

(With an action): Ah! How can this be? The grave is finished! I thank Heaven and earth, for surely this was done through the help of spirits.

(She sings to the tune Wu-keng chuan):

How to measure my resentment and pain!
We three always thought we'd starve together and together die.

Father, Mother, I don't want to bury you, but that can't be. About to bury you, I stop,

For once you're locked within the Springs, the sun will never dawn.
From today we'll be forever separated,
Never again able to lean on each other.

But if I die and am buried with you here, then I can serve you again.

I only grieve that I may die on distant roads.
My corpse then—
How could it be carried here?
From now on,

This grave,

I only hope will be warm and dry.
Will there be glorious descendants for you?
Even if there are high lords among them,
It will be too late to relieve you in your old age.
Silently fall my tears,
As I pray to Heaven above.

(CHANG TA-KUNG and his servant HSIAO-ERH, played by the ch'ou actor, enter, carrying shovels, and sing to the tune Hua-ch'iao-erh):

From all sides mournful winds blow the pine and cypress.
Mountain clouds cold and lonely, the sun gives no light.
Monkeys cry and tigers howl.
How lonely and still!

We hasten on to the cliff
To lend our strength to assist the filial lady.

CHANG: I am Chang Ta-kung, the neighbor of Mr. Ts'ai. Since her old parents-in-law died, the young lady has done everything herself, even carrying earth in her skirt to make the grave mound. It takes many workers to make a grave; how can a woman, all alone, ever finish the work? I must bring Hsiao-erh to help her a little. Ah! Can it be? The mound is finished!

(He recites in shih *form):*

Just see the luxuriant pines and cypress surrounding the grave;
At the lonely grave, fresh earth covers the door to the Springs below.

Wu-niang,

You're all alone on this empty mountain, with no one to give you aid;
Who was it that made this grave?

WU-NIANG *(recites in* shih *form):*

Spirits appeared in my dream—wonderful indeed!
Mysterious troops moved the earth and carried the mud.
When the grave was completed I received personal instructions
To travel to the capital in search of my husband.

HSIAO-ERH *(recites in* shih *form):*
Sir,

From olden times many such things have been recorded.
It must be that her plight has moved Heaven.
The Great Wall was once brought down by the tears of a woman—
Chiang-nü;[2]

Wu-niang,

Your virtuous name will be recorded alongside hers.

ALL: It's just as they say: "The evildoer will be punished, the good meet with just reward; it may be swift, it may be slow, but surely it will come."

WU-NIANG *(sings to the tune* Hao chieh-chieh):

[2] Popular stories tell of Meng Chiang-nü who, while seeking for her husband's bones at the Great Wall where he had died on corvée service, cried so grievously that part of the wall collapsed.

My fingers' flowing blood—
All alone, no way to build the mound—
Moved Heaven to offer silent help.

(They sing the chorus together):

The grave is completed;
After burying your parents, seek your husband.
Change your style of dress and go to the capital.

CHANG *(sings to the same tune):*

I came with Hsiao-erh
To assist you with our strength.
Who could know that spirits would come in silence to help you?

(They repeat the chorus above.)

HSIAO-ERH *(sings to the same tune):*

If you really saw a spirit
Among pines and cypress, by the lonely grave, where is he now?
That little spirit was actually played by me![3]

(Closing poem)
CHANG: Wu-niang,

Your filial heart had the power to move spirit troops.

WU-NIANG:

Without those spirit troops, how could the grave be made?

HSIAO-ERH:

There's no need to wrack your brain over the countless troubles of
    the human world;
Just raise your head—bright spirits hover only three feet away.

---

[3] This type of performers' joke is quite common in *ch'uan-ch'i*. The *ch'ou* actor had indeed played one of the spirits.

SCENE TWENTY-SEVEN

MISTRESS NIU (*enters and sings to the tune* Nien-nu chiao):

The rain's passed,
Waves calmed, trees let fall their leaves—
An autumn scene bright and clear.
Who rode the moon, like a wheel of jade, across the sea,
Crushed it into bits of glimmering glass for miles on miles?
The sound of jade pendants, cool as breezes,
The flute and songs fresh as dew,
Here in this lovely paradise.

MU-MU and HSI-CH'UN (*enter and continue the song*):

We roll up the pearled screen;
In our small pavilion, boundless delight!

(*They recite to the* tz'u Lin-chiang hsien):

Moonlight's turned the world to jade over thousands of miles of
    autumn,
As if its silver glow had shattered to glimmering pieces the glassy
    surface of the sea.

MISTRESS NIU:

In paradise above, cool breezes pass through immortals' robes,
And a divine fragrance drifts down to us—
Who has seen beauty such as this?

HSI-CH'UN and MU-MU:

Next year on this night of brightest moon,
At this time, this scene—will it be the same?

MISTRESS NIU:

Pearl screen rolled up high, we grow tipsy as we drink from carne-
    lian cups.

ALL:

Don't decline to watch the whole night through;
Before we know it, one more year will have passed.

MISTRESS NIU: Mu-mu, Hsi-ch'un, it's Midautumn Night, and the moonlight's clear and bright. Invite my husband to come out and enjoy it with me.

HSI-CH'UN: Come on out! The lady invites the master to come out and enjoy the moon!

TS'AI (*answers from offstage*): I'm sleeping—I don't want to come out.

MU-MU: No wonder he won't come out! He certainly can't look kindly on a face like yours! I'll go invite him.

(*She performs an action.*)

TS'AI (*enters and sings to the tune* Sheng ch'a-tzu):

> I found someone to carry my letter;
> The letter has gone, and my spirit with it.
> In this lovely weather tonight,
> How sad that they're a thousand miles away.

MISTRESS NIU: Sir, it's Midautumn Night and the moon is delightful. I asked you to come out and enjoy it a little. You don't have anything else to do, so why did you decline?

TS'AI: What's so special about the moon?

MISTRESS NIU: Everything! Just look!

(*She recites to the* tz'u Lei chiang yüeh):

> Over the jade pavilion, a rosy sky;
> Clear and pure the cool weather, the clouds all cleared away.
> Drifting fragrance of red cassia refreshes the heart.
> I feel we're living in a paradise.

TS'AI (*continues the* tz'u):

> Shadows penetrate the empty curtains;
> Light steals in through gauze draperies.
> The dew is cool, the sound of crickets incessant.
> Over mountains and passes on this night,
> The moon shines the same on those apart.

MU-MU (*continues the* tz'u):

> Surely you know that separation and reunion, sorrow and joy
> Are just like the moon;
> Sometimes dark, sometimes bright, it waxes and wanes.[1]

---

[1] This and a number of other lines in the scene are derived from the famous *tz'u* "Shui-tiao ko-t'ou" (Prelude to Water Music) by Su Tung-p'o (1037–1101).

And even if life could be an endless revel,
How often will you see the icy wheel above so bright and pure?

HSI-CH'UN (*continues the* tz'u):

How bright this evening!
How far away next year!
Don't let your golden goblets rest.

(*They finish the* tz'u *together*):

We hope forever and ever,
We'll be together, year after year, enjoying the bright moon.

MISTRESS NIU (*sings to the tune* Pen-hsü):

Thousands of miles high in space,
How delightful the beauty of the moon!
Unspoiled by the slightest trace of cloud.
On the twelve railings,
Where light is flooding,
Cool air soaks through pearl screens and silver shutters.
Just as though we
Were dwelling in fairyland.
Laughing, we fill our cups.
In man's life, how often can he see such a scene?

(*They sing the chorus together*):

We only hope
That year after year on this night,
The moon and we alike will be free of clouds.

TS'AI (*sings to the same tune with a modified opening*):

A lonely form,
The bird on southernmost branch is suddenly chilled,[2]
And shadowy forms of crows and magpies are startled into flight,
Their perch no longer safe.
Among green mountains, like ten thousand tiny dots,
Where can they be—
The three paths that lead to my hut?[3]
Deeper and deeper grow my thoughts.
I've plucked the red cassia,
Been loved by the goddess of the moon;
This sympathy for the girl a thousand miles away is all in vain.

[2] From a line in the *Nineteen Old Poems*, the bird perching on the southern tip of a branch is a symbol of homesickness.
[3] T'ao Yüan-ming (365–427), poet of the Tsin dynasty, had three shortcuts leading to his house by which close friends would come to visit.

(They repeat the chorus above.)

MISTRESS NIU *(sings to the same tune with a modified opening):*

Lustrous light!
I want to blow the jade panpipes till they break,
Mount on a phoenix and return to the moon,
But I wonder if the wind is cold in that immortal city?[4]
My jade ornaments are moistened with dew,
Just like Fei-ch'iung as she returned to the moon.[5]
And more,
With these clouds of perfumed hair,
Dazzling arms of jade,
I'm the equal of the moon goddess herself.

(They repeat the chorus above.)

TS'AI *(sings to the same tune with a modified opening):*

How painful to hear
Flutes playing "Passes and Mountains"![6]
At others' doors, the clothes mallets pound.[7]
On this moonlit night, nothing but sounds to break my heart.
Since I traveled far away,
How many times I've seen the bright moon wax and wane!
Everything is just like
That soldier at a border post,
Longing for his wife in her secluded chamber,
And blaming the moon for shining so bright on those who are
    separated.

(They repeat the chorus above.)

HSI-CH'UN and MU-MU *(sing to the tune* Ku lun t'ai*):*

It turns chill,
Mandarin duck tiles grow cold, ice forms on jade pots.
Dew soaks the balcony rail, and still she lingers,
Avidly gazing up at the bright mirror of jade.
And over ten thousand miles,
Is that beautiful white, perfectly round.

[4] The three lines allude both to the lady Nung-yü, who disappeared on the back of a phoenix and became an immortal, and the *tz'u* "Shui-tiao ko-t'ou" by Su Tung-p'o.
[5] Fei-ch'iung is the name of a goddess encountered in a dream by a T'ang scholar.
[6] The lines allude to the poem "Ts'ung chün hsing" (Traveling as a soldier) by Wang Ch'ang-ling (698–755?) describing the homesickness of a soldier (*CTS*, 143:1444).
[7] The sound of mallets pounding clothes to wash them is traditionally evocative of longing for home.

All other lovely nights when the moon is full
Are surpassed by this one night.

HSI-CH'UN (*continues the song alone*):

Give over this night of bright light to the emptying of cups!
We may grow madly drunk,
But on this bright night, we'll be free—drunk, sober, drunk again.
For the party will scatter,
The water clock's silver arrow press on,
The fragrance from golden tripods fade.
The Dipper's turned round and Ts'an moved cross the sky,
And the Milky Way grows bright,
From golden wells, the sound of pulleys ended.

MU-MU (*sings to the same tune with a modified opening*):

I reflect,
How the moon waxes and wanes, is dark then bright,
And in man's life there are partings and reunions, grief and joy;
Never do they stay the same.
In deep courts, peaceful gardens,
Everywhere this clear light shines—
Shines on those whose dreams have come true,
Their spirits high with the love they've found,
As it shines on one alone at Ch'ang-men,
Unblessed by her lord's favor.[8]

HSI-CH'UN (*continues the song*):

And the divine beauty, goddess of the moon,
Sleeps alone through the long night.[9]
How can she bear it—
The stillness of the late hours?
How unpredictable such things!
We only hope that forever and ever,
We'll climb together the small pavilion to watch the moon.

(*They sing together to the tune* Yü-wen):

The cricket's mournful whir urges wives to spinning wheels.[10]

---

[8] A concubine of Emperor Wu (r. 140–88 B.C.) lost his favor and lived alone in Ch'ang-men Palace. She asked Ssu-ma Hsiang-ju (179–117 B.C.) to write a poem describing her loneliness. The poem so moved the emperor that he became intimate with her again.

[9] According to legend, Ch'ang O, goddess of the moon, was condemned to live in eternal loneliness after stealing the Pill of Immortality.

[10] The name for the house cricket, "to urge to the spinning," derives from the idea that its sound is like that of a spinning wheel.

MISTRESS NIU *(continues the song alone):*

Lost in our revelry, I didn't hear their call.

TS'AI *(continues the song):*

No matter to us that everywhere the winter clothes are not yet made.

(Closing poem)
MISTRESS NIU:

On this night, the bright moon is at its fullest.

TS'AI:

Some places are cold and lonely, some places merry.

TOGETHER:

We only hope that forever and ever,
Year after year, over thousands of miles, we'll share this beauty.

(They exit.)

SCENE TWENTY-EIGHT

WU-NIANG (*enters and sings to the tune* Hu tao-lien):

> To bid farewell
> I approach the barren grave,
> Filled with fear of the difficulties on my road ahead.
> I'll paint their portraits to use as an opening;
> When I show it to those I meet, I won't need words to beg.

"The ways of spirits are difficult to understand; their responsiveness to our actions is still without doubt." Yesterday I was all alone on this mountain making the grave mound. Just as I fell asleep, suddenly in my dream there appeared a spirit, who called himself the local god of the mountain. He led spirit troops to add their strength to mine. Then he told me to change my style of dress and go to the capital to seek my husband. When I woke up, I saw that the grave really was already finished. I know now that spirits are supporting me. Truly, "The believer is closer to the truth than the sceptic." Now that my parents-in-law are buried, I have only to change my clothes, take my lute as a beggar's prop, and set forth, singing songs of filial piety as I beg for alms. But after living with my parents-in-law so many years, this separation is too much to bear. I've always been able to paint a little; I'll paint their portraits from my imagination and carry them with me on my back. It will be just as though they were keeping me company. When it's time for sacrifices or the anniversary of their death, I'll unroll the painting and burn paper money and incense, offer cold porridge and water, to express the feelings in my heart.

(*With an action*): I begin to draw.

(*She sings to the tune* San hsien ch'iao):

> Ever since they died,
> I've longed to meet them, but there is no way.
> Only in dreams,
> Brief reunion.

I start to paint,
But can't continue.
Their images in my mind
Make tears flow before brush can ever move.

I draw,

But the pain in their hearts can't be drawn.

I sketch,

But what hunger did to them can't be shown.

I paint,

But those eyes staring out in search of their son can't be painted.
I can only paint disheveled hair,
Clothes ragged and dirty.

All right, then!

For if I painted them happy and well,
It would not be the parents-in-law of Chao Wu-niang.

(She sings to the same tune):

I'd like to make your faces plump,
But famine emaciated your forms.
I'd like to make your faces smooth,
But always they were riddled with lines.
If I paint you so,
How hideous it will be!
But with the grief that fills my heart,
I can't paint happy faces, smiling lips.

It's not that I don't know how to paint good portraits, but since I was married into the family,

For two months only we were free of care;
The rest has all been grief.

Those two carefree months are easily forgotten. Those three or four years,

I remember only their emaciated bodies, withered faces.

This painting—

If their son should receive it,
He wouldn't recognize the father and mother he used to know.

But what of that?

For even if they can't be recognized as the parents Ts'ai Po-chieh
  knew,
They can surely be recognized as the late parents-in-law of Chao
  Wu-niang.

The portraits are finished. I'll burn incense and paper, offer
water and food, then bid good-bye to my parents-in-law.

(She sings to the previous tune):

Father, Mother,

I wouldn't travel so far from you just to find my husband;
I must go, or your family line will end.
When I've found him, I'll return;
I'd dare not stay away long.

Alas!

Along the road
How can I walk?
Father and Mother, I look toward you
To protect me through foreign districts.

(With an action): Alas!

They themselves have no one to turn to;
How can they come and protect me?

This grave—

I only fear that after I'm gone,
Chill and desolate—who will come to sweep it?
And when it's time for spring and autumn sacrifices,
How can there be even a penny offered to them?

But what of that?

Alive they suffered hunger and cold;
Dead they'll become lonely ghosts, from offerings cut off.

Now that I've bid goodbye to my parents-in-law and bowed to
their portraits, I must go say goodbye to Chang Ta-kung. Ah,
here he comes!

CHANG TA-KUNG *(enters and recites in* shih *form):*

Try not to hear the winter cicadas cry amid dying willows.
So many leaves fall scattered by the west wind.
Don't look back as you travel the ancient road to the capital;

"When you go west from Yang-kuan, there will be no more old
friends."[1]

WU-NIANG: I was just coming to your house.

CHANG: Are you leaving today?

WU-NIANG: Yes, I'm leaving.

CHANG: What is that painting?

WU-NIANG: Portraits of my parents-in-law I painted myself. I'll
use it to help me when I beg on the road, and burn incense
and paper money to them whenever I can.

CHANG (*looking at the painting, recites to the* tz'u Che-ku
t'ien):

Wu-niang,

> Those parted by death will surely meet again in dreams;
> You needn't have exhausted your filial heart to show these
>   shadows of them.
> How sad that you never had a chance to paint a happy family
>   celebration!
> This painting's done wrong to the colors in your palate, causes one
>   to weep over the artist's skill.
> Ragged their clothing,
> Disheveled their hair,
> Their brows weighed down by endless resentment and grief.
> Ts'ai could never see here the faces he knew years ago;
> In vain you've shown them as they became after he left.

I heard that you're setting out on a long journey today, and
came to offer you a few strings of cash to help you on the
road.

WU-NIANG: I've bothered you so much already; how can I
trouble you again? There's just one thing I hate to ask of you,
and yet must ask. After I'm gone, the grave—sir, please take
pity and think on my parents as they were in life—please take
care of it for me!

CHANG: That's no trouble. I know you have to leave, but first I
want to offer you several words of warning. Wu-niang, you
grew up in secluded chambers; what have you ever known of
travel? In those days before Ts'ai left, you were young and
beautiful. But now years of famine have taken the beauty

[1] The line is a quotation from the famous parting poem "Wei-ch'eng ch'ü" by Wang
Wei (699–759).

from your face. As they say, "Peach blossoms year after year
are the same. But the faces of people year after year are
changed." When Ts'ai was about to leave, didn't he say, "If I
have the least success, I'll return right away"? Now even after
years of famine and the death of his parents, he has not returned. How can you know what his heart is like today? Just as
they say . . .

(He continues in verse): [2]

> "It's easy to paint a picture of the tiger's skin, but it's bones can't
>   be drawn;
> It's easy to know a man's face, but his heart can't be understood."
> Ts'ai is, after all, a scholar;
> With a single examination, he could have become world-famous.
> He's been away a long time—why?
> Even years of famine and his parents' death haven't brought him
>   home.

Wu-niang,

> When you arrive in the capital, you must take care;
> Humble yourself before others and find out how matters stand.
> When you find your husband, you need not speak of all your tri-
>   als;
> Tell him instead with the music of your lute.
> Don't say right away that you're his wife
> Nor tell him of his parents' deaths.
> And if Ts'ai is moved by you to remember things of the past,
> Let him take pity on his good neighbor Chang Ta-kung.
> Today I'm already seventy years old,
> Just ten years younger than your parents-in-law were.
> Today as you leave, Old Chang is here to see you off;
> When you return, who knows whether he'll be dead or alive?

As I see you off, it's as the poet said,

> "Tear-filled eyes gaze into tear-filled eyes;
> Broken-hearted sees off broken-hearted."

WU-NIANG (*sings to the tune* I to-chiao):

> While they float in endless gloom,
> I'll go forth with no one to support me.
> The road is a thousand miles long,

---

[2] The passage is in a simple form of poetry. Most lines are of seven characters each
and are rhymed.

And so I hold in my heart this dark grave.
When I leave the lonely grave,
I hope you will care for it.

(They sing the chorus together):

We look up toward emptiness
And tears overflow from our eyes.

CHANG *(sings to the same tune):*

The charge I've received
I understand in full.
I myself will watch over this lonely grave,
Never be untrue to your trust.
I only hope you'll make your journey in good health.

(They repeat the chorus above.)

WU-NIANG *(sings to the tune* Tou hei-ma):

Deeply grateful to you
For honoring me with consent,
And the kindness you've always shown,
How could I venture to forget!
I fear only that long road,
My frail body.
Alone, I may become sick,
Strength be spent from weary feet.

(They sing the chorus together):

The solitary grave is desolate and
      still,
Hateful the taste of the road.
In both places, how tragic!
How can this endless grief be de-
      scribed?

CHANG *(sings to the same tune):*

Your husband must surely be
A lofty official of high rank.
When you arrive,
First find out the truth.
I only fear that in your present guise
He will never recognize you.
One lofty, one low—
I'm afraid he'll pile wrong upon wrong.

(They repeat the chorus above.)

(Closing poem)

WU-NIANG:

To see my husband, I leave the solitary grave.

CHANG:

I only fear your husband will deny you.

TOGETHER:

Tear-filled eyes gaze into tear-filled eyes;
Broken-hearted sees off broken-hearted.

(They exit.)

SCENE TWENTY-NINE

TS'AI (*enters and sings to the tune* Chü-hua hsin):

Since I sent a letter to my parents far away,
I watch the geese that fly over passes and streams.
The *wu-t'ung* leaves have filled the courtyard,
Just as depression piles up in my heart.

(*He recites to the* tz'u Sheng ch'a-tzu):

A letter I sent to those far away,
Sent to my family over ten thousand miles.
The letter has gone, and with it my spirit;
Only this lifeless shell of a body remains.

Yesterday I received a letter from home. It said that my family are all well—how happy it made me! I immediately sent back a reply, and now I wonder how the courier's journey is going. Longing constantly changes to anxious depression. It's truly said, "Though there's no thread to stretch over thousands of feet, still my heart is bound to those ten thousand miles away." Such grief I feel!

(*He performs an action, then sits down.*)

MISTRESS NIU (*enters and sings to the tune* I nan wang):

My black-haired young genius
Shows no interest in plucking flowers or playing with willow
  twigs,[1]
Raising goblets and drinking wine.
I know by his furrowed brows there's sorrow in his heart;
But what is it he thinks of all the time?

TS'AI (*continues the song*):

These trifling worries
Would only trouble your heart.

MISTRESS NIU (*continues the song*):

Why not try to tell me?

[1] Flowers and willows are symbolic of women.

TS'AI *(continues the song):*

> I only fear that you'd seek to know everything,
> And that would add to my worries.

MISTRESS NIU: The ancients said, "There's never a frown or smile without its reason." The true gentleman of ancient times "never sighed during meals, and never expressed grief when music was about to be played."[2] To feel sorrow for no cause is said to be an ill omen. Sir, since you came here, you've been neither bright nor dark, as if drunk or in a trance, always lost in anxious thought. What is your problem? Could it be you don't have enough to eat, enough to wear? Perhaps you don't have enough to eat . . .
(She sings to the tune Hung na-ao):

> But you have rare boiled ape lips and baked panther stomachs to
> eat!

Perhaps you don't have enough to wear . . .

> But you have purple gauze robes and white jade belts to wear!

When you go out,

> Attendants on dappled horses precede your carriage,
> Three-layered umbrellas shade your head.

Sir, please don't blame me for speaking like this.

> You were a poor scholar in a thatched hut;
> Now you've become a pillar of the state.
> What do you lack that locks your eyebrows so,
> Mumbling and sighing, never at ease?

TS'AI: You say that I have clothes to wear . . .
(He sings to the same tune):

> I can't move freely in those purple gauze robes;
> I can't step lightly in those black court boots.

You say that I have food to eat . . .

> I grab a few mouthsful, then rush in a panic off to work;
> Drink a single cup of wine while I tremble that I might offend the
> law.
> Better to live like the retired Yen Tzu-ling climbing Fisherman's
> Tower,

[2] *Li Chi* (Book of Rites), 1:12a.

And never have to flee from arrest like the official Yang Tzu-yün
    jumping from office window.[3]
A lifetime spent watching the clock at early court misses out on au-
    tumn moons and spring flowers.
Useless toil and strain have turned my hair to white.

MISTRESS NIU *(sings to the same tune):*
Sir,

    Is it perhaps that my father is overbearing and fierce?

(TS'AI: No.)

    Is it perhaps that my service to you is deficient?

(TS'AI: No.)

    Is it perhaps that three thousand retainers don't fill your painted
    hall?

(TS'AI: No.)

    Is it perhaps that twelve rows of beautiful ladies don't stand before
    your screens?

TS'AI: How could it be that? No.

(TS'AI *performs an action.*)

MISTRESS NIU: Again, no.
(She continues her song):

    How can I guess what is in his heart?
    How can I understand what is in his heart?

(With an action): I think I've guessed it now.

    It must be he has a sweetheart in the pleasure quarters;
    Depressed and heartsick, you can't get her out of your heart.

TS'AI: No.
(He sings to the same tune):

    There is somebody at the end of the world.

I'm not able to see her.

---

[3] Yen Tzu-ling (37 B.C.–A.D. 43) was a scholar of the Latter Han period who refused
to accept official appointment and spent his life as a recluse tending his fields and
fishing. Yang Tzu-yün is Yang Hsiung (53 B.C.–A.D. 18), a scholar-official of the Han
dynasty. During the usurpation of Wang Mang (r. 9–23), he escaped arrest by leaping
from the window of the office where he was collating books. He was almost killed by
the fall.

Pink fades from her cheeks, black from her brows.

MISTRESS NIU: Didn't I say it? It *is* that!

TS'AI: No.

(*He continues his song*):

I suffer only from Sung Yü's autumn melancholy; [4]
I have no wish to go to those empty pavilions in Ch'u. [5]

(MISTRESS NIU: Won't you tell me what it is?)

I've told you already three parts of ten;
From that my heart's feelings you must now guess.

MISTRESS NIU: Why is it you refuse to answer my questions?

TS'AI: Enough! Wife,

Don't nag me into shutting up altogether!
If I told you what my problem is,
Tears would rush forth, cover my cheeks.

MISTRESS NIU: All right, all right! If I don't try to comfort you, you're lost in depression. Then when I ask you, you don't answer. There's nothing I can do! Sir,

(*She continues in* shih *form*):

Why should husband and wife keep secrets from each other?
You shouldn't let these piles of depression fill your inner heart.

But as they say:

"Each family should sweep away the snow from its own door
And not worry about the frost on other people's roofs."

(*She exits.*)

TS'AI: We're certainly not a couple whose "speech is in accord, hearts as if one." I lived in marriage for only two months, have been separated from my parents for years. Day and night my longing for them makes me sigh in bitterness. My new wife, of course, is very wise. She keeps asking me what's wrong, and I really want to tell her, for I know she would consent to my return. The problem is my father-in-law. If he knew that I had a wife at home, he would surely be afraid that

---

[4] Sung Yü, probably of the third century B.C., wrote of the sadness of the autumn season in the opening of his cycle of poems, "Chiu pien."
[5] "Pavilions of Ch'u" indicate courtesans' houses.

once gone, I'd never return, and how could he allow me to leave? For the time being I have to suffer in silence, wait until I can seek a local appointment, and then return to be with my parents; it's the only way. Wife, I'm not being overcautious in keeping these things from you. It's just that I'm afraid your father would insist on keeping me here. Just as they say, "Let husband and wife speak but three parts of ten . . ."

MISTRESS NIU (*enters and, with an action, says*): I understand it all now! "Don't pour out your whole heart to each other." Fine, fine! Go ahead and deceive me, but your parents and wife— how bitter they must be toward you!

(*She sings to the tune* Chiang-t'ou chin-kuei):

> I thought it odd how all day you stamped your feet in silent pain,
> I constantly pondered over the cause of that deep grief,
> Tried to guess the riddle that had no answer.
> As hard as I thought
> I had no way to find out the truth.
> You and I share one pillow, a single coverlet;
> Why should you seek to deceive me?
> You deserted father, mother, and wife,
> Let time pass on and on.
> How they must resent it when your letters never come!
> I have nothing but contempt for your shameless conduct;
> How utterly shallow is your heart!
> And now today,
> You still want to speak only three parts
> And not pour out what's in your heart!

TS'AI (*sings to the same tune*):

> It wasn't my wish to suffer so in silence;
> It's just that your father's power is so oppressive.
> I fear that if he knew my wish to return,
> He'd hold you here.
> I wanted to speak, but choked back my words.

Really, I can't deceive you—

> I want to undo my courtly hairpin,
> Try to obtain a local post.
> If he doesn't prevent it,
> Surely they'll send me to my own home.
> Together we'll return in brocade clothes.

Alas!

My parents are old;
Are they dead? Are they alive? I've no way to know.

I've sent a letter home,

But fear the courier has not got through.

(MISTRESS NIU: Haven't you received an answer yet?)

Though I don't stand guard where beacon fires burn for three
straight months,
Still a letter from home would be worth more than ten thousand
pieces of gold.[6]

MISTRESS NIU: Now I know! I'll go tell Father, and then you
and I can return together.
TS'AI: Don't tell him! How could he let you go? Don't let anybody know my secret.
MISTRESS NIU: It's all right. My father is grand tutor, and that's
a position which involves public morality; surely he wouldn't
do anything wrong!
TS'AI: Don't tell him. It won't do any good.
MISTRESS NIU: It's all right; leave it to me. He won't refuse.

(Closing poem:)
MISTRESS NIU:

"The egret hidden in snow can't be seen till it rises in flight;
Nobody knows about the parrot in the willows until it begins to
talk."

TS'AI:

"Even if the affair could be painted in bright purple or red,
People would still find something to criticize."

(They exit.)

[6] The two lines allude to the poem "Ch'un wang" (Spring vista) by Tu Fu (*CTS*, 224:2403).

SCENE THIRTY

PRIME MINISTER NIU (*enters and sings to the tune* Hsi ti chin):

How strange is my son-in-law!
Never do his frowning brows relax.
My heart's constant worry
Is all for my daughter.

"When you enter a house, no need to ask whether the family there prospers or declines; one look at their faces and you'll know." When I took in Ts'ai Po-chieh to be my son-in-law, I had good reason to be pleased. What bothers me is that ever since he came here, his brows are constantly locked in a frown and his face bears an anxious expression. There has to be a reason. When my daughter comes out, I'll ask her.

MISTRESS NIU (*enters and sings to the previous tune*):

I wondered what was on my husband's mind;
Today I have finally learned the truth.
We want to go together to his distant home;
I must find out what Father thinks.

NIU: My daughter, I've grown old in official service—now, alas, my hair is white! I've noticed that relations between you and your husband are strained and I constantly worry about you. Why is your husband so unhappy? You must know.

MISTRESS NIU: Father, he had been married only two months when he came here for the examinations. Now he's been separated from his family for three or four years and hasn't had any news from them. While he's unable to carry out his duties to his parents, how can he have any heart for conjugal affection! Now he wants to return home and is asking to take leave of his majesty and your excellency. Together we'll go to serve his parents and be true to the proper conduct of son and daughter-in-law.

NIU (*recites in parallel prose*):

I am a high lord and you are a sheltered beauty. What need has he to concern himself with that poor "husk wife"? How can you be willing to serve that old peasant? He's been away from his parents a long time; why doesn't he just send a letter to let them know how he's doing? You've been pampered all your life; how could you ever travel those thousands of miles? Don't let your husband delude you! Just obey your father's command.

MISTRESS NIU *(recites in parallel prose):* Father,

 In reading the canon I've never read of a true wife who failed to pay her respects to her parents-in-law. Think over the inviolable rules of conduct; how can a proper son fail to serve his father and mother? When I reflect on the principle of "Where he leads, she follows,"[1] I know that it is my duty to take care of them from morning to night. There, in cotton skirt and thorn hairpin, his first wife takes care of his parents all alone; how then can I, surrounded by gold screens and embroidered cushions, cling to the pleasures of our mansion here? Father, you hold the lofty rank of prime minister and are in charge of administering the regulations of the court. How can you break another's bonds of love and duty toward father and wife? You'll make Po-chieh commit the sin of neglecting his parents out of passion for his wife, and myself the sin of disobeying my husband's command and failing to serve my parents-in-law.

Please don't be angry, but just have pity!
NIU: You're talking nonsense! They already have a daughter-in-law; why should you go?
MISTRESS NIU *(sings to the tune* Shih-tzu hsü):

A daughter-in-law it's true they have.
But surely I am also
The wife of their son!
And how can a wife not serve her husband's parents?

(NIU: But what would you do if you went?)

A true daughter-in-law
Serves them with food,
Makes sure they're not too cold or too hot,
Gives support to their steps,
Takes care of the sacrifices and cooking.

[1] The quotation is from the *Book of Kuan-yin-tzu* by Yin Hsi of the Chou dynasty.

NIU: Even if there is a lot to be done there, since they already have one daughter-in-law, the son need not return.

MISTRESS NIU: Father,

"Children are raised in preparation for one's old age
Just as one stores up grain in case of famine."

NIU: If "Children are raised in preparation for one's old age," then weren't they wrong to send their son away to the examinations in the first place?

MISTRESS NIU (*sings to the tune* T'ai-p'ing ko):

He sought to pass the examinations
And hoped to return home in brocade clothes,
Never knowing he'd be held by you as son-in-law.

(NIU: "If it's destined, they'll meet though a thousand miles apart." Such things can't be accomplished by force.)

He cursed our bridal chamber filled with flowered candles;
Never were we "destined to meet though a thousand miles apart."
He wanted to keep his place on the golden list;
"It was crisis that brought us together."

NIU: Go ahead then, ignore what I tell you! It makes no difference to me how unhappy Ts'ai is.

MISTRESS NIU (*sings to the tune* Shang kung-hua):

His unending desolation—
How can I bear to see it?

(NIU: Let him be unhappy! There's no need for you to be.)

A husband and wife
Surely should share their happiness!

NIU: Have no fear; if he stays here, he'll become a high official. It's all up to me.

MISTRESS NIU: Father,

For several years he's had no news of them;
"Reaching the Phoenix Pond in ten years" has no value to him.

NIU: You accept what your husband says and ignore everything I say. The girl's been bewitched by him!

MISTRESS NIU (*sings to the tune* Chiang huang-lung):

You must understand,
It's not that I'm bewitched.

A married woman follows her husband;
How could I defy universal morality?

(NIU: There's nothing wrong with your going there, but I have
no other relatives; how can I let you leave me?)

As you think of your daughter,
How would you have them not think of their son?

(NIU: I'd be willing to let you go, but since they already have
one daughter-in-law there, I'm afraid you won't be treated
well.)

Don't talk of that!
For even if I should suffer mistreatment,
What would it matter compared with the suffering of his parents?

NIU: Well then, let Ts'ai go by himself.
MISTRESS NIU: Father,

That certainly wouldn't be
"Where husband leads, wife follows,"
"The hen must fly with the rooster."

NIU: My daughter, his family is poor and lowly; how could you
demean yourself to serve them?
MISTRESS NIU (*sings to the tune* Ta-sheng yüeh):

In marriage, "high" and "low" have no meaning;
If there were high and low, you wouldn't have married me to him.
If parents are lowly, son of high rank,
Surely he shouldn't cast them off!

(NIU: Though their son mustn't cast them off, you needn't
concern yourself with the matter.)

I am their own son's own wife;
Can it be said we're nothing to each other?

(NIU: Why do you persist in arguing against me like this?)

Father, you are the prime minister of the land!
How can you utter these words that would corrupt all morality of
    our society,
That are against all principles?

NIU (*in a rage):* Impudent girl! All she wants is to contradict
me; it seems my words aren't good enough for her ears.
Daughter,

(He continues in shih *form):*

> You consent to your husband and disobey me;
> It must be he's completely befuddled your mind.
> "You gave your heart to the bright moon,
> Never knowing what you saw was but a reflection in the muddy
>   gutter."

(He exits.)

MISTRESS NIU: "When you drink with a good friend a thousand cups are too few; when you talk without rapport half a sentence is too much." My father cares nothing for benevolence and right, and he actually thinks I'm offending him on purpose. Ts'ai Po-chieh was right when he told me not to speak to my father; now how can I face him? I'd better sit here for a while and think what to do.

(She performs an action.)

TS'AI *(enters and sings to the tune* Ch'eng jen hsin):

> I pretended to be foolish and dull;
> Before long she saw through me.
> I want to return home, but will her father let us go?
> I expect that he
> Will not consent.

(With an action) My wife,

> Why are you sitting here alone?

It must be your father won't give permission.

> Clever as your tongue may be,
> Never will your father agree.

MISTRESS NIU *(sings to the same tune with a modified opening):*

> My father
> Has no fear
> Of people's ridicule.
> This matter he sees all wrong.
> So now the roots of disaster sprout,
> Higher and higher they will grow.
> Disaster descends—how can it be avoided?
> He said that I followed my husband,
> And cursed me for not obeying a father's command.

TS'AI *(sings to the tune* Hung shan-erh):

You didn't heed my warning not to tell;
Now there's nothing to be done.
I know your father's nature,
So how could I not know this would be?
Why was it I acted the fool to hide my secret?
Only because of this.
But you determined to let my secret out;
It's you who beckoned disaster on.

MISTRESS NIU (*sings to the same tune with a modified opening*):

I never thought he would hold us here,
That it would be so hard to oppose him.
I've heard your constant sighs; my only wish to make some peace,
Never thinking that from my good will such troubles would arise,
Like merciless wind and waves.
I led you into traps of Heaven and earth;
How can I expect to avoid your blame?

(*With an action*)

It was only I who brought on this grief,
But both of us are hurt.

TS'AI (*sings to the tune* Tsui t'ai-p'ing):

It slips by us,
Time—how easily it moves on!
Even if I could return now, already it is late;
Yet I have no way to return.
Bound by fame and fortune,
I rush about at the ends of the world.
Of what can I be sure?
Most likely I'll grow old and die in the capital city,
Filial devotion ended as if by one stroke of a pen.
How it oppresses me,
Wounds my soul in a thousand ways!
And in secret my tears fall.

MISTRESS NIU (*sings to the same tune*):

I tell you no lie!
Let me die instead.
For if I don't die,
You'll never be able to return.
Of what value is my life?
Your whole family's been hurt by me.
It was all a mistake!
And should we continue as husband and wife, never would we be
    as one,

My heart filled with grief, yours with worry.
But if I cast off this life of mine,
Your filial name will be made,
Your parents saved.

Sir, at the beginning it was my father's command that I serve
you. I never knew you had aged parents and a young wife.
And so it came about that your heart has been filled with dis-
content and you've been unable to fulfill your responsibilities.
When I think about this, I realize that the one who wronged
your parents is I. The one who wronged your wife is also I.
And the one who caused you to be unfilial and untrue is also
I. Guilty of so much! If I were to cling to my despicable life
now, it would be unacceptable by every standard of morality.
Nieh Cheng's sister stood by her brother's corpse and gave up
her life so that his name would not be defiled.[2] Wang Ling's
mother thrust a dagger through her heart, sacrificing her own
life to ensure the virtue of her son.[3] How can I regret the loss
of my own life when to live is to cause your every responsibility to be unfulfilled? I should die to express my gratitude to
you. Then not only will you be freed from anxiety, but above
all the lives of your parents will be saved. Your reputation for
filial conduct will be made sound, and later generations will
have an example of this principle of morality. How then could
I regret my death?

TS'AI: My wife, you have understood only a part of the truth.
"Body, hair, and skin are given us by our parents; we mustn't
presume to injure them."[4] And how can you place your father
in a position where he will be at fault? Furthermore, people
will say you went along with your husband and ignored your
father's command. You mustn't do it!

MISTRESS NIU: Yes, that's all true.

TS'AI: Just wait—perhaps your father will change his mind.
Let's be patient a little longer.

---

[2] Nieh Cheng, a political assassin of the Warring States period, disfigured his face
and committed suicide after the deed so that his sister would not be involved. She,
however, wanted him to receive credit in history for his assassination of a tyrant and
so revealed his identity. She died weeping by his corpse.

[3] See Scene fifteen, note 13.

[4] The quotation is from the opening passage of the *Hsiao Ching* (Classic of filial
piety), p. 2a.

MISTRESS NIU: Though he doesn't agree with us now, I know that everybody else will say we're right.

(Closing poem)
MISTRESS NIU:

"When somebody cuts down a *wu-t'ung* tree,"

TOGETHER:

Of course the busybodies will come out to talk."

(They exit.)

SCENE THIRTY-ONE

WU-NIANG (*as if walking along a road, enters and sings to the tune* Yüeh yün kao):

How wearisome the road,
Step after step, never nearing the end!
And before even reaching the district of Lo-yang,
Already my money is gone.
I think of the lonely grave I've left;
Now I have only a single shadow to gaze upon.
Whom have they there to think of them?
Whom have I here to flee to for help?
How true that, "West of Yang-kuan, there are no old friends."
Indeed, "You don't know the pain of being poor until you leave home."

(*She recites to the* tz'u Su mu che):

I tremble at the mountains to be climbed,
Grieve at the thought of rivers I must cross.
Memories of my parents-in-law
Moisten my robe with tears.
I look back—where is that lonely grave?
Lost in desolation, I as well as they,
Both with grief impossible to tell.
My lovely skin's grown pale,
My delicate feet wearied.
I play my lute to cast off my despair,
But when I've finished playing, even stronger it returns.
And when I look upon the faces of their portraits,
Distraught and worn they gaze back at me,
With distress that they're unable to speak.

How helpless I am as I journey to seek my husband! All alone, lute in hand, portraits on back, I climb towering cliffs, sleep by streams, eat nothing but wind. How hard it is to endure! I feel that if, when I reach the capital and find my husband, everything between us is as of old, then these hardships won't have been suffered in vain. But if he's in a lofty chariot with team of four, attendants in front and behind, and refuses to recognize me in my ragged clothes, then what trouble I'll be in!

(She sings to the previous tune):

Deep within me, thoughts arise—
How uncertain the outcome of this trip!
I fear he'll be of exalted rank,
And refuse to recognize me as his own.
If he pays no heed to me,
I will have suffered all this in vain.

But no!

He could never forget our love;
All groundless are these fears of mine!
He must remember that "single night as husband and wife that
held a hundred nights of love."
How could we ever become strangers?

(She sings to the same tune):
But one thing I fear—

He'll be in a mansion's innermost depths;
How can I ever enter there?
Or if he's in a lofty chariot with team of four,
I'll have no way to greet him.

I know what I'll do—

When I reach his side,
I'll hold up the portraits of his parents.
But I only fear that their faces so worn
Will make it hard for him to believe.
Yet never would he reach the point of "treating strangers better
than kin."
I must be sure only to "guard against the evil of those I meet."

(Closing poem)

I face the portraits, wordless, choked with sobs.
How difficult the path over thousands of mountains and streams!
They say that in the capital the flowers are like brocade;
I only fear that when I arrive, it will not be spring.

(She exits.)

SCENE THIRTY-TWO

PRIME MINISTER NIU (*enters and sings to the tune* Fan pu-suan):

How painful my daughter's words!
Doubts rise in my mind.
Now when I think it over, I see I was wrong,
And so I've made a plan to reunite them all.

"Good medicine's bitter to taste, but it cures the disease; honest words are harsh to hear, but they help us to do right." Yesterday my daughter told me that she and Po-chieh wanted to go back to his hometown to serve his parents. I didn't want to let her go, and when she tried to persuade me, I couldn't control my anger. Now I've thought things over and realize that every word she spoke was true. I'd like to let her go, but after the sheltered life she's always led, it would be impossible for her to make a journey like that. Besides, in my old age I have no one else by my side, and I can't bear to let her leave me. I've thought of a plan. I'll send a messenger to Ch'en-liu, providing amply for his expenses on the road, to bring Ts'ai's parents and wife here. I think that would be the best way. I'll call out my daughter and son-in-law and ask them what they think of this plan. Daughter! Son-in-law! Come here.

TS'AI and MISTRESS NIU (*enter and sing to the previous tune*):

Tears like pearls scatter from our eyes;
Tightly woven strands of sorrow bind us.
If only we'd known then what regret we'd feel now,
How obvious it would have been that we should never marry!

NIU: My daughter, come here. Last night I thought over very carefully what you said. You were absolutely right! But when I consider the situation, it would still be hard to let you leave. I want to send off two messengers today to go and bring Po-chieh's parents and wife here. How would the two of you feel about that?

MISTRESS NIU: I think that would be fine!

TS'AI: If you would do that, how grateful I would be!

NIU: Where is the attendant Li Wang?

LI WANG (enters): "By yellow pavilion I wait for instructions, suddenly hear a summons from the painted hall." Yes, sir!

NIU: Come here. I'm sending you to Ch'en-liu.

LI: Damn! It's too far to Ch'en-liu—I won't go!

NIU: Watch your mouth!

LI: What's this trip for? If there's money in it, I'll go.

NIU: Ts'ai Po-chieh's wife and parents are in Ch'en-liu. I want you to invite them to come here.

LI: I won't go!

TS'AI and MISTRESS NIU: If you bring them here, you'll get a big reward from us.

LI: The young lady may talk about a big reward now, but if I do bring them here and the two wives start fighting for position, I'll never get a reward.

NIU: I order you to go, Li Wang—don't try to refuse. I'll assign a couple of boys to go with you.

LI: All right, I'll go.

NIU: Besides this letter, I'm providing you with everything you'll need for the trip. Don't be negligent in carrying out this commission.

TS'AI and MISTRESS NIU: Li Wang, search everywhere for them, and if you're able to find them and bring them here, look after them most carefully on the road.

LI: Don't worry—I'm an experienced traveler.

NIU (sings to the tune Ssu-pien ching):

> Search everywhere in Ch'en-liu;
> Dedicate yourself to this task.
> And when you've invited them forth,
> Take good care of them on the road.

(They sing the chorus together):

> Put an end to our anxious, mournful thoughts;
> Send us a letter as soon as you can.
> "Our eyes search for the battle flag;
> Our ears strain to hear the good news."

TS'AI (sings to the same tune):

> People scattered in the chaos of famine leave not a trace;
> Whether they're dead or alive we can't be sure.

And perhaps this trip itself,
With its unendurable hardship, will be all in vain.

(They repeat the chorus above.)

MISTRESS NIU *(sings to the tune* Fu-ma lang*):*
Li Wang,

Don't tell them that in the Niu mansion there dwells a young
bride!

(NIU: My daughter, what's wrong with telling them?)

They'd hate me for the wrong I've done them,
And before they even left,
The neighbors would hear
And curse my name.

(They sing the chorus together):

When they reach the capital,
We'll have a great reunion feast!

LI *(sings to the same tune):*

Provide for me well and you'll make my spirit strong!
Over myriads of mountains and streams
I'm experienced in travel.

(He bows.)

I bid farewell to my gracious master.
No need to worry about this trip!

(They repeat the chorus above.)

(Closing poem)
NIU:

By the end of six months, you must send us news.

TS'AI and MISTRESS NIU:

Take good care of them on the road.

LI:

I only hope I can return in good time.

TOGETHER:

That will be more precious than the finest gold.

(All exit.)

SCENE THIRTY-THREE

ACOLYTE *(played by the* mo *actor, enters and recites in* shih *form):*

Old in years, content in heart, I live without a care.
Hemp clothes and straw mat are fine enough for me.
So many people tell me they'll leave the world and come;
But on this hallowed ground not one of them do I see! [1]

I am an acolyte in this Amitabha Monastery. Today we're having an assembly of the Pure Land sect. People from all over are coming, some to save the souls of their dead parents, others to seek protection for their own lives. What a beautiful monastery this is! How does it look?

(He continues in parallel prose):

 Just see the ornateness of the Buddhist temple, the dignity of the lotus throne. Like a craggy mountain, the great hall—its golden walls gleam. Winding round and round, the passageways—in bright colors they're painted. The high pagoda rises a thousand stories high, breaking into the clouds above; high in the sky is heard the intermittant sound of clear bells that hang in its eaves. The towers decorated with seven jewels shine like crystal in the rays of the sun. All through the day constantly echo pealing bells.

Pine trees protect the Buddhist monastery;
The dust of the world can't penetrate here.
Bamboo surrounds this Buddhist retreat;
Bright sunlight can't cast a glare.

 The majesty of the wise countenances of these *arhats* can compare to that of the millions of Buddhas at Snow Mountain.[2] The purity of the austere conduct of these *bhikshus* is like that of the thousands of followers who lived in Jetavana Park. Amid banners, see how high the stone altar is raised! All is quiet in the flower courtyard—only the sounds of those at chess. Enough talk of this pure monastery; let me tell of the dignified assembly hall. See the ethereal vision of pearled pennants and jeweled cano-

[1] The poem is by Ling Ch'e (746–816) (*CTS,* 810:9133).
[2] The reference to the Buddhas of Snow Mountain has not been traced.

pies. Off and on sound the musical stones and golden
bells. All nine grades of red lotuses are set in dragon-
shaped vases; in this Pure Land, though years may pass,
never does one age.[3] Crimson buds of flame blossom on
the thousand branches of phoenix candles—constantly il-
luminating the Buddhist heaven both night and day. In
perfect order, the pages of the Buddhist texts are turned
together; with a rustling sound, the divine flowers scatter
down on the congregation.[4] In this forest of sandalwood
trees is burned "pure clean incense" and "way and virtue
incense." In the temple kitchen is offered up "joys of
meditation food" and "pleasure in the Law food." Each
person seems to be an inhabitant of the immortal islands;
everyone has purified his consciousness and perception.
As they beat the drum of the Great Law and sound the
conch of the Great Law, immortal music is performed.
The sweet dew gate is opened, the sweet dew city entered;
spirits lost in the shades attain speedy deliverance.[5] We
send word to those who sojourn in the sea of travail,
"Come to the assembly at Ling-shan."[6]

Because of the big assembly today, there may be high officials
and other important people coming here to visit. I'll take out
the register and try to solicit some money to help with our expenses. The words are just out of my mouth, and already I see
two patrons coming!

(*Two rogues, played by the* ching *and* ch'ou *actors, enter and sing to
the tune* Lü-lü chin):

Making trouble wherever we go,
Two rascals are we.
Not a scrap of food left over at home;
So what could keep us there?
All our lives we've played the fool,
And now we can't repent.
We've wandered here to the "forest of monks,"
This Buddhist assembly to see.

---

[3] The Pure Land Sect of Buddhism believed that those born into the various levels
of the Pure Land would never age.
[4] Flowers are said to fall from the sky when a Buddhist master expounds the scriptures in a particularly brilliant manner.
[5] The "sweet dew gate" is a reference to the practice of providing hungry ghosts
with food and drink; "sweet dew city" describes the clarity of the master's discourse.
Both help lost souls to advance in the spiritual world.
[6] The lines refers to a famous assembly held at Vulture Peak in India.

ACOLYTE: Gentlemen, please sit down and have some tea.

CHING and CH'OU: Does this assembly cost very much?

ACOLYTE: Yes, indeed! Please excuse me for annoying you with a request, but since Heaven has blessed us with this visit by two such worthy gentlemen, I can't help asking you to donate a little something—just to help out with the expenses.

CHING: Let's have a look at the subscription book! Brother, money is, after all, just a thing of chance—so why not spend it?

CH'OU: Right you are! People like us never pass a day without spending several strings of cash.

CHING: I'll donate five ingots.

CH'OU: Me too!

CHING and CH'OU: Of course we didn't bring cash with us here. In a little while you can come with us and we'll give it to you.

ACOLYTE: Thank you, gentlemen!

CHING: Look! Do you see over there? There's a woman coming. She's not bad looking either!

CH'OU: Yes, I see a woman with a lute on her back. She looks like your sister!

ACOLYTE: As they say, these two can "see clearly even at a distance."[7]

WU-NIANG (enters and sings to the previous tune):

> The road I travel,
> How hard to bear!
> No money left,
> Destitute and helpless,
> I play my lute,
> Beg alms from those I meet.
> To save the souls of my parents-in-law from deep burial,
> I've come to this Buddhist assembly.

I've finally reached Lo-yang! They say that the Amitabha monastery is having an assembly today, so I've come to beg a few cents and use them to pray for the souls of my parents-in-law.

ACOLYTE: Don't come any closer, little lady!

---

[7] Ch'ien Nan-yang suggests that the text may be in error here and that the line should read, "You can see more clearly close up," a common saying of the time. Ming editions amended the text in this way.

CHING and CH'OU: What do you have there?

WU-NIANG: These are portraits of my parents-in-law.

CHING and CH'OU: Where do you come from?

WU-NIANG (*sings to the tune* Hsiao-chin chang):

> Listen and I'll tell you:
> I'm the wife of a well-bred man,
> Yet it was he who brought me down.
> He went to take the examinations,
> And never returned to his hometown.
> In famine's ravage,
> I lost my parents-in-law;
> I made the grave for them myself.
> Now I'm on my way to seek my husband.

(CHING and CH'OU: Where is your husband?)

> I seek and don't know—
> Where is he now?

CHING: What's the lute for?

WU-NIANG: I'll play some songs, beg for alms, then go into the temple and pray for the souls of my parents-in-law.

CHING and CH'OU: What songs can you play? Can you play "Yeh-ssu-erh?"

WU-NIANG: I don't know that one.

CHING and CH'OU: Can you play "Pa-ch'iao-shou?"

WU-NIANG: I don't know that either. I only know a few songs about filial piety.

ACOLYTE: These two gentlemen have been giving out money here and saying, "Why not spend it?" You go ahead and play for them, and they'll give you a generous reward.

WU-NIANG (*recites to the* tz'u Chiang-nan hao):[8]

> In raising children
> How toilsome are the first three years!
> Before the child can talk and walk,
> How the parents suffer!

(*With an action, she sings to the previous tune*):

> In raising children,

'And the three wearisome years of carrying them in one's arms, on
    one's back.
Everyone knows how parents sacrifice their own comfort for their
    children's sake,
Perform thousands and thousands of toilsome duties.
Really, in a thousand ways they show their loving care,
In a thousand ways show their loving protection.
If the slightest discomfort bothers their child,
The parents worry and fuss, don't know where to turn,
Until he's well again.
Then when he's well again, their joy returns anew.

CHING and CH'OU: Well played! That was great.

ACOLYTE: It sure was!

CHING and CH'OU: When you've got money, why not spend it?
We'll give you a nice jacket.

(They perform an action.)

WU-NIANG *(recites to the previous* tz'u*):*

    Day by day the child grows,
    And so grows the happiness of his parents.
    They teach him to walk and to talk, they teach him proper con-
        duct,
    And long for the day when he'll be a man.

(She sings to the previous tune):

    When the child takes his first few steps,
    Mother and father exchange a happy glance.
    Slowly he learns to walk and talk;
    He hankers after food and drink
    From morning to night.
    Always their anxious thoughts are upon him,
    So many, many worries!
    They choose for him a good tutor,
    But worry that their son may be stupid and slow.
    And if he shows but a little talent,
    With what joy do they reward him!

CHING and CH'OU: Well played!

ACOLYTE: Very fine!

CHING and CH'OU: When you have money, why not spend it?
We'll give you another jacket.

(They perform an action.)

ACOLYTE: These two must be crazy!

CHING and CH'OU: Play some more!

WU-NIANG (*recites to the previous* tz'u):

How diligently they teach him—
History in the evening, classics in the morning,
With the hope that he'll bring glory to parents and ancestors,
Achieve fame with a single examination.

(*She sings to the previous tune*):

Classics in the morning, history at night,
Composition of poetry and prose—
All for the spring exam to which they urge him on,
In the hope that he'll bring glory to parents and ancestors,
And raise their status in the world.
Always their anxious thoughts upon him,
They think of the day he'll wear a belt of gold round a purple robe.
While their son is on the road,
They fear he's eating only wind and sleeping in dew.
From spirits and diviners they seek out news,
Secretly calculate the time of his return.

CHING and CH'OU: Well played! Well played! When you have money, why not spend it? Here's another jacket for you!

ACOLYTE: How tattered and torn their clothes are underneath! Would you mind my asking—what are you thinking of to take off your jackets when it's so cold?

CHING and CH'OU: So it's cold! We won't let that ruin our style. People like us who are used to spending lots of money are never afraid of the cold. Another song!

ACOLYTE: I wonder what they'll give her next.

WU-NIANG (*recites to the previous* tz'u):

The son sets out;
Surely he'll soon return.
For if one son commits the Five Sins,[9] another is filial,
Each will meet his just reward.

(*She sings to the previous tune*):

The son who keeps father and mother in his heart
Will hasten to return to his family home,
Remembering how baby crows feed their parents.
Don't take my husband as your model

[9] The Five Sins of Buddhism include killing one's mother or father.

And do wrong to your parents!
It's often said of parenthood,
Only when one has children himself does he realize how kind his
    own father was.
One son commits the Five Sins;
Another obeys and serves his parents.
If they don't meet with their just rewards,
How unfair of Heaven and earth!

CHING and CH'OU: You play and sing very well, but we don't have anything left to give you.

ACOLYTE: I knew it!

CHING and CH'OU (*acting as if cold*): We'd look pretty silly going home like this.

CH'OU: This acolyte here will be glad to give us some clothes. (*They grab the acolyte*): So! This acolyte tricked our clothes away from us!

ACOLYTE: You gave them away yourselves. How can you say I tricked you?

CHING and CH'OU: When we told her she played well, you agreed with us. You kept encouraging us—wouldn't you call that a trick?

ACOLYTE: Young lady, please return their clothes—what would you want with them anyway?

WU-NIANG: Here, take them back.

CHING and CH'OU: Though it's true that "If you have money, why not spend it?" it's hard to bear such cold!

CH'OU: I told you that you sang and played very well, but when I think it over, it wasn't any good at all. If you have any doubt, then sing again and we'll see!

WU-NIANG: I can't sing anymore.

CHING: Of course not! She wouldn't dare.

(*Exit poem*):

CH'OU:

Brother, we're not people who hanker after power and wealth.

ACOLYTE:

It was useless to ask them for alms.

WU-NIANG:

Could it be that these clothes don't belong to you at all?

CHING and CH'OU:

Quite right! We haven't a pair of trousers to our name!

(The ching, ch'ou, *and* ACOLYTE *exit.)*

WU-NIANG: "Every second of man's life is determined by destiny." I came here to beg a few coins to use to pray for the souls of my parents-in-law, never knowing that I'd meet with those two madmen to annoy me so. I see off in the distance a crowd of men and horses; it must be an official coming here. I'd better stand in attendance.

*(*TS'AI, *on horseback, along with the* STEWARD, *and another* ATTENDANT *played by the* ch'ou *actor, enter.)*

TS'AI *(sings to the tune* Lü-lü chin*):*

The times are hard,
Fate how perverse!
For my parents on the road,
I fear disaster.

STEWARD and ATTENDANT *(continue the song):*

This is the Amitabha monastery;
Stop the carriage!

(They sing the chorus together):

With hearts devout, to pray to the Lotus Throne,
We come to join the Buddhist assembly.

STEWARD *(pushes* WU-NIANG *aside):* Get out of sight! A high official approaches.

(He strikes her.)

WU-NIANG *(with an action):* "When you pass under low eaves, you have to bow your head."

(She exits.)

TS'AI *(dismounts, enters the temple, and sees the portraits):* What is this painting doing here?

ATTENDANT: There was a nun here a minute ago—maybe she left it.

TS'AI: Call her back to get it.

ATTENDANT: Sister, come get your painting!
(He performs an action): She's gone off—I can't see her.

TS'AI: Well, if we can't find her, then we'll keep it for her.

(The STEWARD takes the painting.)

ABBOT *(played by the* ching *actor, enters and sings to the previous tune):*

Wine I can drink,
And I gobble up my meatless meals.
I drink till I'm smashed,
Then find a new acolyte to cuddle.
When I expound scriptures and recite prayers,
I'm really at a loss.
So learned gentlemen, I beg you,
Stay away from this Buddhist assembly!

(TS'AI and the ABBOT greet each other.)

TS'AI: My father and mother are on their way here, and I'm worried about their safety and health on the road. I've come to seek protection for them; I wish you to read some scriptures to ensure their safety.

ABBOT: I see. Please offer incense and communicate your desire.

TS'AI *(offers incense and sings to the tune* Chiang-erh shui):

Before Buddha I testify:
This petition of Ts'ai Yung please consider.
Does all go well with my parents on the road?
Only the great compassion of the Bodhisattva can keep them safe.

(They sing the chorus together):

Dragons and angels have heard your request;
Dragons and angels will shelter and protect,
Shelter and protect them as mountains they climb, rivers they
    cross.

ABBOT *(sings to the same tune):*

Before Buddha I testify;
Listen to my heart's desire.

Please give protection to the parents of Ts'ai Yung.
On your ineffable powers we rely.

(They repeat the chorus above.)

STEWARD *(sings to the same tune):*

My master's days are filled
With endless distress and doubt,
For he worries over his parents on the road.
Such filial love will surely move the spirits above.

(They repeat the chorus above.)

ATTENDANT *(sings to the same tune):*

I heard of this assembly here,
And came to have some fun.
Dish me out some vegetables and bread,
Or I'm off to the kitchen to get them myself!

(They repeat the chorus above.)

(Exit poem)

ABBOT:

If it's so destined in your life, Buddha's blessings are bestowed.

TS'AI:

Let my parents' journey have no hardship, no delay.

STEWARD:

"Chancing upon this bamboo temple, I held conversation with a
    monk,

ATTENDANT:

Found freedom from my empty life, if but for half a day." [10]

(All exit.)

WU-NIANG *(enters and sings to the tune Lü-lü chin):*

Who was that
But Ts'ai Po-chieh!
Attendants led the way

---

[10] The two lines are from the poem "T'i Ho-lin-ssu tseng-she shih" (Inscribed on the monks' quarters at Ho-lin monastery) by Li She (fl. 806) (*CTS*, 477:5429).

As the First Winner came near.
I think the portraits of his parents
Are now in his keeping.
It seems that Heaven seeks to reunite us,
And this Buddhist assembly is the start.

I asked the gentleman who was here just now, and it was none other than Ts'ai Po-chieh! How wonderful! It seems we will be able to meet again. It must have been he who took the portraits of my parents-in-law. Now I'll go to his house and see what happens. It may be we can really be reunited! Ah! It really seems Heaven is bringing us together again! Just as they say, "If the old fisherman hadn't led the way, how could I have viewed these billowing waves?"[11]

(She exits.)

[11] This saying, common in *ch'uan-ch'i,* describes the working of fate to lead one to a desired goal.

SCENE THIRTY-FOUR

MISTRESS NIU (*enters and sings to the tune* Shih-erh shih):

To no one can I speak what's in my heart,
And these past days, the pain has grown.
Only when my father had a change of heart
Was my husband's sadness lightened a little.
But still we don't know how their journey goes,
So how can my mind be at ease?

"In life, eight or nine out of ten things go wrong, but there are seldom even two or three that we can tell to other people." Since Ts'ai Po-chieh and I were married, he's been in constant depression. I finally tricked him into telling me the reason, and then told my father about it, asking permission to return with Po-chieh to his home. My father refused, but later changed his mind and sent some men to go and bring Po-chieh's parents and wife here. Now I'm so worried about their journey! In addition to that, the serving boys have all been sent out and, though we have several servants left, none of them is much good. How can I ever find a really good one to serve Po-chieh's parents when they finally arrive? I'll call the steward and discuss it with him.

STEWARD (*enters and recites in* shih *form*):

"When you're enjoying a book, how quickly it's finished!
When you're awaiting a beloved guest, how slow he is to come!
In the world, those who are truly happy are few;
Yet how fast is the passage of time!"

My lady, what is your command?

MISTRESS NIU: Go out into the town and look for a good woman to become a servant here.

STEWARD: That's easy! Here comes a woman now! I wonder what sort of person she is.

WU-NIANG (*enters and sings to the tune* Jao ch'ih yu):

I eat the wind and sleep by streams;
When will I ever find refuge?
Of Heaven I ask, how will this end?

MISTRESS NIU (*with an action, continues the song*):

> Adorned with simple dignity,
> Demeanor worthy of an artist's brush!
> Graceful manner, beautiful and rare!
> Call her forward, I'll find out who she is.

STEWARD: Sister, my mistress requests that you approach.

WU-NIANG: Madame, my greetings to you!

MISTRESS NIU: Sister, why have you come here?

WU-NIANG: A poor beggar, I hope for your aid.

STEWARD: My lady, wouldn't she do? She's a beggar—why not give her a home?

MISTRESS NIU: Sister, are you accomplished at anything?

WU-NIANG: Yes, I know all the superior arts—the *ch'in,* chess, calligraphy, and painting—and the minor skill of needlework. As for food, drink, and all sorts of delicacies, there is nothing I don't know how to prepare.

STEWARD: Madame, why not take her in?

MISTRESS NIU: You must suffer a lot on the road, sister. How would you like to stay in my house and live in comfort?

WU-NIANG: I'm very grateful for your offer, but I fear I'm un-qualified to fill your needs.

STEWARD: Well spoken!

MISTRESS NIU: Sister, did you become a nun in childhood, or was it after you married?

WU-NIANG: The truth is, my husband came here to the capital a long time ago. Left at home, his parents both died. I buried them myself, and now all my possessions are gone, leaving me no means of support. I traveled here, begging with my lute, but still I haven't found my husband.

MISTRESS NIU: I almost made the mistake of taking her in![1]

STEWARD: Ask her who her husband is.

WU-NIANG (*with an action*): What should I say?

MISTRESS NIU: Sister, what is your husband's name?

WU-NIANG (*with an action*): I wanted to tell you. His name is Ts'ai Po-chieh.

MISTRESS NIU and STEWARD: Where is he from?

---

[1] It is unclear whether Mistress Niu suspects Wu-niang's identity at this point or is merely reacting against taking in a married woman as a servant.

WU-NIANG: He comes from Ch'en-liu. Do you perhaps know him?

MISTRESS NIU: How could I know him? Steward, since she's a married woman, it wouldn't do to keep her here. Just give her some money and food and let her go.

STEWARD: Sister, the mistress will give you some money and food and then you must leave.

WU-NIANG: Alas! I shouldn't have told them about my husband. What can I do?

(She performs an action.)

When I was on the road in search of my husband, everybody told me he was living in the mansion of Prime Minister Niu. How can it be you don't know him? Madame, you must be making fun of me!

MISTRESS NIU: Why would I make fun of you? Steward, is there such a man here?

STEWARD: No, there isn't.

WU-NIANG: But everyone said that he lived at Prime Minister Niu's. If he's not here, he must be dead! Alas! My husband, if you've died, where can I turn for help?

(She cries.)

MISTRESS NIU: The poor woman! All right then, you can stay here and I'll have somebody look for your husband. How would that be?

STEWARD: That's a good idea.

WU-NIANG: Thank you, madame!

MISTRESS NIU: While you stay here, you mustn't be dressed like that. I'll give you a change of clothes. Steward, bring out my dressing case and some clothes.

STEWARD: Yes, my lady. *(He exits, then returns.)* Here's the dressing case and clothes. As they say, "Precious swords are sold to valiant gentlemen; rouge and powder are presented to beautiful ladies."

(He exits.)

WU-NIANG: I must observe six years of mourning for my parents-in-law, and still another six years for them on behalf of my absent husband. How can I take off these mourning clothes?

MISTRESS NIU: Don't worry about that. My father would be sure to take offense at your wearing that costume here.

WU-NIANG: Alas! What shall I do?

(*She looks in the mirror and sings to the tune* Erh-lang shen):

> How sallow my face!
> A lonely phoenix, I sigh at the thought of our severed mirror.

MISTRESS NIU: Even if you won't make up your face, at least change your clothes.

WU-NIANG (*picking up the clothes*): Alas!

> I think of my wedding day, those kingfisher-feather hair ornaments and gauze skirts;
> Who could have known that after he went away,
> Not even a thorn hairpin and cotton skirt would be left to me?

MISTRESS NIU: Even if you won't make up your face, at least put a pin in your hair.

WU-NIANG (*picking up a hairpin*): Alas!

> Paired phoenix on gold hairpin—
> How they mock my solitary state!

(MISTRESS NIU: If you won't wear the hairpin, put some flowers in your hair to ward off ill fortune.)

> Flowers in my hair?
> As I take the peony she offers me,
> My heart is filled with resentment toward this moon goddess.

MISTRESS NIU (*sings to the same tune with a modified opening*):

> Ah!
> How grieved is her heart, how pained her face!
> Her emotion is sincere; how could it be feigned?
> For your parents-in-law your tears fall.

Sister,

> Though I too have parents-in-law,
> A single cup of tea I've been unable to offer them.

Sister,

> Though we're both alike unable to serve our parents-in-law,
> You at least aren't disgraced in the eyes of the world.
> One question I have:
> Your parents-in-law—
> What was it caused their death?

WU-NIANG (*sings to the tune* Chuan lin ying):

> Years of famine filled with hardships,
> And my husband away at the capital.
> In secret I tried to satisfy my hunger with husks.
> My parents-in-law died; I sold my hair to give them burial.
> Alone, I built the solitary grave,
> The earth I carried in my skirt.
> All this is the truth—
> From the wounds on my fingers,
> Traces of blood still stain my clothes.

MISTRESS NIU (*sings to the same tune*):

> I hear her sorrow, and my own sorrow grows.
> My tears fall in rows like hemp.
> My husband also long ago left his parents' side.
> He tried to leave his post, but my father interfered.

(WU-NIANG: Were there others in his family?)

> Although he had a wife there,
> I fear she may not have been so attentive to his parents.

(WU-NIANG: Where are they now, madame?)

> At the ends of the earth!
> And though we've sent messengers to bring them,
> How can we know if they're safe on the road?

WU-NIANG (*sings to the tune* Cho-mu li):

> All that she says
> Increases my distress more and more.

(With an action)

> And yet it seems that she is not a jealous woman.

(With an action): Madame,

> You say he has a wife there;
> When they bring her here, might not there be trouble between
>   you?

MISTRESS NIU (*continues the song*):

> If she were as capable as you are,
> How willing I would be to place her above me!
> Now I only grieve
> At all they must suffer on the road,
> And so I watch for them with staring eyes.

WU-NIANG (*sings to the previous tune*):

Mistake within mistake,
Misunderstanding on misunderstanding,
Like divining at the "door of ghosts."[2]

Madame,

If you wish to meet the wife of Ts'ai Po-chieh . . .

(MISTRESS NIU: Where is she?)

I am none other than she!

MISTRESS NIU (*with an action, continues the song*):

If what you say is true, and really you are she,
Then what you suffered was all because of me,
And your difficulties were all because of me.
Toward me your resentment must be directed,
As my resentment is toward my own father.

(*She sings to the tune* Chin-i kung-tzu):

Both are his wives alike—
I in comfort, you in hardship,
You extolled as filial, I an object of scorn.
My father-in-law died because of me.
My mother-in-law died because of me.
Let me wear your mourning clothes, my fine adornments remove.

(*They sing the chorus together*):

The situation now so filled with difficulty,
The lover that perverse fate destined for us
Won't be able to escape from the pain.

WU-NIANG (*sings to the same tune*):

At the beginning he had no choice—
Forced to take part in the examinations,
All attempts to refuse ignored by his father.

MISTRESS NIU (*continues the song*):

Unable to decline his office,
Unable to decline the marriage.

(*They finish the song together*):

Three denials that produced a calamity as great as Heaven itself.

---

[2] "Door of ghosts" is a diviners' term; the whole line means to be unlucky or unsuccessful.

(They repeat the chorus above.)

MISTRESS NIU: Elder sister, please don't take offense. You wouldn't agree to change your clothes, and I'm afraid that Ts'ai Po-chieh will be embarrassed to acknowledge you with your clothes so ragged. Sister, Ts'ai Po-chieh has always been devoted to literature; why don't you go into the study and write a few words to move him? After he's read them, I'll talk to him and bring you together.

WU-NIANG: That's a good idea. *(With an action):* Even if I can't write very well, I'd better follow this plan. Thank you, madame! I depend solely on your help.

MISTRESS NIU: Don't say such things!

(Closing poem)
MISTRESS NIU:

> When a sense of injustice floods one's heart,
> How meaningless are conventional words!

WU-NIANG: Truly,

> "A single leaf of floating duckweed returns to the vast sea;
> In human life who then will never meet again!"

(They exit.)

SCENE THIRTY-FIVE

STEWARD (*played by the* mo *actor, enters and recites in* shih *form*):

Young people must apply themselves to study;
It's the pursuit of literature that establishes one in the world.
Those wearing purple and vermilion who fill the court
Are every one men of letters.[1]

I am a steward in Master Ts'ai's home. Though my master is appointed to serve in the loftiest offices of the court, he often stays here in his study. Whenever there's a recess from court, his hand never rests from turning the pages of his books. Now that it's evening, he should be coming home. I'd better straighten up the study and await his arrival. What does this fine study look like?

(He continues in parallel prose):

 His bright window is wonderfully clear, his desk cleared for study perfectly neat. Bright window wonderfully clear; incense smoke wafts by the green gauze curtains. Desk cleared for study perfectly neat; the tigerskin that covers his chair unspotted by one speck of dust. On his walls hang three or four ancient paintings. On the stone bench rest one or two marvelous *ch'in*. If you were to count up his books, the number would exceed forty thousand; to load them up would require three thousand chariots.[2] Rue-scented leaves have chased away all bookworms from his pages. Over hibiscus-powdered pages the dragon guests play.[3] His inkstones—phoenix beak, horse liver, and mynah eye—are exquisite and rare. His pens—tips of rabbit down and deer tail, tubes of ivory or rhinocerous horn—are extraordinarily fine. Here stand piles of paper, imprinted with golden flowers made from blocks

[1] The four lines are from the collection *Shen-t'ung shih* (Poems by child prodigies).
[2] The allusion is probably to the Tsin dynasty scholar Chang Hua (232–300); when he moved it took thirty carts to carry his books. Ch'ien Nan-yang suggests that the character "thousand" may be a mistake for "ten."
[3] Hibiscus powder was used for adding color to paper. Legend tells of Emperor Ming Huang of the T'ang dynasty who saw a tiny Taoist figure moving about in his ink; he told the emperor that scholars always have "dragon guests" in their ink. The phrase is therefore a symbol for ink.

of jade. There in rows are arranged his penholders, their elegant patterns on bronze green with antiquity. Truly, it doesn't rank beneath the libraries of the East Wall. Indeed, it rivals Han-me lin in the West.[4]

Hey, wait a minute! Yesterday at the Buddhist assembly we picked up a portrait. I don't know what its story is. My master told me to keep it for a while; now I'll hang it here. My master is learned and intelligent; maybe he'll be able to figure out its story.

(He exits.)

WU-NIANG (enters and sings to the tune T'ien-hsia lo):

One small blossom flew into the emptiness of an ancient park,
Then borne by the wind, drifted to the curtains over the door.
No wonder that the lovely lady is startled from her spring dream!
For she fears that the east wind will cause the fallen blossoms to
blush.[5]

"Three or four blossoms are blown down from the trees, but it's wrong of people to blame the dawn breeze." I thought that it was because Ts'ai Po-chieh longed for fame and fortune that he didn't return. It turns out that it was because he was forced to stay here. Yesterday I arrived here as a beggar, and I'm grateful to Mistress Niu for taking me in. She was worried that my husband would refuse to recognize me when he saw me in such a ragged condition and suggested that I write something to touch his heart. I thought it best to follow her suggestion, and so have come to his study. But wait—where can I write it?

(She performs an action): Oh! The portrait of my parents-in-law is hanging here! I'll just write on the back.

(She writes, then sings to the tune Tsui fu-kuei):

I was destined to be his bride and share life with him;
We were not two who "Not destined for each other, would never
meet though face to face."
I shared with him phoenix pillow and luan-bird quilt,
Yet now must depend on rabbit-hair pen and silkworm paper to
touch his heart.

[4] The two lines are from the poem "En-chih tz'u shih yü li-cheng tien shu-yüan yen fu te lin-tzu shih," by Chang Yüeh (667–730) (CTS, 87:945).
[5] The song describes Wu-niang's feeling of shame at being out in the world by herself.

Enough!

> I should cast all this to the east wind,
> And think of our past as but a spring dream.

(She performs an action, then writes the following poem):

> K'un Mountain produces beautiful jade,
> Elegant and fine, possessing all the beauty that jade should have.
> How sad that one small flaw
> Mars this stone that would be worth fifteen cities![6]
> If a man is neither Confucius nor Yen Hui,[7]
> It's rare that his reputation be without flaw.
> How foolish was the prefect of Hsi-ho!
> Why could he not be like Kao Yü?
> Sung Hung was able to follow the path of right;
> How stupid then was Huang Yün![8]
> Kao Yü grieved over the sound of wind in the trees,[9]
> And Sung Hung linked his branches with but one tree.
> I send word to that traveler in the clouds:
> Take care lest you break the constant standards of right!

(She sings to the previous tune):

> He obtained the favor of imperial appointment written with flowery pen and ink so rich,
> Only because our flute songs were interrupted, our phoenix tower emptied.

Lady Niu was afraid that with my ragged appearance, Pochieh would refuse to recognize me. But I must wear these mourning clothes.

In what other way could I appear?

If I did not write this poem to move the heart of Ts'ai Pochieh,

I'm afraid it would be hard to win his affections back.

(With an action)

---

[6] During the Warring States period, the king of Ch'in offered to exchange fifteen cities for a rare piece of jade owned by the king of Chao.

[7] Yen Hui was one of the most virtuous of Confucius' disciples.

[8] The allusions are explained in the following scene when Ts'ai Po-chieh reads this poem to Mistress Niu.

[9] Lines attributed to Kao Yü, a contemporary of Confucius, state that just as the trees cannot be still when the wind blows, so a son can no longer serve his parents when they die. The phrase expresses sorrow at being unable to care for one's parents.

Though he may not recognize this portrait, their appearance
    being so changed,
If he recognizes my writing, his heart will ache.

(Closing poem)

I've not yet divined what's in my husband's heart,
So I must depend on this one poem.
The day his heart gives its assent to me
Will be the day my good fortune has come.[10]

(She exits.)

[10] The two lines are based on a poem attributed to Emperor T'ai-tsung of the T'ang
dynasty.

SCENE THIRTY-SIX

TS'AI (*enters and sings to the tune* Ch'üeh-ch'iao hsien):

We feasted at P'i-hsiang Hall,
Reveled at Shang-lin Park.
Drunk, we're helped to our horses.
Golden lotus candles illumine the corridors,
As the moon rises over the courtyard plum trees.

(He recites in shih *form):*

At evening I leave the Vermilion Gate,
At dawn enter the Purple Pavilion.
How much better to be in my study
Enjoying the greatest pleasure in the world!

(He continues in parallel prose):

 From early morning court to the late hours of the night, I'm on duty at Ch'ang-lo. Having summoned me to talk about spirits, the emperor moves his mat forward; transmitting light, T'ai I comes to share his bramble staff.[1] Only when stars cover my head as I dash through the darkness can I leave the palace. What time is left me to "annotate the *Book of Changes* with red ink made with dew?"[2]

I'm glad that for several days there's been no pressing business at court, and we have some extra free time. Now I'm able to express myself in poetry and calligraphy and devote myself to pen and ink. It's true that, "To be a success, one must read thousands of books; the time we have we must use with care." *(He looks at a book):* What book is this? It's the *Yao tien* section of the Book of History.

[1] Emperor Wen (r. 180–157 B.C.) of the Han dynasty was so fascinated with the scholar Chia I's discussion of the spirit world that he gradually moved his mat forward to hear better. Tradition tells how the spirit T'ai I admired the scholarship of Liu Hsiang (77–6 B.C.) of the Han dynasty. One night when Liu Hsiang was at work collating books, T'ai I visited him, carrying a staff that provided light for the two. The two allusions describe Ts'ai's high standing at court and the late hours he must keep to carry out his responsibilities.

[2] The quotation is from the poem "Pu hsü tz'u" (Walking in emptiness) by Kao P'ien (*CTS*, 344:3860).

(He reads a little, then puts it down): It says here, "Shun's father was stupid, his stepmother was deceitful, and his half-brother, Hsiang, was proud, but Shun was able to live harmoniously with them by means of filial piety."[3] No matter how badly his parents treated him, Shun was still able to live harmoniously with them by means of filial piety! In what way have my parents ever been at fault toward me? And yet I've abandoned them and now can't even see them. How can I bear to read the Book of History? I'll look through Spring and Autumn Annals instead.

(He performs an action): "I have a mother . . . since she hasn't tasted your soup, I would like to put it aside."[4] When a man of antiquity ate even one mouthful of soup, he thought of his mother! Now I'm an official, enjoying rank and wealth; how could I have abandoned my parents? Ah! It's senseless to read these books. If it can't be practiced, what good does it do? Is there one sentence in classical literature that doesn't talk about filial piety and right? At the beginning, it was for the sake of learning filial piety and right that my parents taught me to read. Who could know that instead I'd be led astray by books? Ah! How could I be called a filial son?

(He sings to the tune Chieh san ch'eng):

> Alas, my parents instructed me
> To read the works of ancient sages.
> A learned man, I've abandoned my parents,
> While countless illiterates care for their parents to the end.

Books!

> Only because within you "there's a mansion of gold,"
> You made me abandon the home where my parents dwell.
> And still I long for them.

Enough!

---

[3] The quotation is from the *Shu Ching* (Book of History) (Legge, 3:26). The legendary Emperor Shun, originally a commoner, was summoned to the throne because of his virtuous conduct.

[4] The story is from the *Tso Commentary on the Spring and Autumn Annals* (Legge, 5:2). Ying K'ao-shu, a border warden, set aside part of his food while eating with Duke Chuang of Cheng (r. 743–701 B.C.). He explained that his mother always shared his food, and since she was not present he was putting some aside for her. This so moved the duke that he was reunited with his own mother, whom he had vowed never to see again.

After all, it's literature that has wronged me,
And I who have wronged my parents.

(He sings to the same tune):

> Instead of becoming a guilt-ridden guest in official halls,
> How much better to be a country gentleman keeping to the right
>   all my life!
> I can't forget the "Song of White Hair"; [5]
> Why am I separated from my black-haired wife?

Books!

> Only because within you, "there's a lady with face like jade,"
> You made me abandon my poor "husk wife."
> And still I long for her.

Enough!

> After all, it's literature that has wronged me,
> And I who have wronged my wife.

I don't want to read any more. I'll just look at the ancient landscapes I have hanging on my walls and try to forget my depression for a little while.
(He performs an action): Those are the portraits the steward picked up at the temple yesterday. How did they come to be hanging here?
(He performs an action): I wonder what their story is!

(He sings to the tune T'ai-shih yin):

> Let me examine them carefully;
> Whose brushwork could this be?
> As I look, my heart is stabbed with pain.

(He looks more carefully.)

> How like my parents they are!

But no! For my wife is an excellent seamstress, and if these were my parents,

> How could they be dressed in rags?

In the letter they said,

---

[5] The "Song of White Hair" was composed by Cho Wen-chün; see Scene Eight, note 4.

In my absence they'd all been well;
How could they look so harassed and sad?

And when I think how I had no way to send a letter there,

How could someone have brought these portraits here?

There's no lack of people in the world who look alike!

Everyone knows that Confucius himself was mistaken for Yang Hu![6]

(He sings to the same tune):
I know what it must be!

A sidewalk artist's
Low-class portrait
That makes fun of the peasant's sallow face.

Yet my parents too,

If there were no daughter-in-law by their side
Would look just so, harassed and sad.

(His heart jumps.)

Could it be that this is a divine Buddhist icon?

For if it's not, then why with just a look,

This sudden pounding of my heart?

They don't look like divinities or Buddha, but perhaps the painter is at fault.

For a portrait depends solely on the artist's wish;
Everyone knows how Mao Yen-shou wronged Wang Ch'iang.[7]

But wait a minute! If it's a Buddhist painting, then there must be a colophon on the back.
(He sees the poem): Ah! This poem couldn't have been here before, for the ink is not yet dry. It must have just been written!
(He grows suspicious): Who has entered my study, and why?

---

[6] Confucius was once mistaken for the tyrant Yang Hu by the people of the state of Kuang (Legge, 1:217).
[7] Wang Ch'iang, a palace lady of the Han dynasty, refused to bribe Mao Yen-shou, the court painter. He therefore painted an unflattering portrait of her. The emperor, on the basis of the portrait, selected her to be given away as a bride to the Hsiung-nu chieftain.

(He calls out.)

MISTRESS NIU *(enters and sings to the tune* Yeh yu-hu)*:*

> Worried that the time to speak in full had not yet come,
> I suggested she use poetry to point out his faults to him.
> Let pen and ink open wide his heart,
> Red and green find entrance to his eyes;
> How much better than words to convey her message!

TS'AI *(in anger):* Very strange!
MISTRESS NIU: What's strange?
TS'AI: Who has been in my study?
MISTRESS NIU: Nobody.
TS'AI: Yesterday when I went to the temple to offer incense, I picked up the portraits that are hanging here. Somebody has written a poem on the back.
MISTRESS NIU: Couldn't it have been written there by the artist?
TS'AI: How could that be? The ink is still wet; it was just written!

MISTRESS NIU *(in an aside):* I understand!
(To TS'AI): Sir, please read it to me.

*(*TS'AI *reads the poem.)*

MISTRESS NIU: I don't understand it; would you explain it to me?
TS'AI: It alludes to several stories.
MISTRESS NIU: How do they go?
TS'AI: The prefect of Hsi-ho was Wu Ch'i of the Warring States period. After he was appointed prefect of Hsi-ho by Marquis Wen of Wei,[8] his mother died and he didn't hurry home to mourn her. Kao Yü was a man of the Ch'un-ch'iu period. While he was traveling about the empire, his parents died. When he returned and learned of their deaths, he slashed his throat.
MISTRESS NIU: And the other stories?
TS'AI: Sung Hung lived in the reign of Emperor Kuang-wu.[9] The princess of Hu-yang was offered him in marriage, but Sung Hung refused, saying to the emperor, "The friends of

---

[8] Marquis Wen of Wei ruled from 424 to 420 B.C.
[9] Emperor Kuang-wu reigned from 25 to 57.

one's poor and humble days mustn't be forgotten; a poor husk wife should not be divorced." Huang Yün lived during the reign of Emperor Huan.[10] A high official proposed that Huang marry his niece, and Huang divorced his own wife to do so.

MISTRESS NIU: Sir, which of the two carried out the filial way? The one who didn't hurry home to mourn, or the one who slashed his throat?

TS'AI: The one who didn't hurry home to mourn violated the Way.

MISTRESS NIU: And which of the two carried out the way of rectitude? The one who refused to cast off his original wife, or the one who divorced the first to take another?

TS'AI: The one who divorced the first to take another violated the Way.

MISTRESS NIU: Whom do you wish to emulate?

TS'AI: I don't even know if my parents are dead or alive! But I certainly would not emulate the one who divorced his wife to take another.

MISTRESS NIU: Though you would not emulate him, what if you had a poor "husk wife," ragged and ugly? Wouldn't she be a disgrace to your wealth and position? Wouldn't you feel obliged to divorce her?

TS'AI: No matter how ragged and ugly, as long as she is my wife it would always be wrong to break with her.

(*In anger, he sings to the tune* Hua-ch'iao-erh):

How foolishly you speak!
How plain the smallness of your mind!

I would never emulate Huang Yün—

Cast off a plum grown bitter,
To seek a peach that's sweet.

The ancients said, "There are seven grounds for divorcing a wife."[11]

If she's not jealous, immoral, or a thief,
Then there are no grounds for divorce.

[10] Emperor Huan reigned from 146 to 167.
[11] The seven traditional grounds for divorcing a wife were the following: disobedience to parents-in-law, barrenness, licentiousness, jealousy, serious illness, talking too much, and thievery.

You mentioned the man who abandoned his wife;

> All mankind blames him.

While the one who refused to abandon his wife

> Is praised by all.
> However ugly she became,
> How could I ever divorce her?

MISTRESS NIU (*sings to the same tune*):
All this is true, but,

> You are rich and of high rank
> And still in your youth.
> Look at the purple robe that clothes your body,
> The gold belt encircling your waist.

Whoever becomes your wife

> Receives a royal title,
> Attested by a document on purple paper covered with golden
>   flowers.
> Refined she must be
> And very beautiful.
> If she were ugly,

Sir,

> How could you not divorce her?

TS'AI (*sings to the same tune*):

> How wild your words!
> You provoke me till my heart boils.

Ah!

> It seems you make fun of me,
> Or wish to deceive me.
> You've brought forth lines of tears;
> How they rush down my cheeks!

My wife, who wrote the poem?
MISTRESS NIU: What's it to you?
TS'AI (*continues his song*):

> The author ridicules me;
> I can't forgive that!
> Tell me now, I must know;
> I can't let the matter drop.

MISTRESS NIU *(sings to the same tune):*

> Carefully I consider in my heart—
> Clearly his feelings are not fickle,
> And the reunion between husband and wife
> Can take place this very day.

Sir, don't you know who wrote this poem?

TS'AI: No, I don't.

MISTRESS NIU *(continues her song):*

> So distressed were you;
> Still you haven't understood.

The writer of the poem

> Is your own wife,
> The lady Chao!
> I've been waiting to tell you;
> How could I let the matter drop?

WU-NIANG *(enters and sings to the tune* Chuan):

> I hear the uproar;
> It must be my husband reacting to the poem.

(MISTRESS NIU: Sister, come in.)

> Whose voice is that calling me sister?
> It must be the summons of his wife,
> And already the truth has been revealed.

MISTRESS NIU *(with an action, continues the song):*

> Here is the writer of the poem—now do you know her?

(TS'AI: My wife, from where has she come?)

> From Ch'en-liu she's come in search of you.

TS'AI *(recognizing* WU-NIANG, *continues the song):*

> It's you, but in such ragged clothes!
> And all are clothes of mourning.

Ah!

> It must be
> That my parents are no longer alive!

WU-NIANG *(with an action, sings to the same tune with a modified opening):*

From the time you left
The land was cursed with disaster.

(TS'AI: Disaster!)

We thought all three of us would starve to death.

(TS'AI: Did Chang Ta-kung help you?)

Only Chang Ta-kung took pity on us;
Alas, your parents had no one else to turn to.

(TS'AI: What then?)

(WU-NIANG *performs an action.*)

One after the other they died.
I cut my hair to raise money for their burial.

(TS'AI: And were they buried?)

I made the grave myself,
Carried the earth in my skirt.

TS'AI *(continues the song):*

I hear you speak,
And choked with grief, can stand no more.

(TS'AI *falls to the ground.* WU-NIANG and MISTRESS NIU *revive him.*
TS'AI *rises and bows to the portraits, weeping.*)

TS'AI *(sings to the tune* Shan-t'ao hung):

Ts'ai Yung is unfilial!
Father, Mother, I abandoned you!

Father, Mother! The day I left you, you didn't look like this.

If I had known how you were aging, growing weak,
Never would I have remained here at court.

Wu-niang,

I was the cause of your torment,
I was the cause of your bitter toil!
I thank you for providing burial for my father,
For my mother.
How hard to repay such love!
And they say, "Sons are raised to provide for one's old age"!

(They sing the chorus together):

Boundless grief!
Unending sorrow!
Calamities sent from Heaven man has no way to escape.

WU-NIANG (*sings to the same tune*):

From their remembered faces,
I painted these portraits myself.
A beggar playing on a lute,
Forced to brave the long, long road.

Husband,

You speak of my torment,
Speak of my bitter toil.
If you don't believe how I suffered, look at your father,
Look at your mother—
How emaciated they became after you left!
All alone, how hard it was to endure!

(*They repeat the chorus above.*)

MISTRESS NIU (*sings to the same tune*):

With words like a net,
My father trapped a son-in-law,
Forced him to marry me.
How then could he carry out the filial way?

Sister,

I was the cause of the suffering you endured;
I was the cause of that long road you traveled.

Husband,

It's I who wronged your father,
Wronged your mother,
Wronged your good name, causing you to be called unfilial.
I've failed to be "the virtuous wife" who "saves her husband from
    folly."

(*They repeat the chorus above.*)

TS'AI (*sings to the same tune*):

I'll take off my official cap,
Remove my official robes.

WU-NIANG (*continues the song*):

Make haste to resign your post—
In one day, or two at the most!

MISTRESS NIU (*continues the song*):
Husband,

I won't shirk trouble,
Won't shirk toil.
We'll go together to bow before your father,
Bow before your mother.
With my own hands I'll sweep their grave,
And our homage will bring glory to their souls beneath the earth.

(*They repeat the chorus above.*)

(*They sing together the tune* Wei-sheng):

Years of separation with no news of each other.
How long the road between us over myriad mountains and
    streams!
And the seeds of this misfortune were planted by the three re-
    fusals.

TS'AI: Tomorrow the three of us will return to attend the
grave of my parents and carry out the filial way. What do you
think?
WU-NIANG: I'm afraid her father won't give permission.
MISTRESS NIU: When my father sees how devoted you are to
the filial way, he can't but give permission.

(*Closing poem*)
TS'AI:

The three refusals of parents and ruler
Broke apart the bonds of parents and son.

TOGETHER:

"Tonight let the silver lamps shine bright,
For still we fear this meeting's but a dream." [12]

[12] The lines are from the *tz'u* "Che-ku t'ien" (Partridge sky) by Yen Chi-tao (fl. 1073).
See *Sung Liu-shih ming-chia tz'u* (*Tz'u* by sixty famous authors of the Sung dynasty)
(Shanghai, Commercial Press, 1936), *ts'e* 1, "Hsiao-shan tz'u," p. 4b.

SCENE THIRTY-SEVEN

CHANG TA-KUNG (*enters and sings to the tune* Yü mei-jen):

> The green mountains were always there, will endure forever;
> How many men's lives they've seen buried here!
> Who will sweep the moss from this lonely grave?
> Only the cold wind offers paper money blown from neighboring
>   mounds.

(*He recites to the* tz'u Yü-lou ch'un):

> How dark the long night that will never see another dawn!
> How still the empty mountain, as countless autumns pass!
> Do those who sleep beneath the Springs ever awaken?
> Mournful the wind that sighs through catalpa and pine.

Chao Wu-niang left this grave in my care. For the past few
days I've been too busy to come. Oh! What's this?

(*With an action, he sings to the tune* Pu-pu chiao):

> See how the grave's been covered by drifting leaves.

(*He performs an action of shooing away.*)

> Foxes and rabbits in chase run by.

(*He looks off*): People must have been coming here to chop
down trees.

> Why have the catalpa and pine grown so sparse?

(*He slips and falls.*)

> Moss seals the bricks;
> Bamboo encroaches on the muddy path.

Never mind! What can be done?

> I fear your grave will never last a hundred years.
> For you, who will look after these three feet of earth?

I see a man coming—who could it be?

LI WANG (*enters and sings to the previous tune*):

I've crossed streams and climbed mountains—how hard it's been!
And now I've reached this deserted hamlet.
Far off I see an old man;
I'll ask if he knows
Where Ts'ai's parents live.
I hasten my steps,
And approach a desolate grave.

CHANG: Brother, where are you from?
LI: I come from the capital.
CHANG: From whose residence?
LI: From the residence of his excellency Ts'ai.
CHANG: His excellency Ts'ai . . . What his excellency Ts'ai is that? Why did he send you here?
LI: I was sent by Ts'ai Po-chieh to escort his old mother and father and his wife back to the capital.
CHANG (*performs an action and, in anger, sings to the tune* Feng ju sung):

Don't speak of Ts'ai Po-chieh;
His very name is evil!

(LI: What do you mean by evil? It's improper of you to speak so!)

First Winner in the examinations, for six or seven years a high official,
He abandoned his parents and deserted his wife.

(LI: Where are his parents?)
CHANG (*performs an action*):

The brick-covered earthen heap before your eyes
Is the place where his parents lie buried.

(LI: So his parents are dead! What was the cause?)

After Ts'ai left, in years of drought,
They had no one to turn to.

(LI: Then who looked after them?)

They depended on the care of their daughter-in-law,
Who pawned all her ornaments and clothes.

LI: Yet even pawning must come to an end eventually.
CHANG: Just so! This young lady used the money she got

from pawning her things to buy grain to support her parents-in-law.

> Secretly she fought off starvation by eating husks alone;
> Yet her parents-in-law knew nothing but suspicion toward her.

LI: They must have thought it was good food she was eating in secret.

CHANG: That's right.

(*He sings to the tune* Fan-kun):

> I saw myself how the mother and father
> Both came to death.
> With no money to provide for their burial,
> She cut off her hair and sold it to buy a coffin.

(LI: If she was that poor, how could she provide a grave for them?)

> To this empty mountain she came alone,
> Carried earth in her skirt,
> And the blood that flowed from her fingers
> Moved spirits to descend and lend her their aid.

LI: Where is this young lady now?

CHANG (*sings to the tune* Feng ju sung):

> She's on her way to the capital now.

(LI: What can she use for the expenses of the road?)

> She plays a lute and begs for alms.

LI: Alas! Ts'ai Po-chieh sent me here to get his parents. Now I find they're both dead and his wife is gone. I've made this trip for nothing!

CHANG (*calls out*): Madame Ts'ai! Master Ts'ai! Your son has become an official and has sent someone to bring you there! Alas!

(*He continues his song*):

> No voice can answer my calls—where are their spirits now?
> All I can do is let tears fall, cover my cheeks.

LI: I'll start back now. I'll tell his excellency Ts'ai to commend his parents' souls to Heaven by doing good works.

CHANG (*laughing*): While they lived, he was unable to serve them. When they died, he was unable to assist at their burial.

And now that they're buried, he's been unable to offer sacrifices to them.
(He continues his song):

> Thrice unfilial, sins that offend Heaven itself!
> All his services and observances would be in vain.

Where is your master now?
LI: He lives in the home of his father-in-law, Prime Minister Niu.
CHANG *(sings to the tune* Fan-ch'ao):

> On your return
> Give Ts'ai a message from me.

(LI: What is it?)

> How nicely you bow to the parents of others!
> Yet the death of your own parents didn't rate a single bow from
>   you.

LI: Sir, you mustn't be so hasty in casting blame. He tried to resign his post, but the emperor refused to permit it. He tried to decline the marriage, but Prime Minister Niu wouldn't allow it. And he longed to return, but was unable.
CHANG *(sings to the tune* Feng ju sung):
In that case,

> All he did was not of his own will,
> Just as if spirits directed every step of his life.

It's true that he originally refused to go to the capital for the examinations, but his parents wouldn't accept his refusal.

> He was a victim of the three refusals of parents and ruler.

Seen in this way,

> Though thrice unfilial, he is not to blame.

(LI: Sir, you were about to put blame on a person who didn't deserve it.)

> It must be that his parents were destined for misfortune,
> For everything in our lives is by destiny ordained.

Brother, I am Chang Ta-kung. It was to my care that Ts'ai entrusted his family when he left. Now if you see a woman on the road dressed in nun's garments and carrying a lute and a portrait, that will be the wife of Ts'ai Po-chieh. Please help her with the expenses of the road, and take care of her on her journey. And give your master this message from me:

(Closing poem)
CHANG:

In helpless solitude your parents died;
Should you return now, it's already too late.

LI:

"The night still, the water cold, no fish took the bait;
As I return only bright moonlight fills my boat."

(Both exit.)

SCENE THIRTY-EIGHT

PRIME MINISTER NIU (*enters and sings to the tune* Feng ju sung man):

> I hoped that the creeping vine and strong pine would remain a
> pair—
> All the more because dusk approaches the mulberry tree!
> His *ch'un* tree and day lily both were slain;
> How could he forget the peaches and plums of his native moun-
> tain?[1]
> Though he hit the peacock, he knew nothing of the lady behind
> the screen;
> Once he mounted the dragon, how hard it became to keep my
> daughter here![2]

"Just one wrong move and my knight was lost!" Without
thinking things through carefully, I insisted that Ts'ai Po-
chieh become my son-in-law. Who could have imagined that
his parents would both die and his wife come here in search of
him? They say that my daughter wants to go back with him; I
don't know if it's true or not. I'll call the steward and ask him
about this.

STEWARD (*enters and recites in* shih *form*):

> The next move his, he sits in deep thought;
> Staring at the chessboard, how carefully he ponders!
> For he fears he'll make just one wrong move;
> Then all his efforts will have been in vain!

Yes, sir! What is your command?

NIU: Steward, I've heard that Ts'ai Po-chieh's wife has come
here and that my daughter wants to go back with them; is it
so?

---

[1] The "creeping vine and strong pine" represent Ts'ai and Mistress Niu (See Scene
Eighteen, note 2). Dusk in mulberry trees represents old age (here, of Prime Minister
Niu himself) (see Scene Two, note 11). The *ch'un* tree and day lily are symbolic of
parents (See Scene Four, note 2). Finally, peaches and plums are sometimes used as
symbols of beautiful women and here refer to Ts'ai's first wife.

[2] "To mount the dragon" refers to the marriage of a man; see Scene Thirteen,
note 3.

STEWARD: I've heard that too. But probably old Mu-mu will know the details.

NIU: Old Mu-mu, come here!

MU-MU (*enters and sings to the tune* Kuang-kuang cha):

> The daughter and son-in-law wish to return;
> What does the father-in-law think?
> Why do they suddenly summon me?
> They must want me to come up with a plan.

NIU: Mu-mu, come here. Is it true my daughter wants to go home with Ts'ai?

MU-MU: Yes, she does! His parents both died and their daughter-in-law took care of them all by herself. Now, what would be wrong in your daughter going to sacrifice at their graveside?

NIU: It won't do! How can my daughter dress in mourning for other people?

MU-MU (*sings to the tune* Nü-kuan-tzu):

> It's only right that a daughter-in-law serve her parents-in-law;
> How could you refuse to let your daughter go?
> From the start it was you who kept Ts'ai here;
> Now whom can you blame?

(NIU: And what if I don't let my daughter go?)

> There are standards one must follow;
> How can you presume on your power?
> Don't think that "Within the court the grand tutor's power is like
>   fire,"
> For more than that, "Travelers' talk spreads news better than sign-
>   boards."

(*They sing the chorus together*):

> We think it over—
> This won't be easy to solve!

STEWARD (*sings to the same tune*):

> His excellency is only concerned for his delicate daughter;
> He fears for her on a journey over thousands of mountains and
>   streams.

Sir,

> It's always been said, "A girl faces outward from the moment she's
>   born."

And your daughter already has a husband!
"Where the husband leads, the wife follows."
Of this you must have no doubt!

Sir,

The seeds planted at Lan-t'ien led to a marriage that was wrong.
"Now that we're out at sea in a sinking boat, it's too late to mend
the leak."

(They repeat the chorus above.)

NIU *(sings to the same tune):*

I was careless at the start;
Who could know the complications that would arise?
Now I think of my delicate daughter, always sheltered—
How can she travel ten thousand miles?
And I with no other kin—
How can I bear separation?

But no!

I mustn't let my daughter suffer such worry,
Nor let others gossip about her.

(They repeat the chorus above.)

NIU: Mu-mu, let her go if she wants! What do I care what people will say?
MU-MU: Here they come.
TS'AI, WU-NIANG, and MISTRESS NIU *(enter and sing to the tune* Wu
kung-yang):

All day our tears fall;
Because of our parents, this pain in our hearts.

MISTRESS NIU *(continues the song alone):*

We must go together to watch over the grave,
And so we must leave the imperial city.

TS'AI *(continues the song alone):*

Though we have determined on a plan,
Still I fear your father won't accept.

(They sing the chorus together):

If he refuses to let us go,
We will say it is the ruler's command.

(NIU *and the three greet each other.*)

NIU: Is this Ts'ai Po-chieh's wife?

WU-NIANG: Yes, I am she.

NIU, STEWARD, and MU-MU: What a virtuous lady!

MISTRESS NIU: Father, I have something to say to you. The ancients said, "One marries a wife in order to take care of one's parents"; this is called service to parents-in-law. Confucius said, "While they are alive, serve them as is proper. When they die, bury them as is proper and sacrifice to them as is proper."[3] My elder sister, as the wife of Po-chieh, was able to devote all her efforts to serving her parents-in-law while they were alive. When they died, she was able to provide burial for them as was proper, and then carry out the duties of piling up the mound of earth and planting trees by the graveside. But I, your daughter, though also the wife of Po-chieh, was unable to offer them comfort while they lived. When they died, I was not able to be there to mourn for them, nor was I able to serve them in their long night. How can I be counted as human? I've sinned against my parents-in-law; the conduct of my elder sister shames me! Now, Father, I ask in your presence—let my elder sister take precedence over me!

NIU: How virtuous my daughter is!

STEWARD and MU-MU: Indeed!

WU-NIANG: She doesn't feel that "People of different status can't be judged by the same standards"!

(*She continues in parallel prose*):

 She is a renowned beauty raised in elegant surroundings, while I am but a humble woman wearing a bramble hairpin and a cotton skirt. What's more, *her* marriage was by order of imperial decree! Impossible that she should yield precedence to me!

NIU: Come here. Since you have neither parents nor parents-in-law, you are like a daughter to me. Besides, you married Ts'ai first, and you're older than my daughter. Don't decline any more!

TS'AI: Just call each other sister!

ALL: That's the best way.

[3] Legge, 1:147.

TS'AI: Now I must bid goodbye to my father-in-law and return with my wives to my native village to carry out the filial way. When the mourning period is over, we'll all come back.

NIU: My daughter, I can't bear to see you go, but because your parents-in-law are in their graves, I know I mustn't detain you.

MISTRESS NIU: Father, I leave you only for a time; I have no choice but to go. Father, take care of yourself, and don't worry about me. I'll probably be gone for three years.

NIU (*crying*): My daughter, now you go to bow before the grave of your parents-in-law.

MISTRESS NIU: Father, please calm yourself.

NIU: Enough! Girls will always face outward—what pain it's brought to me!

ALL: Sir, please calm yourself.

TS'AI (*bowing in parting, sings to the tune* Ts'ui-p'ai):

Bear in mind how my parents both lost their lives,
And I became guilty of unfilial conduct that offends the very
  heavens;
Now I must leave the imperial court.
Moved by the kindness of my father-in-law,
I'd dare not be ungrateful!
To fail to return home
Would be a betrayal of their spirits beneath.

(*They sing the chorus together*):

We bid goodbye, to return together to the grave,
Hearts filled with grief, tears overflowing our eyes.

WU-NIANG (*sings to the same tune*):

Bear in mind how I left my village, my home, behind;
Thank you sir, for letting your daughter leave.
Not only will we bring glory to our native town,
But my parents-in-law, in their dark world,
Can finally close their eyes in peace.
I myself will watch over your daughter;
There's no need to ask me!

(*They repeat the chorus above.*)

NIU (*sings to the same tune*):

After you're gone, what will be your fate?
When you return, will I be dead or alive?

Po-chieh,

> Already I am old.
> You, after all, are now without parents,
> And I without other children.
> If you remember how we are now kin,
> You'll surely return as soon as you can.

(They repeat the chorus above.)

MISTRESS NIU *(sings to the same tune):*

> As I gaze at my father's aged face and white hair,
> Pain brings tear after tear from my eyes.

Father,

> Either way it will be hard for me;
> If I wrong my parents-in-law,
> People will censure me.
> If I abandon my father,
> There'll be no one to care for him.

(They repeat the chorus above.)

TS'AI *(sings to the tune* I-ts'o chao):

> Wait for us with easy heart;
> What need to worry so?

NIU *(continues the song):*

> Write to tell me the news;
> Keep sending letters through the post stations.

MISTRESS NIU: Mu-mu,

> My father is aged.

While I'm gone,

> Look after him well!

(They sing together):

> On the journey
> We hope to remain safe and well.
> For separation through death there's no hope at all;
> When parting in life, the outcome still can't be predicted.
> Now we leave;
> When will we be back in the capital city?

NIU: My daughter, the three of you take good care of your-selves on the journey.

TS'AI, WU-NIANG, and MISTRESS NIU: Thank you, Father!

(They sing together to the tune K'u hsiang-ssu):

The most painful thing is to part in life; so hard it is to go!
After we go, when will we ever be together again?

(All exit.)

SCENE THIRTY-NINE

LI WANG (*enters and sings to the tune* Liu ch'uan yü):

> Fast as arrows flew my feet.
> No one could imagine the hardships I've endured.
> "The night still, water cold, no fish took the bait;
> As I return only bright moonlight fills my boat."
> I reach the outer porch;
> I wonder where my master is?

My master sent me to Ch'en-liu to seek out Ts'ai Po-chieh's parents and wife. As it turned out, his parents had both died, and his wife was already on her way here. My trip was for nothing! Wait a minute! Maybe I should go tell Ts'ai first before I speak to the master.

(*He performs an action*): Why is his room all locked up? I know—probably Ts'ai's gone to court and his wife locked the door herself for some peace and quiet.

(*He calls out*): Open the door! Why does no one answer? Why is it so still? Where has the old master gone? Why isn't there a single person in sight?

NIU (*enters and sings to the tune* Wan hsien teng):

> I hear a voice outside the door;
> Who makes such a clamor there?

Ah, Li Wang, you're back!

LI: Yes, sir.

NIU: My daughter and Ts'ai have both left.

LI: Where did they go?

NIU: To his home.

LI: Did Ts'ai's wife come here?

NIU: Yes, and I met her. Is it true that her parents-in-law have died?

LI: Yes, indeed.

(*He sings to the tune* Feng t'ieh-erh):

> When I reached Ch'en-liu,
> I met an old man,
> Sweeping the grave of Ts'ai's parents.

His parents

Both died during the famine.
And his wife
Was on her way here.
So my trip was made for nothing!

NIU (*sings to the same tune*):

Now I'll go
To submit a memorial to the throne.
I'll tell of the filial way of the Ts'ai family;
I'm sure the emperor will make a proclamation,
Bestowing noble titles
And summoning them here.
I'll make a trip to Ch'en-liu myself.

LI: Sir, this Mistress Chao must be an exceptional woman.
NIU: Indeed, yes! The whole family is exceptional. Ts'ai Po-chieh never forgot his parents, Chao Wu-niang took care of her parents-in-law with filial devotion, and my daughter helped them to attain perfection in their virtuous conduct. The emperor will surely bestow commendations!

(*Closing poem*)
NIU: Truly,

The emperor himself will send down a proclamation
To make known to the whole world their filial and virtuous names.

(*They exit.*)

SCENE FORTY

TS'AI (*enters and sings to the tune* Mei-hua yin):

It wounds my heart; the loved faces I look for are here no more.
All that's left is this ancient cemetery, neglected and overgrown.

MISTRESS NIU and WU-NIANG (*enter and continue the song*):

To the green mountain
Was added one more grave.

(*They sing the chorus together*):

Tears flow as we think of that long night which never ends in
dawn.
Spirits that lie beneath the Springs, can you hear our cries?

TS'AI (*recites to the* tz'u Yü-lou ch'un):

Far away, how many tears I shed in longing for my parents,
Unable then to let them scatter on the soil of my native town.
Finally I'm able to let them fall on native soil,
But my parents in their grave will never see my tears.

MISTRESS NIU (*continues the* tz'u):

Deserted grave amid dying grass, covered all in cold mist.
Green moss and yellow leaves, drifting artemisia.
Just before cockcrow, I prepare to make the morning call,
Suddenly wake to find they've passed to the other world.

WU-NIANG (*continues the* tz'u):

To every person death must come,
But who could understand this sorrow of yours?

(*They finish the* tz'u *together*):

So sad to see how, dressed in faded hemp, he bows before the
grave!
He wasn't able "in clothes of brocade to return to his hometown."

TS'AI (*pours a libation, then sings to the tune* Yü yen-tzu):

I wronged you—
For the sake of success and fame, I wronged you, Mother and Father.

Because I was unable to return to my hometown,
You have had to return to the yellow earth.

Father, Mother,

The forces of Heaven and earth all cast out the unfilial son;
Ruined my name, shameless my conduct—how much better to die!

Ah but,

I fear that if I die, sacrifice to you will end.

(They sing the chorus together):

We gaze at the portraits, their weary faces and emaciated forms,
And think of their spirits suffering endless torment of bitter re-
    membrance.

MISTRESS NIU *(sings to the same tune):*

An unfilial daughter-in-law,
With shame I recall how it was I who wronged my husband.
Never in life can I escape others' scorn!

Die I would,

But what shame I'd feel to meet my parents-in-law there!

Father-in-law, Mother-in-law,

Alive, I was unable to serve you;
Shall I serve you now on the road to Yellow Springs?

But one thing more. If I should die,

My old father at home—
Who will look after him?

(They repeat the chorus above.)

WU-NIANG *(sings to the same tune):*

From today we'll dwell in a hut by the grave;
I pray that your parents will shield us from harm.

(With an action)

If the spirits of Mother and Father are able to receive this sacri-
    fice,
Let them forgive my husband!

Ah!

What value have these offerings to the dead?
If only we had been able to offer food to the living!

How can we know whether they receive it?
How can we know where they are now?

(They repeat the chorus above.)

CHANG TA-KUNG *(with an action, enters and sings to the same tune):*

Like pavilions and towers of glimmering silver,
The green mountain has become a lovely painting.
Like the pale white of your clothes, Heaven and earth too,
Have added a silk sash that billows in the wind.
You stamp your feet, beat your breast, how bitter your wail!
The fall of snowflakes makes the scene even more lonely and chill.

You mustn't weep so! Learn to accept adversities in life.

Repress your feelings, accept what comes; always men have done
so.

(They repeat the chorus above.)

TS'AI: Here's Chang Ta-kung!
(He performs an action): How grateful I am for your help! Just
now I was going to finish paying my respects at the graveside,
then come with my wives to express my thanks to you.
CHANG: I've done nothing to deserve your gratitude!
(He continues in shih *form):*

The river's water has flowed to the east, never to return again;
The broken mirror's past repair, no face will it reflect.

WU-NIANG *(in* shih *form):*

On you alone continuance of the line depends;
Be careful lest your grievous cries cut short your life.

MISTRESS NIU *(in* shih *form):*

Clouds cover the mountain peaks; my home can't be seen.
Snow blankets the deep forest; no traveler's horse could advance.

TS'AI *(in* shih *form):*

There must be a reason why you've made this long journey here;
Perhaps to collect my bones when they lie scattered by this grave.[1]

---

[1] The four lines are from the poem "Tso-ch'ien chih Lan-kuan shih Chih-sun Hsiang"
by Han Yü (768–823) (*CTS* 344:3860).

CHANG: Sir, don't go on like this. I have no way to console you, but please, on such a cold day accept one cup of weak wine.

TS'AI (*sings to the tune* Yü-shan kung):

> How kind your offer,
> Your concern for us on this cold day!

But sir,

> My parents suffered three years of hunger and cold;
> Can't I bear one day of chill?

(CHANG: Please!)

> The longing in my heart
> This fragrant wine can't soothe.

(They sing the chorus together):

> We're moved by the kindness of your heart;
> It's hard to refuse this wine,
> For we know that to buy it, you had to struggle through the snow.

MISTRESS NIU (*sings to the same tune*):

> What trouble for you, sir,
> Out of concern for us on this cold day!

CHANG: Madame, please!

MISTRESS NIU: Sir,

> We stand here amid burial mounds,
> Not in a warm pavilion heated by a glowing brazier!

On days like this,

> I wonder who will take care,
> Take care of my own father at home.

(They repeat the chorus above.)

WU-NIANG (*sings to the same tune*):

> In those days I was dressed in rags,
> I thank you, sir, for all the support you gave.
> And alas, before I can repay your past kindness,
> Again you come to care for us!
> It's not only I who is moved by your virtue;
> Mother and Father, in dark world below, will remember your
>   kindness forever.

(They repeat the chorus above.)

CHANG *(sings to the same tune):*

> Life is like the morning dew,
> And fate determines our life, our death, our glory, our ruin.

Sir,

> You've other duties than to weep so for your parents;
> It's you who must see that the family line continues.
> Now that you have this golden belt and purple robe,
> Don't miss the chance to bring glory to your family.

(They repeat the chorus above.)

TS'AI, WU-NIANG, and MISTRESS NIU: For all your trouble, we owe you so many thanks!

(Closing poem)
TS'AI, WU-NIANG, and MISTRESS NIU:

> We'd never dare forget the gratitude we owe to you.

CHANG:

> Set your mind free of this endless anguished grief.

TOGETHER:

> No need to say that "Men are judged only by their position";
> Indeed, "Everyone ignores the humble and courts the high."

(They exit.)

SCENE FORTY-ONE

PRIME MINISTER NIU (*enters and sings to the tune* Liu kun):

Upon a courier steed,
Upon a courier steed,
I go to Ch'en-liu to announce the decree.

ATTENDANT and GROOM (*played by the* ching *and* ch'ou *actors, enter and continue the song*):

We invite his excellency
To make a brief stop.

NIU (*continues the song*):
Hey!

Where are we?
Why do we stop?

ATTENDANT and GROOM (*continue the song*):

This is the post station;
Here we'll change horses.

NIU: If this is the post station, then change the horses.
ATTENDANT and GROOM: Where is the stationmaster?
STATIONMASTER (*played by the* mo *actor, enters and sings to the same tune*):

They tell me,
They tell me
A high official's suddenly arrived.

Yes, sir!

I come too late to meet you;
I beg you forgive my offense!

NIU (*continues the song*):

Don't bother with etiquette;
Just hurry up with the provisions!

STATIONMASTER (*continues the song*):

Come with me to get them;
I'd dare not delay!

Brothers, I shouldn't presume to ask, but where is his excellency going?

ATTENDANT and GROOM: You'd never guess! This is Grand Tutor and Prime Minister Niu.

STATIONMASTER: Where is he going?

ATTENDANT: He's carrying a proclamation to Ch'en-liu to honor the home of a filial son with an official insignia.

NIU: Just hurry up and give us our provisions and saddle the horses.

STATIONMASTER: Yes, sir.

ATTENDANT: Friend groom, on the road we never seem to have enough to eat. We'd better get more this time.

GROOM: I have a plan. When he gives me the provisions, you take them away from me on the sly. Then we can say he never gave them to us.

STATIONMASTER (*gives them provisions*): Four jugs of wine, three catties of meat, and two pecks of rice.

(*The* GROOM *takes the provisions. The* ATTENDANT, *without letting the* STATIONMASTER *see, takes them from him.*)

GROOM: Sir, the stationmaster refuses to give us our provisions!

NIU: Bring that crook here!

(*The* ATTENDANT *drags the* STATIONMASTER *forward. He kneels down.*)

GROOM (*pointing to the* ATTENDANT): You took them!

NIU: The regulations state the stationmaster must supply us with provisions. What do you mean by refusing to give them out? Have you no fear?

STATIONMASTER: I did give them out.

ATTENDANT: So where are they?

STATIONMASTER: The groom took them.

GROOM: I don't know what he's talking about.

NIU: Give the ass a good beating!

(*The* ATTENDANT *beats the* STATIONMASTER.)

STATIONMASTER: I'll give you the provisions.
NIU: Keep an eye on him.

(The STATIONMASTER *doles out provisions again.)*

ATTENDANT: Friend groom, what else can we take?
GROOM: Let's say he didn't give them out again. Then we'll strip off his clothes and hat and beat him up.
GROOM *(after hiding the provisions):* So! You still refuse to give them out! We'll rid you of your clothes and hat then!

(Closing poem)
STATIONMASTER: Sir,

   This poor stationmaster's lost all his clothes!

NIU:

   These knaves think of nothing but their stomachs.

GROOM:

   High officials don't worry themselves about right and wrong.

ATTENDANT:

   We can use the torn hat to wrap up the meat!

(They exit.)

SCENE FORTY-TWO

TS'AI, WU-NIANG, and MISTRESS NIU (*enter and sing to the tune* Hsiao-yao lo):

Who shows us pity in our chill solitude?
We can only let our tears fall upon the lonely grave.

(*They sing the chorus together*):

Like the snap of fingers, three springs have passed by.
Their spirits fade away in obscurity,
Locked so deep within the palace of night
That we know not where to call to summon them forth.

TS'AI: My wives, do you see?
(*He continues in* shih *form*):

A pair of trees, branches intertwined—whose hand set them there?

MISTRESS NIU:

White rabbits, as if tame, scamper over the burial mound.[1]

WU-NIANG:

Even unknowing animals and plants become omens of good fortune;
When the depths of ill fortune are reached, good fortune must begin.

CHANG TA-KUNG (*enters and recites*):[2]

An edict has been sent down from the emperor;
Suddenly in the outskirts of the town rumors fly.
They say that someone's door is to be honored with insignia;
Still we don't know whose!
Ah! What's this?
How marvelous the sight of white rabbits scampering by the grave!
And that pair of trees with branches interlocked!

---

[1] Such auspicious omens were said to have been manifested at the grave of the historical Ts'ai Yung's parents.
[2] The passage is rhymed, but the lines are of various lengths.

All is brought forth in response to the filial way;
Such omens can't be false!

Sir, congratulations!

TS'AI, WU-NIANG, and MISTRESS NIU: Why, sir?

CHANG: They say that by proclamation a filial son's door will
be honored with an imperial insignia. The messenger has already been received by the prefectural officials. I think it must
be because of you that he comes.

TS'AI: But there are so many filial sons! And besides how am I
worthy of such a title? Even the filial piety that the Duke of
Chou and Tseng-tzu showed to their parents was nothing
more than their duty as sons. Why should it merit being honored with an imperial insignia?

WU-NIANG and MISTRESS NIU: How true!

CHANG: My ladies, what can you mean? It was said in antiquity,
"Acts of filial piety and respect toward elders make themselves
known even to the spirits above. They shine everywhere
within the four seas; everything is touched by their power."[3]
Look at those ancient trees with branches intertwined, and the
white rabbits scampering about as if tame. With these auspicious signs, it's certain that good fortune is on the way.

(*He sings to the tune* Liu yao ling):

Rare trees have joined their branches,
And see on the grave mound,
Rabbits run as if tame.
Even animals and plants manifest your virtue.
The proclamation then
Must surely be because of you!

(*They sing the chorus together*):

Thus does Heaven express its sympathy.
Thus does Heaven express its sympathy.

TS'AI (*sings to the same tune*):

If such imperial favor is really for me,
I have no wish
That benefits fall on me.
For in my heart there's only sorrow that my parents have no
     share.

---

[3] *Hsiao Ching* (Classic of filial piety), p. 8a.

All it does is wrong
This lonely grave.

(They repeat the chorus above.)

WU-NIANG *(sings to the same tune):*

How can we know if it's true?
Thank you, sir,
For taking such care to bring us the news.

Sir,

How much you've suffered for our sake!
Yet who will come
To place an insignia on your door?

(They repeat the chorus above.)

MISTRESS NIU *(sings to the same tune):*

Who is it carries the decree?
My depression's so deep I can't refrain
From asking him one question.

(TS'AI: What is the question you ask in your depression?)

I must ask if my own father
Remains in good health,
Is dead or alive.

(They repeat the chorus above.)

COUNTY MAGISTRATE *(played by the* ch'ou *actor, enters and sings to the same tune):*

As the imperial message draws near,
The streets are alive with excitement,
Everywhere the people swarm.
When I heard the news I rushed forth
To prepare the incense table
To receive the imperial favor.

(They repeat the chorus above.)

TS'AI: What high minister is it who has come all the way to Ch'en-liu?
MAGISTRATE: Sir, it's Prime Minister Niu, and he personally carries an imperial edict. It will be read in public here. The edict orders the placing of imperial insignia at your gate and

promotes you in official rank. Both your wives are to receive titles of nobility. I came here first to prepare things and to request your excellency and the two ladies to change to more auspicious clothing.

TS'AI, WU-NIANG, and MISTRESS NIU: We mustn't!

MAGISTRATE: The former kings prescribed the proper duration for the wearing of mourning clothes. The virtuous man must accept its end, while the unvirtuous must strive to last through it.[4] Your period of mourning is over; can it be wrong to remove your mourning clothes?

TS'AI, WU-NIANG, and MISTRESS NIU: True!

ALL: "Without the cold wind that chilled us to the bone, how could we have experienced the fragrance of the plum blossoms of early spring?"[5]

TS'AI: See far off that crowd of horses and men drawing near? It must be the proclamation! We must go forward to greet them!

PRIME MINISTER NIU and an ATTENDANT *(played by the* ching *actor, enter and sing to the previous tune)*:

Cold winds have covered our temples with frost;
Astride carved saddles, with bridles of jade,
We've journeyed all through the world of red dust.
Finally arrived, we're full of joy.
To meet again
Ends all our pain.

(They repeat the chorus above.)

NIU: Where are we?

MAGISTRATE: This is the Ts'ai family farm. Please dismount.

(NIU dismounts and the ATTENDANT performs an action.)

TS'AI, WU-NIANG, and MISTRESS NIU *(in changed clothing enter[6] and sing to the previous tune)*:

Our hearts are pounding, our steps hurried,
Because favor from his majesty

---

[4] The lines are based on a passage in the *Li Chi* (Book of Rites) 20:192.

[5] The two lines are common in Yüan-Ming drama, expressing the idea that only after suffering does one appreciate good fortune.

[6] No stage direction is given previously for the exit of the three. There is some confusion as to whether this scene was originally divided in two and, if so, at what point. Perhaps this led to the dropping of the stage direction.

Has arrived at our humble gate.
In long robes, tablet in hand, our sashes hanging low,[7]
Our hats, our robes,
Are each one new.

(They repeat the chorus above.)

NIU: Kneel as I read the decree: "It is our belief that good customs are the foundation of moral development, and that filial piety and righteousness are the foundation of good customs. With every day that brings us further from the time of the ancient sages, so do their pure customs grow more and more corrupted. Social morality is in a state of decay, and this fills our heart with distress. Therefore, when a man is able to fulfill the ways of both filial piety and righteousness and encourage others to reform their own behavior, how can we fail to commend him so that the whole world will be inspired by his example?

"Counselor Ts'ai Yung practiced the filial way with the utmost honesty. Neither wealth nor rank could free his mind from grief, and the one longing that never left his mind was to care for his parents. Though it conflicted with his ambition, he chose instead a righteous name. Though he relinquished his position, his reputation was the more enhanced.

"Mistress Chao, his wife, all alone as she served her parents-in-law, wore her body down with suffering and toil. She was able to fulfill her heart's desire—to take care of them in life and provide burial for them after their death. Truly did she achieve perfection in the virtues of purity and submissiveness. Finally we have seen a real 'husk wife'!

"Mistress Niu remonstrated with her father to act according to the principles of right and assisted her husband in his proper conduct. With no jealousy in her heart, how excellent was the humble spirit in which she yielded!

"To carry out both filial piety and righteousness is a double perfection. Upon these three we hereby confer our sincerest commendations. Let the multitudes of the world follow their example, take them as a model. For if customs are improved and conduct reformed, our era can compare with the great dynasties of antiquity. And so we graciously reward them, that

[7] The tablet referred to is that held by officials when in audience with the emperor.

the whole world may know of their filial piety and righteousness. Ts'ai Yung, we appoint as General of the Gentlemen of the Household. Mistress Chao, we entitle the Lady of Ch'en-liu. Mistress Niu, we entitle the Lady of Honan. All must leave for the capital this very day. Let the departed father, Ts'ai Ts'ung-chien, be given the sixteenth order of merit, and the mother, Mistress Ch'in, be given the title Lady of Ch'in. Ah!

> How strong were his feelings over the wind in the trees![8]
> Truly, on such filial piety all morality is based.
> How sad were his thoughts when frost or dew fell![9]
> It is fitting that he be favored with our rain of grace.

It is our hope that these commendations will give you consolation in your time of distress." Let us give thanks for his benevolence!

(He bows, then rises.)

TS'AI *(bowing to* NIU): How can I be worthy of such praise!
NIU: Don't be so modest!
MISTRESS NIU: I've been separated from you for so long—how glad I am that you're still in good health!
NIU: My daughter, I'm glad that both of us have kept well and that we're able to see each other again!
(He indicates the ATTENDANT): Here is an official sent to accompany me.
TS'AI *(greets the* ATTENDANT): I'm honored that you consented to visit my humble home.
NIU *(indicating* CHANG): And who is this?
TS'AI: Chang Ta-kung, somebody to whom we're extremely grateful.
NIU *(greets* CHANG): Ta-kung, you gave so much help to my son-in-law's parents, and we haven't been able to repay you for your kindness before. Po-chieh, I have an ingot of gold with which we can repay a small part of what we owe him for his great virtue.
TS'AI: I would be most grateful!
CHANG: Sir, to help others and take pity on one's neighbors is

---

[8] Wind blowing in the trees evokes a son's filial feeling; see Scene Thirty-five, note 9.
[9] When frost and dew fall, one is reminded of the seasonal sacrifices and wishes to be with his parents; see *Li Chi*, p. 137b.

but the correct way of the ancients. Why should you reward me for that?

TS'AI: Please go ahead and accept it! I myself can only work like a dog or horse in your service to repay you.

CHANG: No need to speak so!

(He takes the gold.)

NIU *(sings to the tune* I-feng shu*):*

> I myself carried the imperial decree,
> Traveled thousands upon thousands of miles.
> I thought of how excellent are the characters of my kin;
> My daughter and son-in-law I came to seek out.

My daughter,

> Though you lived through years of pain,
> This unforeseen glory's at last arrived!

(They sing the chorus together):

> Glory to the home,
> Advancement in rank,
> And a name for filial piety and right becomes known to the world!

TS'AI *(sings to the same tune):*

> Without filial piety a son has no virtue at all.
> It was you, father-in-law, who gave me support.

Ah!

> Far, far better to have kept them from death!
> What need would I have then of glory and fame?
> Alas, my parents paid with death in hunger and cold;
> For this, my return in fortune and fame!

(They repeat the chorus above.)

WU-NIANG *(sings to the same tune):*

> I should paint their portraits again,
> For now they've been given noble titles.
> Their frowning eyebrows I'll smooth,
> But their emaciated faces will be hard to round out.
> Is it only my heart that's filled with thanks?
> I know that those below treasure this favor in their hearts.

(They repeat the chorus above.)

MISTRESS NIU *(sings to the same tune):*

Separated from you, Father, how I suffered
Without ever having news of you!
Always sad thoughts of my parents-in-law,
And tears that fell again and again for my own father;
And now I can face my parents-in-law without shame,
And again I can stay by my father's side.

(They repeat the chorus above.)

CHANG, ATTENDANT, and MAGISTRATE *(sing together to the tune*
Yung t'uan-yüan):

Everywhere in the world his fame has spread, no equal has he;
How much better than bringing glory to his own home alone!
If no one were able to hold true to the principles of filial piety and
    right,
The glorious ages of the past could never be matched.
Though this praise from the emperor is glorious indeed,
You need feel no shame to accept it as your due.
Your name will be recorded in history for all time.
And now you must go
All together back to the capital.
Having given thanks for the imperial kindness,
To the family hall return,
And in happy celebration,
Convene a splendid feast—
For you'll be together now for all seasons!

(They sing to the tune Wei-sheng):

How bright our culture, so wise the government!
Of filial men and virtuous women we sing.
Cosmic forces all harmonious,
Our emperor sits with hanging robes, and all is at peace.[10]

(Closing poem)
TS'AI:

For three years I've dwelt in a graveside hut.

WU-NIANG:

Today from the Ninth Heaven there came a vermilion decree.

[10] The line describes the traditional wise emperor who need take no action to create
harmony in the empire. It is based on a line in the *I Ching* (Classic of changes).

CHANG:

If name is to be honored, if rank is to be high,

ATTENDANT:

Filial must be the son, virtuous the wife.

(All exit.)

APPENDIX

Synopsis of *The Lute*

Scene One. In this prologue to the play, the *mo* actor recites two *tz'u* that present the author's theory of literature and summarize the action of the play.

Scene Two. Ch'en-liu. Ts'ai Po-chieh expresses pride in his scholarly accomplishment and qualifications for official responsibilities, but in consideration of his parents' old age, determines to stay at home to serve them. He invites them out to the garden to drink the newly matured spring wine and celebrate their long life. Spring is in full blossom, and the family, including Ts'ai's wife, Wu-niang, congratulate each other on their contentment and familial harmony. At the same time, the parents urge their son to embark on an official career.

Scene Three. The capital. A steward in the mansion of Prime Minister Niu describes the wealth and power of his master and the beauty and virtue of Mistress Niu, his daughter. He is joined by a maid, Hsi-ch'un, and housekeeper, Mu-mu, and the three amuse themselves with jokes and games. Mistress Niu catches them at their fun and scolds Hsi-ch'un for her frivolous behavior, then leads her back to the house to work on embroidery.

Scene Four. Ch'en-liu. Ts'ai Po-chieh has declined an invitation from the district official to attend the capital examination. His father, along with their neighbor, Chang Ta-kung, attempts to persuade him to go, while his mother wants to keep him at home to take care of the family. Only after Ts'ai's father has accused him of being reluctant to leave his new bride and Chang has offered to take care of the family in his absence does Ts'ai consent to go.

Scene Five. Ch'en-liu. As Ts'ai is preparing to leave, Wu-niang reproves him for forsaking his filial duties. He bids goodbye to his parents, enjoining both Chang and Wu-niang to take care of them. In a private farewell to Wu-niang, he assures her that he can never be tempted to take a second wife in the capital and promises to return as soon as possible.

Scene Six.   The capital. Two matchmakers deliver marriage proposals for Mistress Niu to her father. He sends them away, saying he will marry his daughter only to the First Winner in the examinations. Reminded by this that his daughter is of marriageable age and will soon be mistress of her own home, he summons her and scolds her for allowing the female servants to play outside.

Scene Seven.   On the road. On his way to the capital, Ts'ai grieves over the separation from his family and home, while two other travelers, also on their way to the examination, enjoy the beauty of the scenery and their anticipation of achieving fame and fortune.

Scene Eight.   Ch'en-liu. Wu-niang expresses her loneliness for her husband and her anxiety for his parents. She determines to devote herself to their care, thereby diminishing his fault in leaving them.

Scene Nine.   The capital. The officials make elaborate preparations for the entertainment of the winners in the examination, of which Ts'ai is first. After a good deal of comic dialogue and action involving the fall of one of the winners from his horse and the composition of poems by the successful candidates, Ts'ai is congratulated for his great success. He, however, continues to express guilt over having left his parents.

Scene Ten.   Ch'en-liu. The Ts'ai family is beginning to suffer from the famine that has struck the area. Mother Ts'ai blames her husband for sending their son away, leaving them helpless in time of calamity. Wu-niang tries to make peace between the two and promises to pawn her jewelry to get money for food.

Scene Eleven.   Prime Minister Niu tells the steward that, at the emperor's suggestion, he will invite Ts'ai, the First Winner, to marry his daughter. The matchmaker is summoned and, after a humorous dialogue in which she talks about her trade, she is sent to propose the marriage to Ts'ai.

Scene Twelve.   The capital. As Ts'ai grieves over the separation from his family, the matchmaker, accompanied by the steward, enters and proposes the match. Ts'ai firmly declines, saying he already has a wife. When the matchmaker warns him of the danger of offending the prime minister, Ts'ai states that he will petition the emperor to be permitted both to decline the marriage and to resign from office.

Scene Thirteen.   The capital. The matchmaker informs Prime Minister Niu of Ts'ai's refusal. Enraged at such impudence, he sends the matchmaker back to insist on the marriage. He also plans to petition the emperor to refuse Ts'ai's request to resign his office and return home.

Scene Fourteen. The capital. Mistress Niu is appalled at her father's insistence on making the unwilling Ts'ai her husband. Though Mu-mu tries to persuade her of the excellence of the match, Mistress Niu feels that a marriage in which one partner is unwilling can end in nothing but mutual resentment.

Scene Fifteen. The capital. Ts'ai petitions the emperor for permission to leave his office and be appointed to a local post in his own district. He asks also to be allowed to decline the marriage. His petition is denied on the grounds that the highest expression of filial piety is in service to one's ruler and that the proposed marriage to Mistress Niu is a great honor.

Scene Sixteen. Ch'en-liu. A miniature comic plot about the village head is presented in this scene. He has been pilfering grain from the official granary under his supervision and must find a way to replenish the stores before the arrival of officials who are to distribute grain to those suffering in the famine. Though he succeeds in borrowing a portion of the needed grain, the amount is still insufficient; he proceeds to appear before the officials in various disguises, each time requesting a share of the grain for relief.

When Wu-niang arrives to ask for grain for her parents-in-law, the granary is empty, but she finally receives a share of the grain which the village head is forced to give over. This, however, he steals back from her as she is on her way home. As she attempts suicide out of despair, she is discovered by Father Ts'ai. Moved by her devoted service, he also tries to kill himself. Chang Ta-kung enters and offers them half the grain he has received from the public granary.

Scene Seventeen. The capital. The matchmaker announces to Ts'ai that the "happy day" has come and that he must go to Prime Minister Niu's for the wedding; reluctantly, he goes with her.

Scene Eighteen. The capital. In the splendor of the prime minister's mansion all acclaim the excellence of the match as Ts'ai marries Mistress Niu; he, however, continues to protest and grieve.

Scene Nineteen. Ch'en-liu. As conditions in the Ts'ai family grow daily more critical, Wu-niang secretly eats only the husks in order to save the rice itself for her parents-in-law. Mother Ts'ai suspects that she has been buying good food for herself and eating it in private, but Father Ts'ai maintains confidence in her devotion and honesty. They determine to spy on her while she is eating.

Scene Twenty. Ch'en-liu. Wu-niang laments over the hardships of the famine and forces herself to eat husks. She expresses bitterness toward Ts'ai, who has deserted the family. Her parents-in-law enter and discover what she is eating; appalled at their former suspicions and her suffering, both fall down in a faint. Father Ts'ai soon revives, but his wife remains unconscious. Later, the neighbor Chang enters, and Wu-niang tells him her mother-in-law has died; Chang offers to provide the money for funeral expenses.

Scene Twenty-one.   The capital. Ts'ai, now living in the mansion of his new father-in-law, grieves over his separation from parents and wife and plays the *ch'in* in a vain attempt to relieve his pain. When his new wife enters, he finds it impossible to play the cheerful songs she requests, and she begins to suspect he is thinking of another woman. After she urges him to drink wine with her, they make love and enjoy the beautiful summer evening.

Scene Twenty-two.   Ch'en-liu. Ts'ai's father is seriously ill; as Wu-niang prepares medicine and urges him to drink it, she blames Ts'ai Po-chieh's desertion for his father's illness. Father Ts'ai also condemns Ts'ai severely, while blaming himself for urging him to go, thus causing so much hardship for Wu-niang. The scene ends as Father Ts'ai bequeaths his staff to Chang Ta-kung, enjoining him to give Ts'ai a good beating should he ever return.

Scene Twenty-three.   The capital. Ts'ai grieves over his situation, blaming father, emperor, and prime minister for compelling him to act against his conscience. He confides in the steward and asks him to find a trustworthy messenger to take a letter home to his family. He plans to wait until his appointment expires, then find a way to return home.

Scene Twenty-four.   Ch'en-liu. Father Ts'ai has died, and Wu-niang, having no money for burial expenses, cuts her hair and goes out in the streets to offer it for sale. Just as she despairs of finding a buyer, Chang Ta-kung enters and offers to help again with the expenses.

Scene Twenty-five.   The capital. A swindler, who first describes his great skill, makes a plan to go to Ts'ai with a fake letter from his parents, in the hope of being entrusted with a reply, gift to them, and traveling money, which he can then pocket. The plan works perfectly; after rejoicing at the letter, which states that his family is well, Ts'ai writes a reply and gives money to the swindler to take to his family.

Scene Twenty-six.   Ch'en-liu. Having no money to hire help to dig the grave for her parents-in-law, Wu-niang must do the work herself. Alone on the mountain, weary from her labor, she falls asleep. Spirits sent by the Jade Emperor, in pity for her devoted service, finish the grave, then appear in her dream and tell her to go to the capital in search of her husband.

Scene Twenty-seven.   The capital. Mistress Niu admires the beautiful moonlight of mid-autumn and invites Ts'ai to come out and enjoy it with her. Reluctantly he joins her, and they watch the moon, each responding differently; Mistress Niu is moved by its romantic beauty, while it envokes in Ts'ai thoughts of his family far away.

Scene Twenty-eight.   Ch'en-liu. Wu-niang visits the grave of her parents-in-law and paints their portraits to carry with her on her journey to the capital. Chang comes to say goodbye and warns her to be circumspect when she reaches the capital, as her husband, now rich and honored, may be ashamed to acknowledge her.

Scene Twenty-nine.   Mistress Niu, upset by her husband's depression and lack of warmth toward her, demands an explanation. He refuses to tell her, but she discovers the cause when she overhears him grieving over the separation. She upbraids him for deserting his family and insists that they go together to Ch'en-liu. Although he warns her not to tell her father, she is confident of the prime minister's moral rectitude.

Scene Thirty.   The capital. Prime Minister Niu questions his daughter about Ts'ai's depression. When she explains its source and asks permission to return to Ch'en-liu with her husband, Niu is furious that the two would wish to devote themselves to such humble people and refuses to let Mistress Niu go, accusing her of lack of filial devotion to himself. Ts'ai learns that his wife has informed Niu of his situation and scolds her; she is ashamed both of revealing his secret and being a hindrance to his performance of his filial duties all along. The scene ends with the couple expressing hope that Niu will have a change of heart.

Scene Thirty-one.   On the road. Wu-niang travels to the capital, carrying a lute which she plays while begging, and the portraits of her parents-in-law. She laments over the hardships of the road and worries about how Ts'ai will receive her when she finds him in the capital.

Scene Thirty-two.   The capital. Prime Minister Niu has realized that his first reaction to his daughter's wish was wrong, but he is still reluctant to let her leave him in his old age. He has decided to send a messenger to bring Ts'ai's family to the capital. Ts'ai and Mistress Niu are pleased with this plan, and the messenger, Li Wang, is sent.

Scene Thirty-three.   A monastery outside the capital. The monastery is holding an assembly, and two comic rogues attend, pretending to be gentlemen. When Wu-niang arrives, they promise to reward her well for playing her lute and singing. She sings several songs about filial piety, for which they give her their own jackets, but when they start shivering from the cold, she is forced to return them.

Ts'ai arrives at the monastery to pray for the safety of his family on the road, but does not meet with Wu-niang, who has concealed herself. He does, however, pick up the portraits of his parents, which she has left behind, without recognizing them. She has learned who he is and sets off to his home, confident of reunion.

Scene Thirty-four. The capital. Mistress Niu is just asking the steward to find a good maid to serve her parents-in-law upon their arrival when Wu-niang enters, dressed as a nun. She is invited to join the household as a maid, and gradually her true identity is revealed. The two women describe their suffering and express resentment toward Ts'ai, though admitting that he was helpless in the situation. Mistress Niu advises Wu-niang to write a note and leave it in Ts'ai's study to prepare him for her appearance.

Scene Thirty-five. The capital. Wu-niang, finding the portraits of her parents-in-law hanging in Ts'ai's study, writes an unsigned, allusive poem on the back, in which she remonstrates with him for his desertion of the family.

Scene Thirty-six. The capital. Ts'ai tries to relieve his anxiety by reading, but finds in every book references to filial piety that depress him all the more. Seeing the portraits, he is deeply moved as he discerns a resemblance to his parents, but he reassures himself that they could never have become so ragged and emaciated. He then reads the poem and angrily calls Mistress Niu to learn who has been in his study. They discuss the meaning of the poem and Mistress Niu determines that Ts'ai is a man of high integrity who would not divorce his poor and humble first wife. She calls in Wu-niang, who is reunited with her husband. Ts'ai learns that his parents are dead, and the three make plans to return to Ch'en-liu to observe the mourning period.

Scene Thirty-seven. Ch'en-liu. Chang Ta-kung is sweeping the grave of Ts'ai's parents when the messenger from Niu arrives in search of the Ts'ai home. When he speaks of Ts'ai, Chang curses him severely for his unfilial conduct, but softens somewhat when he learns the causes of his delay in returning. Learning that Ts'ai's parents are dead and that Wu-niang is on her way to the capital, the messenger starts back to inform Niu.

Scene Thirty-eight. The capital. Prime Minister Niu reluctantly consents to his daughter's wish to return to the graveside with Ts'ai and Wu-niang. They say goodbye, promising to return when the three years of mourning are over.

Scene Thirty-nine. The capital. The messenger returns and finds that Prime Minister Niu already knows of the death of Ts'ai's family and is about to submit a memorial to the throne, asking that Ts'ai and his two wives receive imperial commendation for their filial and virtuous conduct.

Scene Forty. Ch'en-liu. Ts'ai and his two wives mourn at the graveside and offer sacrifices to the spirits of his parents. Chang arrives to offer them wine, is warmly thanked by them, and tries to console Ts'ai in his grief.

Scene Forty-one. On the road. Prime Minister Niu, on his way to Ch'en-liu to present the imperial commendation to Ts'ai, stops at the post station to change horses and receive supplies. In a comic passage, his two servants trick the post official into giving them a double apportionment of food and strip off his clothes.

Scene Forty-two. Ch'en-liu. At the end of the period of mourning, Ts'ai and his two wives come to the grave and find it surrounded with auspicious signs—trees with intertwined branches and tame white rabbits. Prime Minister Niu brings the imperial commendation for Ts'ai and his two wives and posthumous titles for his parents. He also gives Chang a gift of money as a reward for his help. The four plan to return to the capital, where Ts'ai will resume his official career.

TUNE TITLES IN THE
P'I-P'A CHI

TZ'U TITLES

Che-ku t'ien　鷓鴣天
Chiang-nan hao　江南好
Ch'in-yüan ch'un　沁園春
Ch'ing-p'ing yüeh　清平樂
Hsi-chiang yüeh　西江月
Huan-ch'i sha　浣溪沙
Lei chiang yüeh　酹江月
Lin-chiang hsien　臨江仙
Mu-lan hua　木蘭花

Nan-hsiang-tzu　南鄉子
P'u-sa man　菩薩蠻
Sheng ch'a-tzu　生查子
Shui-tiao ko-t'ou　水調歌頭
Su mu che　蘇幕遮
T'a-so hsing　踏莎行
Tieh lien-hua　蝶戀花
Yü-lou ch'un　玉樓春

SONG TITLES

Che-ku t'ien　鷓鴣天
Ch'en-tsui tung-feng　沉醉東風
Ch'eng jen hsin　稱人心
Ch'i-t'ien lo　齊天樂
Chiang-erh shui　江兒水
Chiang huang-lung　降黃龍
Chiang-t'ou chin-kuei　江頭金桂
Chiao-chiao ling　僥僥令
Chieh-chieh kao　節節高
Chieh san ch'eng　解三酲
Chin ch'an yen　錦纏雁
Chin chiao-yeh　金蕉葉
Chin-ch'ien hua　金錢花
Chin-i kung-tzu　金衣公子
Chin lung-ts'ung　金瓏璁
Chin-so kua wu-t'ung　金索掛梧桐
Chin-t'ang yüeh　錦堂月
Cho-mu-erh　啄木兒
Cho-mu li　啄木鸝
Chu-ma t'ing　駐馬聽

Chu Ying-t'ai chin　祝英台近
Chu Ying-t'ai hsü　祝英台序
Ch'u-p'o　出破
Ch'u tui-tzu　出隊子
Chuan　賺
Chuan lin ying　囀林鶯
Ch'uan-po chao　川撥棹
Ch'uan-yen yü-nü　傳言玉女
Chung-kun ti-ssu　中袞第四
Chü-hua hsin　菊花新
Ch'üeh-ch'iao hsien　鵲橋仙
Erh-fan yü-chia ao　二犯漁家傲
Erh-lang shen　二郎神
Fan-ch'ao　犯朝
Fan hu-ping　犯胡兵
Fan-kun　犯袞
Fan pu-suan　番卜算
Fen tieh-erh　粉蝶兒
Feng-huang ko　鳳凰閣
Feng ju sung　風入松

Feng ju sung man　風入松慢
Feng t'ieh-erh　風帖兒
Feng-yün hui ssu ch'ao yüan
　風雲會四朝元
Fu-ma lang　福馬郎
Hao chieh-chieh　好姐姐
Hei-ma hsü　黑麻序
Hsi ch'ien ying　喜遷鶯
Hsi-nu chiao　惜奴嬌
Hsi ti chin　西地錦
Hsia-shan hu　下山虎
Hsiang liu niang　香柳娘
Hsiang-lo tai　香羅帶
Hsiang pien-man　香遍滿
Hsiao-chin chang　銷金帳
Hsiao-shun ko　孝順歌
Hsiao-yao lo　逍遙樂
Hsieh-p'ai　歇拍
Hsiu-tai-erh　綉帶兒
Hu tao-lien　胡搗練
Hua-ch'iao-erh　鏵鍬兒
Hua-hsin tung　花心動
Hua-mei hsü　畫眉序
Hung hsiu-hsieh　紅綉鞋
Hung na-ao　紅衲襖
Hung shan-erh　紅衫兒
I-chien mei　一剪梅
I-chih hua　一枝花
I Ch'in-o　憶秦娥
I-ch'un ling　宜春令
I-feng-shu　一封書
I nan wang　意難忘
I pu-chin　意不盡
I to-chiao　憶多嬌
I-ts'o chao　一撮棹
Jao ch'ih yu　繞池游
Ju-p'o ti-i　入破第一
Jui-ho hsien　瑞鶴仙
Kan-chou ko　甘州歌
Kao-yang t'ai　高陽台

Ko-erh　哥兒
Ku lun t'ai　古輪台
K'u ch'i p'o　哭岐婆
K'u hsiang-ssu　哭相思
Kua chen-erh　桂眞兒
Kuang-kuang cha　光光乍
Kuei-ch'ao huan　歸朝歡
Kuei-chih hsiang　桂枝香
Kun ti-san　袞第三
La-mei hua　臘梅花
Lan hua-mei　懶畫眉
Liang-chou hsü　梁州序
Lin-chiang hsien　臨江仙
Liu ch'uan yü　柳穿魚
Liu kun　劉袞
Liu p'o-mao　劉潑帽
Liu yao ling　六么令
Lo-chang-li tso　羅帳裏坐
Lo ku ling　羅鼓令
Lü-lü chin　縷縷金
Man chiang hung　滿江紅
Man p'ai ling　蠻牌令
Man-t'ing fang　滿庭芳
Mei-hua t'ang　梅花塘
Mei-hua yin　梅花引
Nien-nu chiao　念奴嬌
Nü-kuan-tzu　女冠子
Pao-lao tsui　鮑老催
Pao-ting-erh　寶鼎兒
Pei hun-chiang lung　北混江龍
Pei tao-tao ling　北叨叨令
Pei tien chiang-ch'un　北點絳唇
Pen-hsü　本序
Po-hsing　薄幸
P'o ch'i-chen　破齊陣
P'o ti-erh　破第二
Pu-pu chiao　步步嬌
Pu-suan hsien　卜算先
Pu-suan hou　卜算後
P'u-hsien ko　普賢歌

P'u-t'ien lo　普天樂
San hsien ch'iao　三仙橋
San hsüeh-shih　三學士
San huan-t'ou　三換頭
San tuan-tzu　三段子
Sha wei　煞尾
Shan-hua-tzu　山花子
Shan-p'o yang　山坡羊
Shan-t'ao hung　山桃紅
Shang kung-hua　賞宮花
Shao yeh-hsiang　燒夜香
Shen chang-erh　神杖兒
Sheng ch'a-tzu　生查子
Sheng hu-lu　勝葫蘆
Shih-erh shih　十二時
Shih-tzu hsü　獅子序
Shuang hsi-ch'ih　雙鸂鶒
Shuang-sheng tzu　雙聲子
Shuang-t'ien hsiao-chiao　霜天曉角
Shui-ti yü-erh　水底魚兒
So-ch'uang lang　瑣窗郎
So nan chih　鎖南枝
Ssu-niang-erh　似娘兒
Ssu-pien ching　四邊靜
Su-ti chin-tang　窣地錦襠
Ta-ch'iu ch'ang　打球場
Ta ho fu　大和佛
Ta-sheng yüeh　大聖樂
Ta ya-ku　大迓鼓
T'ai-p'ing ko　太平歌
T'ai-shih yin　太師引
Tao-lien-tzu　搗練子
T'e-t'e ling　忒忒令
Ti-liu-tzu　滴溜子
Ti-ti chin　滴滴金

T'i yin-teng　剔銀燈
Tien chiang-ch'un　點絳唇
T'ien-hsia lo　天下樂
Tou hei-ma　斗黑麻
Tsui fu-kuei　醉扶歸
Tsui t'ai-p'ing　醉太平
Tsui-weng-tzu　醉翁子
Ts'ui-p'ai　催拍
Tung-hsien ko　洞仙歌
Wan hsien teng　玩仙燈
Wei fan　尾犯
Wei fan hsü　尾犯序
Wei-sheng　尾聲
Wu chih chi　吳織機
Wu Hsiao-ssu　吳小四
Wu-keng chuan　五更傳
Wu kung-yang　五供養
Wu ni-shang　舞霓裳
Yeh chin-men　謁金門
Yeh yu-hu　夜游湖
Yen-erh wu　雁兒舞
Yen kuo-sha　雁過沙
Yen yü chin　雁漁錦
Yen yü hsü　雁漁序
Yung t'uan-yüan　永團圓
Yü chiao-chih　玉交枝
Yü-chia hsi yen-teng　漁家喜雁燈
Yü-ching lien hou　玉井蓮后
Yü mei-jen　虞美人
Yü pao-tu　玉包肚
Yü-shan kung　玉山供
Yü-wen　余文
Yü yen-tzu　玉雁子
Yüan-lin hao　園林好
Yüeh yün kao　月雲高

GLOSSARY

Chang Ch'ang 張敞
Chang Chia-chen 張嘉貞
Chang Hsieh Chuang-yüan 張協狀元
Chang Hua 張華
Chang Kuang-ts'ai 張廣才
Chang Ta-kung 張大公
Chang Yüeh 張說
Ch'ang-lo 長樂
Ch'ang-men 長門
Ch'ang O 嫦娥
Chao Chen-nü 趙眞女
Chao Chen-nü Ts'ai Erh-lang
　趙眞女蔡二郎
Chao Wu-niang 趙五娘
"Chao yin-shih" 招隱士
Ch'ao Ts'o 晁錯
"Che-ku t'ien" 鷓鴣天
Ch'en-liu 陳留
ch'i-t'ai 乞胎
Chia I 賈誼
"Chiang-nan ch'un chüeh-chü
　shih" 江南春絕句詩
chieh 介
Chien-chang 建章
Chien-chu T'ao Yüan-ming chi
　箋注陶淵明集
ch'ih-t'ai 吃胎
Ch'in 秦
ch'in 琴
"Chin se" 錦瑟
chin-shih 進士
Ch'in-ts'ao 琴操
ching 淨
Chiu-fang Kao 九方皋

"Chiu pien" 九辯
Ch'iung-lin 瓊林
Cho Wen-chün 卓文君
Chou 周
ch'ou 丑
Chou Li 周禮
Chu Mai-ch'en 朱賣臣
Ch'u-chou 處州
Ch'u-tz'u 楚辭
Ch'ü Yüan 屈原
chuan-t'a 傳踏
ch'uan-ch'i 傳奇
Chuang-tzu 莊子
"Chüeh-chü erh shou" 絕句二首
ch'un 椿
"Ch'un hsiao ch'ü" 春曉曲
"Ch'un su tso-sheng" 春宿左省
"Ch'un wang" 春望
Chung K'uei 鍾馗
chung-lang 仲郎
chung-lang-chiang 中郎將
Chung Tsu-ch'i 鍾子期
"En-chih tz'u shih yü li-cheng
　tien shu-yüan yen fu te lin-tzu
　shih" 恩制賜食於麗正殿書院
　宴賦得林字詩
Fan Ch'i-liang 范杞梁
Fan Yeh 范曄
Fang Kuo-chen 方國珍
Fei-ch'iung 飛瓊
"Feng-cheng" 風正
"Feng-ho chung-shu she-jen Chia
　Chih tsao-ch'ao Ta-ming kung"
　奉和中書舍人賈至早朝大明宮

fu 賦
fu-ching 副淨
Fu-sang 扶桑
Han Yü 韓愈
Ho-chin 河津
Ho Yen 何晏
Hsi-ch'un 惜春
Hsi-ho 西河
Hsi-k'ao 戲考
Hsiang 象
"Hsiang chün" 想君
Hsiang Yü 項羽
hsiao 孝
Hsiao Ching 孝經
"Hsiao chou yu chin-ts'un"
　小舟遊近村
Hsiao-erh 小二
"Hsiao shan tz'u" 小山詞
Hsiao shang fen 小上墳
Hsiao Shih 簫史
hsien 賢
hsiu-ts'ai 秀才
Hsiung-nu 匈奴
Hsü Hsün (Chen-chün) 許遜
　（眞君）
Hu-yang 胡陽
Hua-liu 驊騮
Huang Hsiang 黃香
Huang Yün 黃允
hun chieh 混介
i-lang 議郎
I Yin 伊尹
Jüan Chi 阮籍
Kao Ming 高明
Kao P'ien 高駢
Kao Yü 皋魚
ku-feng 古風
"Kuan-shan" 關山
Kuan-yin-tzu 關尹子
"Kuei-ch'ü-lai tz'u" 歸去來辭

K'uei 奎
K'un-lun 昆侖
K'ung Jung 孔融
K'ung-t'ung 崆峒
lai 賴
Lan-t'ien 藍田
Lao Lai-tzu 老萊子
lao tan 老旦
li 里
Li Chi 禮記
"Li Sao" 離騷
Li Shang-yin 李商隱
Li-she 櫟社
Li She 李涉
Li Wang 李王
Liang Po-luan 梁伯鸞
Lieh-tzu 列子
Ling Ch'e 靈徹
Ling shan 靈山
Liu Hsiang 劉向
Liu Pang 劉邦
Lu Fang-weng shih-chi 陸放翁詩集
Lu I-tien 陸貽典
Lu K'ai 陸凱
Lu Pan 魯班
Lu Yu 陸游
luan 鸞
Lun-yü 論語
Lü Tung-pin 呂洞賓
Mao Yen-shou 毛延壽
Meng Chiang-nü 孟姜女
Meng Chiao 孟郊
Meng Te-yao 孟德耀
mo 末
Mo-tzu 墨子
Mu 穆
Mu-mu 姆姆
Nan-feng 南風
Nan p'u 南浦
Niang-tzu 娘子

Nieh Cheng　聶政
Niu　牛
Niu Hsiao-chieh　牛小姐
Niu Hsiu　鈕琇
Nung-yü　弄玉
"Pa-ch'iao-shou"　八俏手
Pan Ku　班固
p'eng　鵬
P'i-hsiang　披香
P'i-huang　皮黃
p'i-p'a　琵琶
Po Li-hsi　百里奚
Po Ya　伯牙
"Pu hsü tz'u"　步虛詞
pu ju kuei ch'ü　不如歸去
se　瑟
"Shan-t'ing hsia-jih"　山亭夏日
Shang-lin　上林
Shen-t'ung shih　神童詩
sheng　生
shih　詩
Shih Ching　詩經
Shih Ch'ung　石崇
Shu　蜀
Shu Ching　書經
"Shu Hu-yin hsien-sheng pi"　
　書湖陰先生壁
Shu-sun T'ung　叔孫通
"Shui-tiao ko-t'ou"　水調歌頭
Shun　舜
Sou shen chi　搜神記
Ssu-ma Ch'ien　司馬遷
Ssu-ma Hsiang-ju　司馬相如
Su Ch'in　蘇秦
Su Tung-p'o　蘇東坡
Su Wu　蘇武
Sung Hung　宋弘
Sung liu-shih ming-chia tz'u　
　宋六十名家詞
Sung Yü　宋玉

ta chieh　打介
Ta T'ang Ch'in wang tz'u-hua　
　大唐秦王詞話
Tai Shu-lun　戴叔倫
T'ai I　太乙
T'ai-shan　泰山
tan　旦
T'ao Yüan-ming　陶淵明
"Teng-k'o hou shih"　登科後詩
"T'i Ho-lin-ssu tseng-she shih"　
　題鶴林寺僧舍詩
t'i-mu　題目
t'ieh-tan　貼旦
T'ien-lü ko　天祿閣
Tou I　竇毅
tsa-chü　雜劇
Ts'ai Po-chieh　蔡伯喈
Ts'ai Ts'ung-chien　蔡從簡
Ts'ai Yung　蔡邕
Ts'ao Chih　曹植
Ts'ao P'ei　曹丕
Tse-ch'eng　則誠
Ts'en Shen　岑參
Tseng Shen　曾參
Tseng-tzu　曾子
Tsin Shu　晉書
"Tso-ch'ien chih Lan-kuan shih
　Chih-sun Hsiang"　左遷至藍關
　示姪孫湘
Ts'ui-wei　翠微
"Ts'ung chün hsing"　從軍行
Tu Fu　杜甫
Tu Mu　杜牧
Tung Cho　董卓
Tung Chung-shu　董仲舒
tzu　字
"Tzu-ch'en-tien t'ui ch'ao
　k'ou-hao"　紫宸殿退朝口號
tz'u　詞
wai　外

wang 亡
Wang 王
Wang An-shih 王安石
Wang Ch'ang-ling 王昌齡
Wang Chao-chün 王昭君
Wang Ch'iang 王嬙
Wang Hsi-chih 王羲之
Wang Lin-ch'uan ch'üan-chi
  王臨川全集
Wang Ling 王陵
Wang Mang 王莽
Wang Wei 王維
"Wei-ch'eng ch'ü" 渭城曲
Wei Chieh 衞玠
Wen-chün 文君
Wen T'ing-yün 溫庭筠
Wu 吳
Wu Ch'i 吳起

Wu-shan 巫山
wu-t'ung 梧桐
Yang Hsiung (Yang Tzu-yün)
  揚雄(揚子云)
Yang Hu 陽虎
Yang-kuan 陽關
"Yao tien" 堯典
"Yeh-ssu-erh" 也四兒
Yen Chi-tao 晏幾道
Yen Hui 顏回
Yen Tzu-ling 嚴子陵
Ying K'ao-shu 潁考叔
Yung-lo ta-tien 永樂大典
Yü 禹
yüan-nao 猿猱
Yüeh-chih 月支
Yüeh-t'an 越腅

BIBLIOGRAPHY

TEXTS AND TRANSLATIONS OF THE
P'I-P'A CHI

Bazin, A. P. L. *Le Pi-pa-ki ou l'Histoire du Luth.* Paris: Imprimerie Royale, 1841.

Chang, H. C. *Chinese Literature, Popular Fiction and Drama.* Edinburgh: Edinburgh University Press, 1973. Chang translates six scenes from the play.

Ch'ien Nan-yang 錢南揚, editor. *P'i-p'a chi.* 琵琶記 Shanghai: Chung-hua shu-chü, 1960. Not only does this edition make widely available the most reliable extant text of the play, but the detailed and accurate notes are invaluable. A biography of the author and a discussion of texts are also included.

Hundhausen, Vincenz. *Die Laute von Gau Ming.* Leipzig: Pekinger Verlig, 1930. A complete translation into German, this poetic rendition sacrifices accuracy for literary effectiveness.

Mao Chin 毛晉 (1599–1659), editor. *Liu-shih-chung ch'ü* 六十種曲 (Sixty plays). 12 vols. Shanghai: K'ai-k'ai shu-tien, 1935. A good example of revised play texts of the Ming-Ch'ing period, Mao Chin's edition is more refined in language than the original, and spoken passages are often expanded to clarify the meaning of the songs.

SECONDARY SOURCES

Aoki Masaru 靑木正兒. *Chung-kuo chin-shih hsi-ch'ü shih* 中國近代戲曲史 (History of modern Chinese drama). Translated from the Japanese by Wang Ku-lu 王古盧. 2 vols. Peking: Tso-chia ch'u-pan-she, 1958.

Birch, Cyril. "Some Concerns and Methods of the Ming *Ch'uan-ch'i* Drama." In Cyril Birch, ed., *Studies in Chinese Literary Genres.* Berkeley: University of California Press, 1974. Pp. 220–58.

—— "Tragedy and Melodrama in Early *Ch'uan-ch'i* Plays: Lute Song and Thorn Hairpin Compared." *Bulletin of the School of Oriental and African Studies,* 36 (1973): 228–47.

Chang Ch'i 張琦 (late Ming). *Heng-ch'ü chu-t'an* 衡曲塵譚 (Talks on the evaluation of plays). In *Chung-kuo ku-tien hsi-ch'ü lun-chu chi-ch'eng* (Collection of studies of classical Chinese drama), 4. Peking: Chung-kuo hsi-chü ch'u-pan-she, 1959.

Chang Ching 張敬. *Ming Ch'ing ch'uan-ch'i tao-lun* 明清傳奇導論 (An introduction to Ming-Ch'ing *ch'uan-ch'i*). Taipei: Tung-fang shu-tien, 1961.

Chang Hsiang 張相. *Shih tz'u ch'ü yü-tz'u hui-shih* 詩詞曲語辭滙釋 (Dictionary of words and phrases in *shih*, *tz'u* and *ch'ü*). Shanghai: Chung-hua shu-chü, 1954.

Chang Ti-hua 張棣華. *P'i-p'a chi k'ao-shu* 琵琶記考述 (Research on the *P'i-p'a chi*). Taipei: Cheng-chung shu-chü, 1966.

Chao Ching-shen 趙景深. *Hsi-ch'ü pi-t'an* 戲曲筆談 (Notes on plays). Shanghai: Chung-hua shu-chü, 1962.

—— *Yüan Ming nan-hsi k'ao-lüeh* 元明南戲考略 (Research on Yüan-Ming southern drama). Peking: Tso-chia ch'u-pan-she, 1958.

Chao P'ang 趙汸 (1319–1369). *Tung-shan ts'un-kao* 東山存稿 (Extant manuscripts of Tung-shan). In *Ssu-k'u ch'üan-shu chen-pen erh-chi* (Second edition of the rare volumes in the Ssu-k'u collection). Taipei: Taiwan Commercial Press, 1971.

Cheng Chen-to 鄭振鐸. *Chung-kuo hsi-ch'ü ti hsüan-pen* 中國戲曲的選本 (Anthologies of Chinese plays). In *Chung-kuo wen-hsüeh yen-chiu ts'ung-pien ti-i-chi* (First edition of materials for research on Chinese literature). Hong Kong: Lung-men shu-tien, 1969.

—— *Chung-kuo su-wen-hsüeh shih* 中國俗文學史 (History of Chinese popular literature). Ch'ang-sha: Commercial Press, 1938.

Ch'ien Nan-yang 錢南揚. "Chang Hsieh hsi-wen chung ti liang-chung chung-yao ts'ai-liao" 張協戲文中的兩椿重要材料 (Two important types of research material in the southern play *Chang Hsieh*). *Wen-che chi-k'an*, 2, 1 (1931): 137–44.

—— *Sung Yüan hsi-wen chi-i* 宋元戲文輯佚 (Reconstruction of play texts of the Sung-Yüan period). Shanghai: Shang-hai ku-tien wen-hsüeh ch'u-pan-she, 1956.

—— *Sung Yüan nan-hsi pai-i-lu* 宋元南戲百一錄 (Collected fragments of southern drama of the Sung-Yüan period). Peking: Harvard-Yenching Institute, 1934.

Chin Meng-hua 金夢華. *Chi-ku-ko liu-shih-chung-ch'ü hsü-lu* 汲古閣六十種曲絞錄 (Annotations on the *Chi-ku-ko* edition of the Liu-shih-chung ch'ü). Taipei: Chia-hsin shui-ni kung-ssu, 1969.

Ching-ch'ai chi 荆釵記 (The thorn hairpin). Attributed to K'o Tan-ch'iu 柯丹邱 (fourteenth century). Shanghai: Chung-hua shu-chü, 1960.

Chou I-pai 周貽白 *Chung-kuo hsi-ch'ü lun-ts'ung* 中國戲曲論叢 (Collection of articles on Chinese drama). Shanghai: Chung-hua shu-chü, 1952.

—— *Chung-kuo hsi-ch'ü shih* 中國戲曲史 (History of Chinese drama). Shanghai: Chung-hua shu-chü, 1953.

Chu Chü-i 朱居易 . *Yüan chü su-yü fang-yen li-shih* 元劇俗語方言例釋 (Colloquialisms and dialect phrases in Yüan drama). Shanghai: Commercial Press, 1956.

Chung Ssu-ch'eng 鍾嗣成. *Lu kuei pu hsin chiao-chu* 錄鬼簿新校注 (Record of ghosts, with new annotation). Peking: Wen-hsüeh ku-chi k'an-hsing-she, 1957.

Chü-pen yüeh-k'an she 劇本月刊社 (Drama monthly society). *P'i-p'a chi t'ao-lun chuan-k'an* 琵琶記討論專刊 (Special volume on the discussion of *P'i-p'a chi*). Peking: Jen-min wen-hsüeh ch'u-pan-she, 1956.

Crump, James I. "The Conventions and Craft of Yüan Drama." In Cyril Birch, ed., *Studies in Chinese Literary Genres*. Berkeley: University of California Press, 1974. Pp. 192–219.

—— "Elements of Yüan Opera." *Journal of Asian Studies*, 17 (1958): 417–34.

—— *Li K'uei Carries Thorns*. Center for Chinese Studies Occasional Papers, No. 1. Ann Arbor: University of Michigan, 1962.

Feng Yüan-chün 馮沅君. *Ku-chü shuo-hui* 古劇說彙 (Notes on old drama). Shanghai: Commercial Press, 1947.

Frye, Northrop. "The Structure of Comedy." In *Eight Great Comedies*. New York: New American Library, 1958. Pp. 461–69.

Ho Liang-chün 何良俊 (1506–1573). *Ch'ü-lun* 曲論 (Discussion of drama). In *Chung-kuo ku-tien hsi-ch'ü lun-chu chi-ch'eng* (Collection of studies of classical Chinese drama), 4. Peking: Chung-kuo hsi-chü ch'u-pan-she, 1959.

Hsia, C. T. *The Classic Chinese Novel*. New York: Columbia University Press, 1968.

Hsü Chen 徐㴡 (fl. 1368). *Sha-kou chi* 殺狗記 (A dog is killed). Shanghai: Chung-hua shu-chü, 1960.

Hsü Fu-tso 徐復祚 (1560–c.1630). *Ch'ü-lun* 曲論 (Discussion of drama). In *Chung-kuo ku-tien hsi-ch'ü lun-chu chi-ch'eng* (Collection of studies of classical Chinese drama), 4. Peking: Chung-kuo hsi-chü ch'u-pan-she, 1959.

Hsü Wei 徐渭 (1521–1593). *Nan-tz'u hsü-lu* 南詞敍錄 (Notes on southern drama). In *Chung-kuo ku-tien hsi-ch'ü lun-chu chi-ch'eng*, 3. Peking: Chung-kuo hsi-chü ch'u-pan-she, 1959.

Hu Ying-lin 胡應麟 (1551–1602). *Shao-shih shan-fang ch'ü-k'ao*

少室山房曲考 (Study of drama). In *Hsin ch'ü-yüan* (New anthology of drama). Taipei: T'ai-wan chung-hua shu-chü, 1969.

Huang Li-chen 黃麗貞. *Nan-chu liu-shih-chung ch'ü ch'ing-chieh su-tien yen-yü fang-yen yen-chiu* 南劇六十種曲情節俗典諺語方言研究 (The plots of the sixty southern plays and a study of their folk allusions, proverbs, and dialect expressions). Taipei: Taiwan Commercial Press, 1972.

Huang Wen-yang 黃文暘 (b. 1736). *Ch'ü-hai tsung-mu t'i-yao* 曲海總目提要 (A descriptive bibliography of plays). Shanghai: Ta-tung shu-chü, 1928.

Jen Chung-min 任中敏, comp. *Hsin ch'ü-yüan* 新曲苑 (New collection of writings on drama). Taipei: T'ai-wan chung-hua shu-chü, 1969.

Legge, James, trans. and ed. *The Chinese Classics*, 5 vols. Hong Kong: Hong Kong University Press, 1960.

Li Fang 李昉 (925–996), compiler. *T'ai-p'ing kuang-chi* 太平廣記, 10 vols. Peking: Chung-hua shu-chü, 1961.

Li Yü 李漁 (1611–1679). *Li Li-weng ch'ü hua* 李笠翁曲話 (Comments on plays by Li Yü). Shanghai: Ch'i-chih shu-chü, 1927.

Liu, James J. Y. "The *Feng-yüeh chin-nang*: A Ming collection of Yüan and Ming plays and lyrics preserved in the Royal Library of San Lorenzo Escorial, Spain." *Journal of Oriental Studies*, 4 (1957): 79–107.

Liu Jung-en, trans. and ed. *Six Yüan Plays*, Harmondsworth, Eng.: Penguin, 1972.

Lo Chin-t'ang 羅金堂, ed. *Chung-kuo hsi-ch'ü tsung-mu hui-pien* 中國戲曲總目彙編 (A bibliography of Chinese drama). Hong Kong: Wan-yu t'u-shu kung-ssu, 1966.

Lu K'an-ju and Feng Yüan-chün 陸侃如·馮沅君. *Nan-hsi shih-i* 南戲拾遺 (Reconstructed fragments of southern drama). Peking: Harvard-Yenching Institute, 1936.

Lu Tan-an 陸澹安. *Hsiao-shuo tz'u-yü hui-shih* 小說詞語滙釋 (Dictionary of phrases in fiction). Peking: Chung-hua shu-chü, 1964.

Morohashi Tetsuji 諸橋轍次. *Dai kanwa jiten* 大漢和辭典 (Unabridged Chinese-Japanese dictionary), 13 vols. Tokyo: Tokyo taishukan, 1955–60.

Pai-t'u chi 白兔記 (The white rabbit) (late Yüan). Taipei: T'ai-wan k'ai-ming shu-tien, 1960.

P'eng Ting-ch'iu 彭定求, comp. *Ch'üan T'ang shih* 全唐詩 (Complete T'ang poetry), 12 vols. Peking: Chung-hua shu-chü, 1960.

Shen Te-fu 沈德符 (1578–1642). *Ku-ch'ü tsa-yen* 顧曲雜言 (Miscellaneous notes on plays). In *Chung-kuo ku-tien hsi-ch'ü lun-chu chi-ch'eng* (Collection of studies of classical Chinese drama), 4. Peking: Chung-kuo hsi-chü ch'u-pan-she, 1959.

Shih Hui 施惠 (late Yüan). *Yu-kuei chi* 幽閨記 (Ladies' secluded chambers). Shanghai: Chung-hua shu-chü, 1960.

Tai Pu-fan 戴不凡. *Lun ku-tien ming-chü P'i-p'a chi* 論古典名劇琵琶記 (On the famous classic play *P'i-p'a chi*). Peking: Hung-chih shu-tien, 1956.

T'an Cheng-pi 譚正璧, ed. *Chung-kuo wen-hsüeh-chia ta-tz'u-tien* 中國文學大辭典 (Encyclopedia of Chinese authors). Hong Kong: Shang-hai yin-shu-kuan, 1961.

T'ao Tsung-i 陶宗儀 (fl. 1360). *Cho-keng ch'ü-lu* 輟耕曲錄 (Notes on plays while living at leisure). In *Hsin ch'ü-yüan* (New anthology of drama). Taipei: T'ai-wan chung-hua shu-chü, 1969.

Tsang Mou-hsun 臧懋循 (fl. 1580), comp. *Yüan ch'ü hsüan* 元曲選 (Anthology of Yüan drama). Shanghai: Commercial Press, 1918.

Van Gulik, R. H. *The Lore of the Chinese Lute.* Tokyo: Sophia University, 1940.

Wang Chi-te 王驥德 (1573–1620). *Ch'ü-lü* 曲律 (Drama rules). In *Chung-kuo ku-tien hsi-ch'ü lun-chu chi-ch'eng* (Collection of studies of classical Chinese drama), 4. Peking: Chung-kuo hsi-chü ch'u-pan-she, 1959.

Wang Ku-lu 王古魯. *Ming-tai hui-tiao hsi-ch'ü san-ch'u chi-i* 明代徽調戲曲散齣輯佚 (Collection of scenes from plays of Anhwei style drama from the Ming dynasty). Shanghai: Ku-tien wen-hsüeh ch'u-pan she, 1957.

Wang Kuo-wei 王國維. *Sung-Yüan hsi-ch'ü shih* 宋元戲曲史 (History of Sung-Yüan drama). Shanghai: Commercial Press, 1930.

Wang Shih-chen 王世貞 (1526–1590). *Wang-shih ch'ü-tsao* 王氏曲藻 (Drama study by Mr. Wang). In *Hsin ch'ü-yüan* (New anthology of drama). Taipei: T'ai-wan chung-hua shu-chü, 1969.

Wei Liang-fu 魏良輔 (late Ming). Ch'ü-lü 曲律 (Drama rules). In *Chung-kuo ku-tien hsi-ch'ü lun-chu chi-ch'eng* (Collection of studies of classical Chinese drama), 5. Peking: Chung-kuo hsi-chü ch'u-pan-she, 1959.

Yüan Ming Ch'ing hsi-ch'ü yen-chiu lun-wen chi 元明清戲曲研究論文集 (Collected research on drama of the Yuan, Ming, and Ch'ing periods). Peking: Tso-chia ch'u-pan-she, 1957.

Zbikowski, Tadeusz. *Early Nan-hsi Plays of the Southern Sung Period.* Warsaw: Wydawnictwa Uniwersytetu Warszarskiego, 1974.

Translations from the
Oriental Classics

Modern Asian Literature

Studies in Oriental Culture

Neo-Confucian Studies

The Unfolding of Neo-Confucianism, by Wm. Theodore de Bary and
the Conference on Seventeenth-Century Chinese Thought. Also
in paperback ed.   1975

*Principle and Practicality: Essays in Neo-Confucianism and Practical
Learning,* ed. Wm. Theodore de Bary and Irene Bloom. Also in
paperback ed.   1979

The Syncretic Religion of Lin Chao-en, by Judith A. Berling   1980

Companions to Asian Studies

Approaches to the Oriental Classics, ed. Wm. Theodore de Bary   1959

Early Chinese Literature, by Burton Watson. Also in paperback ed.   1962

Approaches to Asian Civilizations, ed. Wm. Theodore de Bary and
Ainslie T. Embree   1964

The Classic Chinese Novel: A Critical Introduction, by C. T. Hsia. Also
in paperback ed.   1968

Chinese Lyricism: Shih Poetry from the Second to the Twelfth Century, tr.
Burton Watson. Also in paperback ed.   1971

A Syllabus of Indian Civilization, by Leonard A. Gordon and Barbara
Stoler Miller   1971

Twentieth-Century Chinese Stories, ed. C. T. Hsia and Joseph S. M.
Lau. Also in paperback ed.   1971

A Syllabus of Chinese Civilization, by J. Mason Gentzler, 2d ed.   1972

A Syllabus of Japanese Civilization, by H. Paul Varley, 2d ed.   1972

An Introduction to Chinese Civilization, ed. John Meskill, with the assistance of J. Mason Gentzler   1973

An Introduction to Japanese Civilization, ed. Arthur E. Tiedemann   1974

A Guide to Oriental Classics, ed. Wm. Theodore de Bary and Ainslie
T. Embree, 2d ed. Also in paperback ed.   1975

Introduction to Oriental Civilizations
Wm. Theodore de Bary, *Editor*

Sources of Japanese Tradition 1958   Paperback ed., 2 vols. 1964
Sources of Indian Tradition   1958   Paperback ed., 2 vols. 1964
Sources of Chinese Tradition   1960   Paperback ed., 2 vols. 1964